ReFocus: The Films of Doris Wishman

ReFocus: The American Directors Series

Series Editors: Robert Singer, Frances Smith, and Gary D. Rhodes

Editorial board: Kelly Basilio, Donna Campbell, Claire Perkins, Christopher Sharrett, and Yannis Tzioumakis

ReFocus is a series of contemporary methodological and theoretical approaches to the interdisciplinary analyses and interpretations of neglected American directors, from the once-famous to the ignored, in direct relationship to American culture—its myths, values, and historical precepts.

Titles in the series include:

ReFocus: The Films of Preston Sturges
Edited by Jeff Jaeckle and Sarah Kozloff

ReFocus: The Films of Delmer Daves
Edited by Matthew Carter and Andrew Nelson

ReFocus: The Films of Amy Heckerling
Edited by Frances Smith and Timothy Shary

ReFocus: The Films of Budd Boetticher
Edited by Gary D. Rhodes and Robert Singer

ReFocus: The Films of Kelly Reichardt
E. Dawn Hall

ReFocus: The Films of William Castle
Edited by Murray Leeder

ReFocus: The Films of Barbara Kopple
Edited by Jeff Jaeckle and Susan Ryan

ReFocus: The Films of Elaine May
Edited by Alexandra Heller-Nicholas and Dean Brandum

ReFocus: The Films of Spike Jonze
Edited by Kim Wilkins and Wyatt Moss-Wellington

ReFocus: The Films of Paul Schrader
Edited by Michelle E. Moore and Brian Brems

ReFocus: The Films of Doris Wishman
Edited by Alicia Kozma and Finley Freibert

edinburghuniversitypress.com/series/refoc

ReFocus:
The Films of Doris Wishman

Edited by Alicia Kozma and
Finley Freibert

EDINBURGH
University Press

Edinburgh University Press is one of the leading university presses in the UK. We publish academic books and journals in our selected subject areas across the humanities and social sciences, combining cutting-edge scholarship with high editorial and production values to produce academic works of lasting importance. For more information visit our website: edinburghuniversitypress.com

© editorial matter and organization Alicia Kozma and Finley Freibert, 2021, 2023
© the chapters their several authors, 2021, 2023

Edinburgh University Press Ltd
The Tun—Holyrood Road
12 (2f) Jackson's Entry
Edinburgh EH8 8PJ

First published in hardback by Edinburgh University Press 2021

Typeset in 11/13 Ehrhardt MT by
IDSUK (DataConnection) Ltd

A CIP record for this book is available from the British Library

ISBN 978 1 4744 8234 9 (hardback)
ISBN 978 1 4744 8235 6 (paperback)
ISBN 978 1 4744 8236 3 (webready PDF)
ISBN 978 1 4744 8237 0 (epub)

The right of the contributors to be identified as authors of this work has been asserted in accordance with the Copyright, Designs and Patents Act 1988 and the Copyright and Related Rights Regulations 2003 (SI No. 2498).

Contents

List of Figures   vii
Notes on Contributors   viii
Acknowledgments   xi
Foreword   xii
Joan Hawkins

   Introduction: Making Films in Hell   1
   Alicia Kozma and Finley Freibert

Part I   Gender and Genre

1. The Body as Apparatus: Doris Wishman's *Double Agent 73*   15
   Elena Gorfinkel
2. The Girls in the Mirror: Women's Horror Filmmaking and Doris Wishman's *Each Time I Kill*   32
   Alexandra Heller-Nicholas
3. Trans/sexual Negativity and the Ethics of (S)exploitation in *Let Me Die a Woman*   47
   Harper Shalloe

Part II   Cultural History and Adult Film Studies

4. Hardcore Wishman   67
   Whitney Strub
5. Bad Bis Go to Hell: Bisexuality as Transgressive and Lucrative in Doris Wishman's Roughies   78
   Finley Freibert
6. "It's strange, but it's wonderful": Doris Wishman's *Nude on the Moon*   101
   Karen Joan Kohoutek

Part III Comparative Approaches to Authorship

7 Depicting Female Bodies: Doris Wishman, Carolee Schneemann, and Legacies of Subversion 121
Hannah Greenberg

8 Revolutionization of the Erotic Screen: The Films of Doris Wishman and Wakamatsu Koji 144
Molly Kim

9 "You can't say you're not getting a horror film here!": Authorship, Genre, and the Accidental Avant-Garde in Doris Wishman's *A Night to Dismember* 159
Jamie Hook

10 My Teenage Cinematic Love Affair with Doris Wishman 178
Rebekah McKendry

Index 186

Figures

5.1	Examples of 1960s print commodities that marketed sexual identities and practices	82
6.1	Moon residents at the real-life Coral Castle	103
6.2	Establishing shot of the bleak lunar surface	107
6.3	Astronauts surrounded by palm trees	108
6.4	Cathy seen as the Moon Queen	112
7.1	The San Remo apartment building stands out as a symbol of the female body on the horizon in *Bad Girls Go to Hell*	128
7.2	Chesty Morgan caressing, shaking, and animating her enormous breasts during the credit sequence of *Deadly Weapons*	133
8.1	Crystal's breasts displayed non-erotically and seen from both female and male gaze	149
8.2	Sex among rebels	155
9.1	An out-of-place optical or "a Doris Wishman touch"?	163
9.2	Grisly, yet artificial, gore effects	167
9.3	Vicki looks at a photograph of Frankie	170

Notes on Contributors

Finley Freibert is currently a part-time Senior Lecturer in Comparative Humanities at the University of Louisville and an adjunct Lecturer at the Kentucky College of Art and Design. In 2019, he completed a Ph.D. in Visual Studies from the University of California, Irvine. Finley researches and teaches at the intersection of media industry studies, gender and sexuality studies, and bisexual cultural history. His published work has included peer-reviewed research articles in venues including *Film Criticism*, invited scholarly articles for *Flow* and the quarterly journal of the non-profit Bob Mizer Foundation, and in popular LGBTQ+ press outlets *The Advocate* and *Washington Blade*.

Elena Gorfinkel is senior lecturer in Film Studies at King's College London and the author of *Lewd Looks: American Sexploitation Cinema in the 1960s* (2017). She is co-editor of *Global Cinema Networks* (2018) and *Taking Place: Location and the Moving Image* (2011), and edited an issue of *Feminist Media Histories* on "Sex and the Materiality of Adult Media" (2019). Her scholarly essays have appeared in *Screen, Journal of Cinema and Media Studies (Cinema Journal), Camera Obscura, Framework, Discourse, World Picture*, and in several edited collections. She is the recipient of a 2018 Art Writers Grant from Creative Capital/The Andy Warhol Foundation for her current book project "Aesthetic Strike: Cinemas of Exhaustion." She is also at work on a short monograph on Barbara Loden's *Wanda*. Gorfinkel regularly writes criticism in *Sight & Sound, Art Monthly, Cinema Scope*, and *Another Gaze*, among other venues.

Hannah Greenberg has degrees in Film Studies from Mount Holyoke College (BA) and Columbia University (MA). She currently works as the Director of Development & Membership at Anthology Film Archives in

New York City. Greenberg has also guest programmed multiple film series at Anthology, including "Women of the West" in 2018 and "A Real Young Girl: Coming of Age" in 2019. She has been interviewed about her curatorial work in the *New York Times* and the *Brooklyn Rail*.

Alexandra Heller-Nicholas is an award-winning Australian film critic who has written books on *Suspiria* (2015), *Ms. 45* (2017), and *The Hitcher* (2018), as well as *Rape-Revenge Films* (2011), *Found Footage Horror Films* (2014), and her 2019 Bram Stoker Award nominated *Masks in Horror Cinema: Eyes Without Faces*. She has co-edited collections including *Cattet & Forzani* (2018), *ReFocus: The Films of Elaine May* (2019), and *Wonderland*, the catalogue for the 2018 Australian Centre for the Moving Image exhibition on Alice in film. Alexandra is a programmer at Fantastic Fest in Austin, Texas; a board member of the Miskatonic Institute of Horror Studies; and a member of the Alliance of Women Film Journalists. She holds a Ph.D. in Screen Studies from the University of Melbourne and is an Adjunct Professor at Deakin University.

Jamie Hook is a Ph.D. candidate in the Department of Communication and Culture at Indiana University, Bloomington, where he also received his MA in 2012. His research focuses on media adaptation practices across film, literature, and theater during the sexual revolution and explores their role in reorganizing taste cultures and negotiating social stigmas. His work has been published in the Routledge journal *Porn Studies* and the Palgrave Studies in Adaptation and Visual Culture book series. He is scheduled to complete his Ph.D. in the fall of 2020.

Molly Kim is a film scholar specializing in the history of 1970s–80s Korean cinema, Japanese erotic cinema, film censorship, and genre. Her doctoral research focused on the representation of women and sex labor in 1970s Korean hostess films. She currently teaches at the University of Suwon, Korea. Her research has been published the *International Journal of Korean History* and the anthologies *Prostitution and Sex Work in Global Visual Media: New Takes on Fallen Women* and *Women Make Horror: Feminism, Filmmaking, Genre*.

Karen Joan Kohoutek is an independent scholar and poet who has published about weird fiction and cult films in various journals, literary websites, and anthologies. Subjects of recent and upcoming publications include *Mystery Science Theater 3000*'s versions of the *Gamera* films, folk magic in the novels of Ishmael Reed, August Strindberg as a weird writer, and the relationship between Marvel's *Black Panther* and the Black Panther Party. She has also published a novella, *The Jack-o-Lantern Box*, and the reference book *Ici Repose: A Guide to St. Louis Cemetery No. 2, Square 3*, about the historic New Orleans cemetery, through Skull and Book Press.

Alicia Kozma is Chair and Assistant Professor of Communication and Media Studies at Washington College. Her research focuses on gendered labor behind the screen in Hollywood. Her work has been published widely, including in *Camera Obscura, Television and New Media, The Projector*, and the *Journal of Japanese and Korean Film*. She holds a Ph.D. from the Institute of Communication Research at the University of Illinois, Urbana-Champaign.

Rebekah McKendry is an award-winning film and television director with a strong focus in the horror, thriller, and science fiction genres. Her two most recent feature films are the horror/comedy *All the Creatures Were Stirring* (featuring Constance Wu and which was released by RLJ) and the thriller *Granny's Home* (Mar Vista). Rebekah is the co-host of the popular Blumhouse Productions' podcast *Shock Waves*, as well as a film professor at the University of Southern California. Rebekah previously worked as the Editor-in-Chief at Blumhouse Productions and as the Director of Marketing for Fangoria Entertainment. She has a doctorate in Media Studies from Virginia Commonwealth University focused in genre media.

Harper Shalloe is a Ph.D. student in the department of Modern Culture and Media at Brown University. Harper holds a BA in Cinema Studies from New York University, where they were an Undergraduate Fellow at the Center for the Humanities (2016). They have presented work at the annual meetings of the Society for Cinema and Media Studies, the European Network for Cinema and Media Studies, and the Society for Social Studies of Science, as well as at the Oxford Internet Institute. Their article "I Sexually Identify as an Attack Helicopter" recently appeared in *Transgender Studies Quarterly*. Harper's research focuses on how the notion of identification traverses popular culture, critical theory, and technologies of surveillance and security. They are scheduled to complete their Ph.D. in 2022.

Whitney Strub is an associate professor of history at Rutgers University-Newark. He is the author of *Perversion for Profit: The Politics of Pornography and the Rise of the New Right* (2011) and *Obscenity Rules: Roth v. United States and the Long Struggle over Sexual Expression* (2013) and coeditor of *Porno Chic and the Sex Wars: American Sexual Representation in the 1970s* (2016). His work has appeared in such scholarly venues as *Radical History Review, American Quarterly, JCMS*, and *GLQ*, as well as popular outlets including *Slate, Salon, Washington Post, The Nation*, and *Temple of Schlock*.

Acknowledgments

Doris Wishman c. 1961, Sunny Palms Lodge. Image reproduced courtesy of Michael Bowen.

Thomas C. Lynch and Charles A. O'Brien, "A Report to the California Legislature on Obscenity (Sacramento: Dept. of Justice, 1967)." Images reproduced courtesy of the Government Information Collection, Henry Madden Library, Fresno, CA.

Nude on the Moon. DVD. Seattle, WA: Something Weird Video, 2006. Images reproduced courtesy of Something Weird Video.

Double Agent 73. DVD. Seattle, WA: Something Weird Video, 2000. Images reproduced courtesy of Something Weird Video.

The editors would like to thank Robert Singer for his dedication to this project, the generative feedback from our reviewers, and those Wishman scholars whose early work enabled this collection.

Foreword

Joan Hawkins[1]

I met Doris Wishman briefly at the 1998 Chicago Underground Film Festival. She was there with her biographer Michael Bowen to receive a Lifetime Achievement Award. And I remember literally bumping into her in the crowded theater lobby. "My God," I said, "you're Doris Wishman." "I know who *I* am," she snapped. "But who the hell are you?" I told her my name, which she remembered. Throughout the remainder of the festival, whenever she saw me she said hello and warned me not to be so clumsy. To call her irascible is an understatement. But she was also canny and shrewd, talented and wickedly smart. She had no idea who I was, but she remembered my name anyway, in case she ever needed it.

A prolific filmmaker, Wishman has been largely overlooked in film history. This is partly due to the fact that she made exploitation films, a genre generally omitted in traditional academic studies, despite its enormous influence on mainstream film culture. But even in exploitation histories, Wishman has not received the recognition she deserves, far less recognition than male directors like Radley Metzger and Russ Meyer who have attained something like underground auteur status. And for a while she received even less acknowledgment than Roberta Findlay, another underappreciated female exploitation director, even though Wishman made thirty-one films, many more than Findlay, and had more influence. Roger Corman, David Friedman, Larry Cohen, John Carpenter, and John Waters were all inspired by her. The fact that she produced, as well as directed and distributed her own films is an extraordinary achievement for a woman working in a male-dominated arena of an even larger male-dominated industry. The fact that she continued making films until her death in 2002, even without major financial backing, is a testament to both her tenacity and her importance. If you want to know the history of twentieth-century American, low-budget, independent filmmaking, you need to study Wishman.

Like many other women filmmakers, Wishman was completely self-taught. And she was, by needs, innovative, often utilizing techniques that—in other parts of the culture industry—were considered experimental. Her films often feature hand-held tracking shots that cut suddenly to overflowing ashtrays or to a character's knees or hands. Much of her sound is post-dubbed and not always well synched, which gives the movies a sort of vertiginous feel. Interiors are *noit-flat*, and the mise-en-scène takes wild continuity chances, reminiscent of an aesthetic I first encountered in Downtown No-Wave Films. Like the Downtown artists who borrowed from her, Wishman had a definite DIY Punk aesthetic (even in 1961). But more pointedly, she had something of a punk, Downtown, No-Wave attitude, dealing with what Lydia Lunch once called "very negative things in an aggressive way," because that is the way oppressive institutions work.[2] And long before Nick Zedd coined the term, Wishman was making transgressive cinema.[3]

Wishman's work was not only in conversation with that of other contemporary exploitation directors and subsequent experimental filmmakers, but also with contemporary avant-garde figures, who also explored the human condition through graphic sexual representation. Most notably, this volume includes a comparison between Doris Wishman's work and Carolee Schneeman's, a brilliant pairing, I think. But Wishman's work can also be read alongside that of Barbara Rubin (*Christmas on Earth*, 1963), Jack Smith (*Flaming Creatures*, 1963), *and* Kenneth Anger (*Scorpio Rising*, 1963). Part II of this volume, which deals explicitly with Wishman's relationship to the changing sexual landscape of the 1960s and 1970s, should be of interest to anyone engaged in work on this era.

But as I hope is clear from this Foreword, I believe the volume should engage anyone interested in film history. Not only does it fill a notable lacuna in exploitation and underground scholarship, but it also engages with the larger questions of exploitation's relationship to mainstream cinema. It explores the avenues open to women who were driven to independent production (both high and low) and whose important role in shaping American Independent Film is frequently overlooked. It explores the sexual revolution of the 1960s–70s, and the changing mores which have mapped onto the larger social upheavals of that time period in profound ways. Finally, in its inclusion of so many women scholars, it challenges received gendered ideas about genre and genre scholarship. As Doris Wishman's career demonstrated, exploitation isn't just a boys' club.

NOTES

1. Joan Hawkins is an Associate Professor in Cinema and Media Studies at Indiana University Bloomington and specializes in work on taste politics. She has written extensively on horror and the avant-garde. Her best-known book is *Cutting Edge: Art Horror and the Horrific Avant-garde*. Her most recent book is an anthology, co-edited

with Alex Wermer-Colan, titled *William S. Burroughs Cutting Up the Century*. She is currently editing a volume on 1960s Radical Aesthetics and writing a book on independent horror.

2. Nick Soulsby, *Lydia Lunch: The War Is Never Over: A Companion to the Film by Beth B* (London: Jawbone Press, 2020), back cover.

3. Nick Zedd, "The Underground Film Bulletin and the Cinema of Transgression," <https://www.printedmatter.org/catalog/tables/137 1/25/2018> (last accessed August 20, 2020).

Introduction: Making Films in Hell

Alicia Kozma and Finley Freibert

Producer and director Doris Wishman was a pioneering woman in the film industry, leaving an extensive body of work. Between 1960 and 2002 she made thirty-one films, making her one of the most prolific women directors ever. Wishman worked so steadily that she famously quipped, "When I die, I'll be making films in hell!" Despite her bountiful filmic contributions, many people have never heard of her, and she is largely overlooked in film histories and archives, her significant oeuvre virtually untapped by critical and cultural analysis. In large measure this is because Wishman was a woman who worked in a normatively neglected industry: exploitation films. Indeed, she and other women who produced and directed adult and exploitation films have tended to be understudied in comparison to male directors like Radley Metzger, Joe Sarno, and Russ Meyer who have attained masculinized auteur status as the key directors in that milieu. As a reparative to her neglected place in film histories and scholarship, this book breaks new ground in the study of her career and filmic productions.

Beyond classed disregard for exploitation cinema and masculinist bias against women filmmakers, the study of Wishman has also been stilted by the lack of publicly accessible archival holdings and restrictive filmic histories that rely on outmoded constructions of taste and artistic cultures. Furthermore, relatively new techniques of digitally traversing industry publication archives like the University of Wisconsin-Madison's open-access Media History Digital Library or Proquest's Entertainment Industry Magazine Archive turn up minimal results on how Wishman or her films circulated in historical industry discourse. As a specific political intervention into filmic histories and archives, then, this book addresses the critical lacuna in Wishman studies through creative approaches—often employing multimodal analyses—marshalled to circumvent such problems of archival inaccessibility and industry press silences.

Wishman was a practical person, and that practicality seeped into her filmmaking decisions, including her decision to work in exploitation film. As she said, "I could get a gimmick for doing exploitation, whereas if you're doing a regular feature film the cost is unreal. And I felt this was preferable."[1] Specifically, Wishman made sexploitation films. Sexploitation, a concatenation of sex exploitation, flourished in the 1960s and 1970s by leveraging legal decisions codifying nudity on film as not obscene per se. The sexploitation category offered a combustible mix of sex, nudity, sexuality, and desire. Elena Gorfinkel's recent leading-edge book *Lewd Looks* offers a detailed and cogent analysis of sexploitation's role in U.S. cinema and the country's cultural understanding of sex. Gorfinkel describes how the sexploitation cycle systematizes "a soft-core aesthetic ethos and elaborates excessive scenarios of social change represented through changes in sexual practices."[2] Sexual mores and behaviors were indeed changing in the 1960s and 1970s, as sex moved from the private sphere to the public, from the bedroom to the screen. As exploitation film historian Eric Schaefer has calculated, "by the end of the 1960s roughly 5 percent of all U.S. theaters were regularly exhibiting sexploitation films each week of the year, and another 1,500 played at least one or more exploitation films in 1968 and 1969."[3]

Sexploitation films are representative of a type of independent narrative filmmaking once public and pervasive that has all but ceased to exist outside of niche cult labels and the now infrequent production of narrative features in the professional adult film industry. The sexploitation industry was comprised of a network of seasoned and novice filmmakers, producers, distributors, and exhibitors primarily located in New York City and Los Angeles. Performers were usually drawn from adjacent professions including figure models, exotic dancers, and extras; and typical sexploitation films were made in about week on a budget anywhere from $10,000 to $40,000.[4] Wishman's films were similarly constructed. While Wishman wasn't the only woman making sexploitation, she was among the most resilient, comparable to her contemporaries like Roberta Findlay. Wishman is part of a rich underresearched history of female and queer filmmakers that worked in the adult film industry; as Elena Gorfinkel has eloquently stated, Wishman is a "reminder of the massive historical work yet to be done [with respect to] the untold women and countless queer makers and performers who filmed, produced, distributed, presented, and performed in sex films."[5] Wishman's career offers an encapsulation of the evolutions in sexploitation films, from nudist films, to roughies, softcore, and the decline of sexploitation into genres like horror or hardcore pornography. These evolutions are necessarily messy and ateleological, but by examining Wishman's career and body of work it is possible to chart some of the ebbs, flows, and mutations of the cycle.

Wishman's films are complicated, ideological, and often troubling social performances of the contemporary human condition as manifest through desire, sex and sexuality, gender, class, and corporeality. This volume, the first book-length study of Doris Wishman, is a specific and political intervention meant to increase Wishman's presence in film histories. Scholarly consideration of Wishman up to this point has been limited to a handful of book chapters and journal articles. These writings have become sacred texts of sorts for anyone interested in the director and her body of work, and this volume aims to extend that body of scholarship while acknowledging its foundational importance, providing a critical jumping-off point for future Wishman scholarship. To dedicate as much space as possible to her work, the chapters in the volume include very little biography of Wishman; rather, a version of her personal and professional lives is included in this Introduction. It is *a* version, not *the* version, because the details of Wishman's life are as enigmatic and contradictory as many of her films.

THE MISTRESS OF SEXPLOITATION

Something Weird Video founder Mike Vraney once described Wishman as "a perfect example of anarchy filmmaking."[6] It is fitting, then, that much of her biography mirrors the anarchic spirit of her films. Doris Wishman was born on April 23, 1920—maybe. Wishman biographer Michael Bowen reported that as the date on a passport Wishman carried.[7] In a 1994 interview she said her birth certificate listed July 1 as her entry into the world, but in school her birthday was listed as July 23.[8] To complicate matters, the *Social Security Applications and Claims Index* registers her birth date as June 22, 1912, while the *Social Security Death Index* lists June 1, 1912 as her birthday, the date currently present on Wishman's Wikipedia page. While she loathed discussing her age, history can agree on this: Doris Wishman was born.

Her mother died when she was two years old, and her family—father, two brothers, and two sisters—moved from New York City to Westchester County, where Wishman grew up.[9] She came back to New York City to attend Hunter College; she wanted to be an actress. Wishman took acting classes and went on double dates with Shelley Winters,[10] and at some point was a working stage actress in New York City. She quit acting and went to work for Joseph E. Levine and Max Rosenberg; Levine made his mark with Charles Atlas pics and sword and sandal epics.[11] Rosenberg distributed *Garden of Eden* (Max Nosseck, 1954), an early nudist camp film whose successful legal battle against censorship was pathbreaking for nudity on screen. Wishman married a man named Jack Silverman; Jack worked in advertising. The couple moved to Florida in 1959 to be near her family, and four months later Jack tragically passed away.[12]

Wishman suffered a tremendous loss, and "looked for an all-consuming job—something to fill my hours with."[13] She knew distribution; how difficult could production be? She borrowed a total of $20,000 from her sister Pearl and made her first film, the nudist camp romp *Hideout in the Sun* (1960).[14] As it turns out, production is very different than distribution: "There's no connection . . . as far as actually making a film, it has nothing to do with distribution. So it was a little difficult for me at first."[15] *Hideout* was Wishman's first nudist camp picture, a type of sexploitation film that purported to showcase everyday life at nudist camps—always from the waist up and usually focused on women nudists. As Moya Luckett notes, "The breast was the nudist film's *raison d'être* [. . .]."[16] Shooting on location, Wishman's camera moved observantly around the nudist camp, revealing its inhabitants in their natural state, albeit with carefully placed foliage or some other obstacle in front of their groins. She soon moved into "nudie cuties," which freed nudity from encampment and moved it everywhere from a suburban street to the moon.

Wishman made eight films in this vein after *Hideout*: *Nude on the Moon* (1961), *Diary of a Nudist* (1961), *Blaze Starr Goes Nudist* (1962), *Gentlemen Prefer Nature Girls* (1963), *Playgirls International* (1963), *Behind the Nudist Curtain* (1964), *The Prince and the Nature Girl* (1964), and *Behind the Nudist Curtain* (1964). *Playgirls International* and *Behind the Nudist Curtain* were different than the comparatists:

> Wishman purchased the rights to an unwanted European travelogue containing scenes of nightclub entertainment from various exotic vacation spots. After shooting additional nudist footage and editing sections of the purchased film together with this new material, Wishman cut the negative into [the] two different features.[17]

Her nudie cuties do not take themselves seriously, but rather satirize ethnographic film and popular genres of the time like science fiction while trading on voyeurism.

During the decline of censorship regulations in the 1960s, nudie cuties became increasingly passé. As their popularity waned, a new type of sexploitation film evolved. Films like Russ Meyer's *Lorna* (1964) and *Sin the Suburbs* (Joe Sarno, 1964) diverged from the Technicolor nudist camps of Florida and innocently topless suburban housewives to gritty black and white portrayals of sex, nudity, and physical and sexual violence. These films, known as "roughies," ascended. While nudie cuties depended on "erotic looking,"[18] roughies spectacularized sexual violence, deviancy, and criminality. Rape was *de rigueur*, often a punishment for women's actions. Danger, hostility, and aberrance were built into the roughie milieu, due in no small part to their setting, which was frequently the urban cityscape. In the case of Wishman and her contemporaries Barry Mahon, Joe Sarno, and Michael Findlay, the common setting was a narratively anonymous but easily recognizable New York City. The work of these filmmakers was also linked to New York City non-narratively, as they became synonymous with the grindhouse movie theaters and sex work economy of 1960s–70s Times Square.

Wishman moved back to New York City in 1965,[19] and that same year she made her first two roughies: *The Sex Perils of Paulette* and *Bad Girls Go to Hell*. In 1966 she married Jack Abrams. Of Abrams Wishman said, "he was very wealthy and very handsome, and he showered me with gifts. I wasn't in love with him, but it was so exciting. And we eloped. It was real sixteen-year-old-stuff. So I married him, what the heck!"[20] She went on to make five more roughies: *My Brother's Wife* (1966), *Another Day, Another Man* (1966), *A Taste of Flesh* (1967), *Indecent Desires* (1968), and *Too Much Too Often!* (1968). While aesthetically recognizable as roughies, Wishman's films are more experimental in editing style and narrative. Her thematic editing style juxtaposes the mundane with the sensational: sex scenes are interrupted by cuts to hairbrushes or overflowing ashtrays, hurried conversations are heard in voiceover while her camera is trained on a squirrel in the park. It is an avant-garde strategy that is Kuleshovian in its simplicity and effectiveness, as Wishman collapses the perceived distance between women's everyday lives and patriarchal violence. Similarly, Wishman's narrative structure reinserts women's subjectivity in a filmic style that is, at least ostensibly, about women. Elena Gorfinkel notes that Wishman's roughies "reflect a counterpoint to the male-authored narratives of betrayal and recompense so popular in the early roughies made by men, with the rape occurring as the catalyst rather than the outcome of narrative action."[21] Not content with a singular style, Wishman has three non-roughie credits during this period. *The Hot Month of August* (1966) and *Passion Fever* (1969) were two Greek films Wishman purchased and added footage to.[22] *Love Toy* (1968) is her only color softcore feature that is arguably a traditional roughie narrative.

Wishman's non-stop filmmaking pace slowed in the early 1970s. In 1970 she made *The Amazing Transplant*, the story of a man who has the penis of a serial rapist transplanted onto his body and subsequently becomes a rapist himself. *Keyholes Are for Peeking* (1972) is a Peeping Tom-style sex comedy. In 1974 Wishman made two of her most well-known, or perhaps notorious, features: *Deadly Weapons* and *Double Agent 73*, ostensibly spy movies. Both films starred Polish exotic dancer Chesty Morgan (born Liliana Wilczkowska), whose fame stemmed from her seventy-three-inch breasts. In 1975 *The Immoral Three* extended Wishman's loosely constructed espionage genre, as three sisters do whatever it takes to avenge the death of their spy mother. *Satan Was a Lady* (1976) and *Come with Me My Love* (1976) are Wishman's only hardcore films. She vigorously denied ever making them. In a 1974 interview Wishman decried graphic nudity and sexuality: "I don't approve of explicit sex on a screen . . . I'm certainly not a prude or anything like that but I think enough is enough."[23] Wishman and Abrams divorced in 1975.[24] She did not make another film for three years.

Let Me Die a Woman (1978) stands apart from other Wishman films. Riding a tense generic line between documentary and pornography, the film chronicles the lives of a group of trans individuals, dramatizes their experiences, and documents gender alignment surgeries. Recalling the genesis of the film, Wishman said:

> The first film I made was a nudist film, and the women I worked with, who owned and ran the nudist camp, happened to call me, a number of years after I started production. And I said what was she doing, and she said she was working with transsexuals [sic]. And I thought, "Gee, that's a good idea." Because as I said, when you don't have too much money, you have to have gimmick. So she introduced me to a doctor who does the operations and I worked with him.[25]

The film is a heady mix of lived experiences, cultural anxieties, and empathy that was difficult for Wishman: "These people were very unhappy . . . [after it was released] I didn't follow it at all. I wanted to forget about it. Because making the film, as I said, was a sad experience, but it was a good experience."[26] She moved on from the complicated film by latching on to the popularity of the slasher film in the 1980s with *A Night to Dismember* (1989). She shot the film irregularly, and a third of the footage was lost by the laboratory.[27] Wishman finished it with material from other films, voiceover narration and outtakes. It was eventually released on video in 1983 and again in 1989.

By 1994 Wishman had moved back to Florida, where she worked at the Pink Pussycat Boutique, a now defunct sex shop in Miami. Younger generations were exposed to her films on VHS, the bulk of which were remastered and released by Something Weird Video. The popularity of her home video releases and her rising cult film iconicity led to career retrospectives, college lectures, and two appearances on *Late Night with Conan O'Brien*—once in 1998 along with actress Juliana Margulies and again in 2002 beside critic Roger Ebert.[28] She began making films again in the 2000s, first *Satan Was a Lady* (2001; a different project than the film of the same name she made in 1976) and then *Dildo Heaven* (2002). Her second *Late Night* appearance in 2002 was to promote *Dildo Heaven*. During her appearance, O'Brien plays a short clip of the film, which mixes new footage with old: a man walking down the street in 2002 looks into a camera placed in a bush and sees footage from 1975's *The Immoral Three*. Wishman explains the technique, and her career-long practicality in filmmaking: "I needed more footage, and I didn't have money."[29] At the end of the show she asks O'Brien to plug her upcoming film, *Each Time I Kill*. The film would be released posthumously in 2007, five years after her appearance on the show. Wishman passed away from complications from lymphoma on August 10, 2002. She was either eighty-two, or as her family believed, around ninety years old.[30]

"WHAT'S SO GREAT ABOUT DORIS WISHMAN?"[31]

For the purposes of this book, we have decided not to standardize the release years of Wishman's films across all chapters. This decision reflects the anarchic nature of the documentation of Wishman's life and career—exemplified in the numerous conflicting accounts of her birthdate discussed above—yet, our decision is also justified for several additional reasons. First, exploitation film releases are notoriously difficult to track. Many films were released under multiple titles, and often advertised in newspapers without attribution with statements like "Call Theater for Title." Second, the American Film Institute Catalogs are often considered the gold standard when attributing a release date, because AFI researchers performed extensive studies that usually culminated in both a premiere date and city. However, adult films are not represented in post-1970 volumes of the AFI Catalog, and small-scale independent movies, like Wishman's later films, often were not covered in later volumes or AFI's online databases either. Additionally, even when a pre-1971 sexploitation film is listed in the catalog the dates and cities are not always reliable.[32] Third, user-editable platforms like IMDb and Wikipedia are perpetually subject to change; basing dates on their listings does not guarantee the dates will not be changed at some later date. Fourth, there does not appear to be a single book or non-contingent database that lists the dates of Wishman's entire filmography on which to base a standardization. Even Michael J. Weldon's nearly comprehensive *Psychotronic* guides stop at the year 1996, which leaves out portions of Wishman's oeuvre. Given all of these circumstances, we leave a determination of each film's date up to the preference of each chapter author. This decision is a testament to the precarious state of the Doris Wishman archive, and it underscores the conflicting, freewheeling, and sometimes ambivalent nature of her career in general.

This book is divided into three parts that are representative of, and often reparative to, major themes that circulate around Doris Wishman and her films: Wishman as feminist, Wishman as maven of the sexual zeitgeist, and Wishman as accidental artist. Perhaps the most persistent of these themes is a version of the question, "Is Doris Wishman a feminist or not?" Rather than try to interpret or recuperate the director's politics, the chapters in Part I avoid entanglement in this unanswerable, and ultimately unhelpful question, focusing instead on the complicated machinations of how gender unfolds in a selection of her films. In Chapter 1, a reprint of Gorfinkel's germinal "The Body as Apparatus" with a new introduction, the author considers how the female body acts as both a prop and a technology in *Deadly Weapons* and *Double Agent 73*. Beginning with a contextualization of the film's modes of production and marketing strategies as hallmark of exploitation films, Gorfinkel considers how Morgan's body becomes the films' primary prop and exploitation marketing "gimmick." However, the way the films use Morgan's body transforms her from prop to screen and memory technology, assaulting the male characters and arguably the viewer in the process as Morgan moves from actor to prop to gendered technology.

Chapter 2 sees Alexandra Heller-Nicholas apply genre analysis to considerations of gender when examining *Each Time I Kill* in relation to the similarities it shares with other U.S. women-directed horror films that bookended it, *Mirror Mirror* (Marina Sargenti, 1990) and *The Dorm* (Rachel Talalay, 2014). *Each Time I Kill* is discussed as part of the tradition of women's horror filmmaking that interrogates the effects of gendered power relations on identity, alienation, and constructions of femininity. Sidestepping the easy reducibility of feminism with women's authorship, the chapter uses comparative formal and textual analysis of the film's engagement with mirror imagery in relation to the trope of the "transforming girl-outsider."

Harper Shalloe's "Trans/sexual Negativity and the Ethics of (S)exploitation in *Let Me Die a Woman*" builds on the part's themes of gendered body as apparatus, genre, and transformation, underscoring critical links between trans studies and psychoanalysis through the case study of *Let Me Die a Woman* (1978). Shalloe presents the film as a site of struggle pertaining to genre classifications, psychoanalytic sublimation, and recent theorizations of trans negativity in trans studies. The author argues that the process of sublimation—creating something out of nothing—expressed in segments of the film's documentary footage unveils editing as the key formal element in the film. Resultingly, Shalloe suggests that *Let Me Die a Woman*'s "subliminating montage" represent trans desire and sexual contact as the collision of formal elements through montage rather than narrative.

Part II delves into Wishman's intersection with the changing sexual landscape of the 1960s and 1970s. Wishman is a contradictory symbol of the changes wrought by the sexual revolution. While her films are organized around nudity and sex, they are very rarely about nudity or sex. The exception are her hardcore films—*Come with Me My Love* and *Satan Was a Lady*—which she steadfastly refused to acknowledge as her own. In Chapter 4, "Hardcore Wishman," Whitney Strub historicizes Wishman as one of the few women directors during the golden age of adult cinema, and as one of a handful of sexploitation directors who disavowed their hardcore work, including Pat Rocco and Herschell Gordon Lewis. Despite the rise of "porno chic" jumpstarted by *Deep Throat* (Gerard Damiano, 1972) and other hardcore films that prized narrative and production value, Wishman's hardcore films focus on depictions of sex as their primary content, delivering the hardcore sequences with only minimal stitching to a narrative trajectory. Strub's examination of Wishman's adult cinema authorship complicates her presumed relationship to pornography, as the two films evince formal techniques found in her softcore films, while also pointing to the creative influences of performer Annie Sprinkle on the film's production.

Following this focus on historiography and cultural histories of the sexual public sphere, Chapter 5 sees Finley Freibert's examination of bisexuality in the content and marketing of Wishman's roughies in the 1960s in conversation with the place of bisexuality within the historical context of the sexual revolution. To do so, Freibert first reviews gay and bisexual histories, articulating how queer audiences and urban spaces of sexual media consumption are a significant and overlooked social context for sexploitation films. Secondly, the author parses *The Sex Perils of Paulette* (1965) and *Bad Girls Go to Hell* (1965) for their formal and narrative techniques that centralize bisexual women protagonists. Freibert concludes with an analysis of *Too Much Too Often!* that demonstrates the film's bisexual address in its formal, narrative, and advertising elements.

Chapter 6, Karen Joan Kohoutek's "'It's strange, but it's wonderful': Doris Wishman's *Nude on the Moon*," imbricates cultural, production, genre, and social movement histories to articulate the intersections of second-wave feminism and nudie cuties. Trading off the population of science fictions films at the height of the space race, Kohoutek traces how the film—one of Wishman's least studied—flouts traditional conventions of the science fiction and nudist genres in a way that critiques hegemonic gender norms. Providing ample textual analysis and production history, Kohoutek provides a starting point for re-evaluating the film as a political and generic text.

The book's final part considers Wishman as author and artist by putting her work into conversation with other artists and film movements. In much of the popular and scholarly opinion of Wishman she is coded as a director interested in filmmaking solely as an economic proposition, rather than someone who knowingly combines filmmaking artistry with its inherently capitalist nature. Any artistic prowess in her films, then, is assumed accidental. The authors in this part reverse this infantilization of Wishman's cinematic abilities through comparative authorship. In Chapter 7, Hannah Greenberg explores Wishman in conversation with visual artist and experimental filmmaker Carolee Schneemann. Greenberg addresses Wishman's work in the context of sexploitation, Wishman's relationship to the more established avant-garde, and why her work deserves placement in the avant-garde. Focusing on how Wishman and Schneemann both centralize female bodies in their films and demonstrating the complexities of depicting female nudity, Greenberg aligns their work by disrupting cultural hierarchies of high and low culture and situates both directors within a tradition of women's avant-garde filmmaking.

Molly Kim takes a similar comparative approach in Chapter 8, providing a much-needed global framework by analyzing eroticism in Wishman's *Double Agent 73/Deadly Weapons* and Wakamatsu Koji's *Season of Terror* (1969) and *Ecstasy of the Angels* (1972). Koji, a Japanese Pink movie director and radical leftist activist, demonstrated how politics could be voiced through the erotic conventions of Pink films. Wishman as gendered filmmaker suggested new possibilities in the representation of women's agency within the male-dominated field of erotic cinema. Through a comparative filmic analysis, Kim traces how each director's concept of "erotic" was cinematized to cater to the commercial, sexual, and political desires of the time while also serving as the representative faces of rule breaking and progressive cinema.

Jamie Hook's Chapter 9 "'You can't say you're not getting a horror film here!': Authorship, Genre, and the Accidental Avant-Garde in Doris Wishman's *A Night to Dismember*" considers the question of authorship with regard to a film regularly downplayed in Wishman's oeuvre thanks to its production history. Returning to avant-gardism, Hook considers the film through three lenses: (1) as a Wishman film and its attendant engagement with the hallmarks of her earlier filmography; (2) as a piece of paracinematic horror that draws on and departs from trends of the contemporaneous slasher cycle; and (3) as an accidental evocation of avant-garde aesthetics. By doing so the author demonstrates what is conventional and exceptional about the film when situated in each of these contexts and, collectively, indicates the impracticality of ever fully disentangling its respective authorial and generic influences.

Rebekah McKendry, an early Wishman scholar, concludes the volume with an analysis of the impact Wishman's legacy has had on present and future women filmmakers. McKendry writes self-reflexively from her unique position as a filmmaker, popular genre film journalist, and academic about the impact Wishman and her body of work had on her own filmic consciousness. Leveraging a personal anecdote into metaphor, McKendry traces how Wishman's influence, however unlikely, has extended across time and space for cinephiles, filmmakers, and scholars alike.

NOTES

1. Doris Wishman, interview by Peggy Ahwesh, February 11, 1994, reprinted in *The Films of Doris Wishman*, ed. Peggy Ahwesh (New York: Impatient Press and Light Industry, 2019), 6.
2. Elena Gorfinkel, *Lewd Looks: American Sexploitation Cinema in the 1960s* (Minneapolis and London: University of Minnesota Press, 2017), 7.
3. Eric Schaefer, "Introduction—Sex Seen: 1968 and Rise of 'Public' Sex," in *Sex Scene*, ed. Eric Schaefer (Durham, NC: Duke University Press, 2014), 1–22, 8–9.
4. Elena Gorfinkel, "The Body's Failed Performance: Work in Sexploitation Cinema," *The Journal of Cinema and Media* 53, no. 1 (Spring 2012): 78–98.
5. Elena Gorfinkel, "Editor's Introduction: Sex and the Materiality of Adult Media," *Feminist Media Histories* 5, no. 2 (2019): 1–18, 4.
6. Myrna Oliver, "Doris Wishman; Exploitation Film Director, Cult Favorite," *Los Angeles Times*, last modified August 21, 2002, <https://www.latimes.com/archives/la-xpm-2002-aug-21-me-wishman21-story.html> (last accessed November 3, 2020).

7. Douglas Martin, "Doris Wishman, 'B' Film Director Dies," *New York Times*, August 19, 2012, A-13.
8. Wishman, interview Ahwesh.
9. Ibid.
10. Ibid.
11. Rebekah McKendry, "Fondling Your Eyeballs: Watching Doris Wishman," in *From the Arthouse to the Grindhouse: Highbrow and Lowbrow Transgression in Cinema's First Century*, ed. John Cline and Robert G. Weiner (Lanham, MD: Scarecrow Press, 2010), 57–74.
12. Wishman, interview Ahwesh.
13. Oliver, "Doris Wishman."
14. Michael J. Bowen, "Embodiment and Realization: The Many Film-Bodies of Doris Wishman," *Wide Angle* 19, no. 3 (July 1997): 64–90.
15. Wishman, interview Ahwesh, 7.
16. Moya Luckett, "Sexploitation as Feminine Territory: The Films of Doris Wishman," in *Defining Cult Movies: The Cultural Politics of Oppositional Taste*, ed. Mark Jancovich, Antonio Lázaro Reboll, Julian Stringer, and Andy Willis (Manchester: Manchester University Press, 2003), 150.
17. Bowen, "Embodiment and Realization," 72.
18. Gorfinkel, *Lewd Looks*, 134.
19. McKendry, "Fondling Your Eyeballs."
20. Wishman, interview Ahwesh, 16.
21. Gorfinkel, *Lewd Looks*, 149.
22. Bowen, "Embodiment and Realization."
23. Doris Wishman, interview by Donald Davis, 1974, reprinted in *The Films of Doris Wishman*, ed. Ahwesh, 32.
24. Wishman, interview Ahwesh, 18.
25. Ibid., 8.
26. Ibid., 8–9.
27. Bowen, "Embodiment and Realization."
28. McKendry, "Fondling Your Eyeballs."
29. Doris Wishman interviewed by Conan O'Brien, *Late Night with Conan O'Brien*, March 7, 2002, <https://www.youtube.com/watch?v=q-LCPdiThsI> (last accessed November 3, 2020).
30. Douglas, "Doris Wishman."
31. Doris Wishman, 1995, quoted in *The Films of Doris Wishman*, ed. Ahwesh, 8.
32. For example, the AFI date for Wishman's *Too Much Too Often!* is incorrect, as discussed by Finley Freibert in note 50 of his chapter in this volume.

PART I

Gender and Genre

CHAPTER 1

The Body as Apparatus: Doris Wishman's *Double Agent 73*

Elena Gorfinkel

PREFACE: WISHMAN'S THEORY OF THE GIMMICK

This essay was written over twenty years ago and represents my first encounter with both feminist film theory and sexploitation cinema. It originally appeared in the edited collection Unruly Pleasures: The Cult Film and its Critics *in 2000. My discovery of Wishman was occasioned by her reclamation by the New York underground film scene, notably by early supporters—experimental filmmakers Peggy Ahwesh and M. M. Serra, as well as film scholar Michael Bowen—and the Wishman retrospective at the 1998 New York Underground Film Festival, as well as her visit to my feminist film theory seminar at NYU. I watched* Bad Girls Go to Hell *and* Double Agent 73 *at the festival, in a moment when these films were circulating primarily as schlocky desiderata on clamshell-cased VHS, at places like Kim's Video on St. Marks Place in the East Village. Kim's had a "sexploitation" section devoted to the films—most of which were distributed by Something Weird Video—a large walled shelf perched at the border between the cash register and a back nook reserved for the display of hardcore porn. The gift of celluloid scale at the festival may have given Wishman the seriousness that her films had scarcely enjoyed prior.*

Wishman was my "gateway drug" into the history of sexploitation cinema, and the below essay is the heady evidence of that first point of contact. Thus, the essay's theoretical claims, as well as its oversights and limitations, all my own, speak as much to how the field has changed, as to how much my own thinking has shifted its perspective on the subject of adult film and media history in the intervening time. Approaching the works of an independent woman filmmaker through feminist film theory was a way for me to contend with the paucity of attention to Wishman and to the sex cinema in general in film studies of that moment, as much as a means of complicating the exemplary objects film theory used for its theorizations of sexuality, spectatorship, and women's presence in the cinema, in front of and behind the camera. If one could use Hitchcock or von Sternberg to model the apparatus and its sexuating presumptions, then why not Wishman?

A tale of a female spy who must crack a heroin-smuggling ring through the use of her wits, her physical endowment, and her technically amplified body alone, Double Agent 73 *(1974) has long looked like an unwittingly executed counter-cinema. It seems to refract and transmute some of the precepts of a contemporaneously developing Anglo-American screen theory. I am hardly suggesting that sexploitation films such as Wishman's gave grist to the mill of psycho-semiotics or to Laura Mulvey's concept of the male gaze. But such broadened historical genealogies can be revealing, widening the historical frame and the capacity of women's cinema, in all its forms and in its far-flung industrial locations, to propose their own concepts and ideas. No doubt the "working out" of the problem of women's representability took different shapes in the crass terrain of exploitation cinema than in a feminist film theory steeped psycho-semiotics. As I have argued in* Lewd Looks: American Sexploitation Cinema in the 1960s *(2017), sexploitation films were inordinately preoccupied with scenarios of erotic looking and thematized their own conditions of consumption in a decade when permissible screen sex was continually being re-litigated. Wishman's cinema was part of this larger orientation toward specularity as both boon and problem. By the early 1970s, Wishman's* Double Agent 73, *made in the wake of porno chic, had to rely on other resources and generic strategies to compete, and one of those tools is Morgan's body couched in a topical spy thriller container.*

By leveraging her star's body as the site of an ingenious gimmick—a hidden camera resident in Morgan's spectacular embodiment—Wishman worked with and against sexploitation's codes of erotic sensation and commodification. Wishman worked in a largely male-dominated market at the level of both production and consumption. It is no wonder then that her films anatomize metaphorically and literally the psychically dense operations of cinema's fundamentally perverse logics, even as they unabashedly deployed the corporeal heft and seductive force of women's bodies within the terms of sexploitation's formulas, often concerning working, single women navigating a rotten male world. This has given some feminist critics of Wishman and the sexploitation mode itself pause, for good reason. But in looking away, there is a danger of diminishing the labor and ingenuity of women like Wishman who attempted tenaciously to work within systems and industries expressly not made with them in mind, as producers or as consumers, in the interest of sexual expressivity.

Looking at this essay now, I have many reservations about its approach and modeling of a psychoanalytic "black box" through which to understand Wishman's film and the aesthetic of its maker. While the method and style derives more from the idioms of feminist film theory I was immersed in at the time, it also in a contemporary sense points to what cultural theorist Sianne Ngai, in her newest book, calls for in taking seriously and exploring at length the "theory of the gimmick." The necessity of that theorization of such gimmickry on the part of Wishman seems especially pertinent, particularly when it sits at the crosshairs of women's film history, feminist theory, and cinema as capitalist commodity.

While theorizing the Wishman gimmick and arguing out the theoretical heft of her imaginative rejigging of looking relations, regrettably the film's specific historical textures, classed materiality and aesthetic peculiarities are below given less space. Re-watching the film in 2020, it is clear that Double Agent 73 is a much stranger text—aesthetically and performatively—than the account here relays. I would write about the film very differently today, as the film's particular compositional and editorial madness and maudit-lumpen charm emits from a genuine pleasure taken in the working with (sometimes limited) materials. The one-two punch of the film rests also in its very economical editorial arrangement, and use of Wishman's common post-synch dubbing, in which voices rarely coincide with faces speaking the words we hear, creating a slightly hypnagogic feeling of delayed transmission and subterfuge—the relation between shots like a strange game of "telephone." Coupled with the bruteness and unabashed mobility of the camera and zoom lens, Morgan's performance floats somewhere between an arrested, stunned presence and a world-weariness. The outré decor and Wishman's predilection for clashing patterns of wallpaper and Morgan's polyester suits, the vinyl platform footwear and kitsch glassware, such as a steaming ceramic pipe used for one hit-job, all force a toggling of attention between mise-en-scène and action, between banality and hyperbole. Morgan's body, stressed by gravity, bidden to perform, also exacts a quality of fatigued performance, even as the plot's hydraulics moves her improbably from nightclubs to living rooms to speeding cars to parking lots and bathrooms, all organized by the necessity of that flash of the hidden camera by the breast, mobilized and exposed, and the accumulation of the clicks that will document the scene of her labor (professional seduction and snuffing out), proof of work successfully completed for an exacting price. The woozy point-of-view shots of Jane's victims as they are deposed in the face of her corporeal exposure bestow the film with the contradictory tremors of sexual plenitude and mortal danger.

Many forms of time-shifting and anachronism permeate this re-presentation and re-evaluation of Doris Wishman. Not least there is the disjunction between 1980s and 1990s feminist theoretical claims about cinematic representation against the counter-example of Wishman's production twenty years prior in the 1960s and 1970s, as well as in the belated recirculation and recovery of Wishman as a previously unknown underground auteur, in the late 1980s and 1990s and up to the present. It is fitting then that such belatedness also attends the republication of this essay, which attests to how much more work there is still to be done on Doris Wishman and her films, a call to which this edited collection represents one abundant reply.

*

THE BODY AS APPARATUS: DORIS WISHMAN'S *DOUBLE AGENT 73*

> The simple gesture of directing a camera toward a woman has become the equivalent of a terrorist act.
>
> —Mary Ann Doane[2]

Written in 1981, Mary Ann Doane's articulation of the difficulties of a feminist film practice in light of the "impossibility" of representing the female body can serve as an interesting point of departure for a discussion of exploitation film, particularly in the work of director Doris Wishman. In the male-dominated world of exploitation film in the 1960s and 1970s, Wishman was a prolific and active producer of grindhouse fare, making thirty feature films across her career, such as *Nude on the Moon*, *Bad Girls Go to Hell*, *Deadly Weapons*, *The Amazing Transplant*, and *Let Me Die A Woman*, among others. Wishman's identifiable and distinct "female signature" and attention to the gendered and sexed body can be read to operate within a mode of production which appears explicitly overdetermined by its content: largely sensational, hyperbolic, and sexualized in nature. Wishman partook of all of the variegated cycles of exploitation, the nudist camp film, the roughie, the kinky, as well as venturing into the body horror film and the pseudo-documentary.

Wishman's film *Double Agent 73* (1974), which utilizes the female body as a conceptual prop as well as its primary material, can offer feminist film theory an alternative route for theorizing the feminine in relation to spectatorial pleasure. Routed through an analysis of Wishman's film, Doane's provocative statement requires a number of questions posed to it: whose rhetorical "terrorism"? What is the terrorism in service of? And whom does this terrorism address? Wishman not only directs a camera toward the body of her star, burlesque performer, Chesty Morgan (stage name of Liliana Wilczkowska), but directs a camera "inside" her star via a critical plot device: a camera implanted in the breast of the spy Jane, the "Double Agent 73" referring to her measurements. The camera is also revealed to be a bomb and will detonate if Jane does not complete her mission in time. The two gestures of Wishman's direction can be conceived as co-extensive; the interiorized camera facilitates and reinforces the cinematic gaze, which fixes on the excessive body of Morgan with the knowledge of what that body "contains."

While the "invasion" of bodies by foreign elements, be they alien or technological, is largely the domain of science fiction, *Double Agent 73* is located loosely within the genre of detective, crime, and spy films as channeled by 1970s sexploitation filmmaking. The plot device and gimmick of the surgically implanted camera in the breast of its endowed star is significant in how it plays with the traditions of the woman's body as a site of inscription, using the logic of entry into the bodily interior to install an imaging technology. The breast-camera, reconfigured into photographic device and veritable weapon, inverts the logic and meanings of medical imaging technologies which aim to diagnose via an inspection and epistemological capture of hidden, invisible organs. Instead, the body's interiority is employed to investigate, survey, and taxonomize the outer world. Morgan's body becomes an empirical and technical site of evidence gathering, as the installation of mechanical memory, via photography, records the faces of the secret agent's victims. Wishman also hyperbolizes the gimmick of Morgan's eroticized body as appeal to the sexploitation public, as Jane must of course undress each time in order to take a picture.

Wishman's exploitation premise, which ostensibly invites a voyeuristic, patriarchally inflected spectatorship, also has immense ramifications for conceiving of the body as a photographic mechanism. Wishman's ingenious gimmick posits double agent Jane's body not merely as a surface for the inscription of the phallocratic order, but as a technology which itself inscribes, records, and performs an epistemology of its "victims." The problematics and complexities of Wishman's deployment of the woman's body—as seductive tool, as reproductive instrument, as photographic apparatus—seems to re-enact, yet trouble, the division explored by psychoanalytic feminist film theory, which posits the woman as entirely outside of discourse, exterior to language, given access to it only through a mimetic function. Doane comments on Parveen Adams's negotiation of the difference between the girl and the boy in relation to the phallus in Lacanian theory:

> For it is clear that what is being suggested is that the boy's body provides an access to the processes of representation while the girl's body does not. From this perspective, a certain slippage can then take place, by means of which the female body becomes an absolute tabula rasa of sorts: anything and everything can be written on it. Or, more accurately, perhaps, the male body comes fully equipped with a binary opposition—penis/no penis, presence/absence, phonemic opposition—while the female body is constituted as "noise," an undifferentiated presence which always threatens to disrupt representation.[3]

The antagonisms set up between the female body and the field of representation imply the gendering of representation in favor of the male. *Double Agent 73* pressures this presumption into a confrontation between the "undifferentiated presence" of Chesty Morgan as the spy Jane, materialized in the object of her breasts, and the invisible camera, which is signified by the *exposure*, in both senses of the term, of the breasts against her assailants and victims. The "terrorism" of wielding a camera, in Doane's meaning, is doubled, collapsing the gaze with its object. Photography becomes a trope by extension, operating as technological antecedent as well as self-reflexive foil to the cinematic apparatus itself. The photographic act—Jane's given task to identify, ensnare, and kill her targets and then take their picture with the breast-camera—is set in dialogue within the diegesis and conceptually with the cinematic mechanism.

Wishman reimagines the operations of the woman's body as a figure for cinema's work, and she offers an object of examination of how that body is subject to the intersecting operations and demands of exploitation cinema as it rewrites the precepts of the cinematic apparatus, as routed through a history of psychoanalytically inflected feminist film theory. *Double Agent 73* thus presents an alternative within what Gaylyn Studlar describes as a "masochistic heterocosm,"[4] in its theorization of image-making through the represented female body and its address to an exploitation spectator. The fractious act of "terrorism" in representing the female body in *Double Agent 73* can be reassessed within the context of a discussion of masochistic cinematic spectatorship. Wishman's film proffers an alternative model of "body as apparatus," in a body that in turn "terrorizes" the spectator, within the masochistic contract of cinema's "pleasure of unpleasure,"[5] as articulated by Studlar and to be discussed in greater depth below.

The viewing structures and presumptions of exploitation cinema need to be explored as the groundwork for an analysis of Wishman's film. In the oppositions set between mainstream Hollywood cinema and a feminist, or anti-realist avant-garde, feminist film theory had largely neglected addressing the potentialities of an exploitation cinema, whose gimmicks, contrived narratives, and low-budget productions contravene conventions of aesthetics and social respectability. Yet just as the genre of pornography has proven crucial for an understanding of the figuration of women within representational modes, epistemological structures, and cinematic discourses, so too exploitation, particularly in its lack of accountability to the traditions and conventions of Hollywood cinema and the aesthetic dispositions and ambiguities of an art cinema, provides a different way to theorize "woman as image" outside of narrow determinisms. Pam Cook was one of the few feminist film theorists to write about women directors in exploitation, such as Stephanie Rothman. Cook followed Noel Burch's argument about films made before 1919, remarking that,

> instead of inferior products which fail to conform to the classic ideal, these films can be seen as evidence of what might have been, offering alternatives to the representational system that became dominant, and opening up the possibility of saying something different.[6]

The implicit analogy to the operations of exploitation allows an avenue for investigating alternative histories of the gendered cinematic body: exploitation cinema's reliance on sensation, corporeality, and transgression, the films' aggressive marketing strategies, the mode's commodification of sexualized and violent themes to sell the film to distributors and audiences, are indelibly linked to its mode of address and the ways its spectatorship is constructed. Paul Watson comments on the genre of exploitation as an economic one: "Exploitation cinema is a convenient category in which aesthetic and formal considerations organized with capital investment/assets so as to ensure that their economic potential will be utilized to maximum effect."[7]

Wishman, proud proponent of the exploitation gimmick, utilized the image of her star, performer Chesty Morgan, and instrumentalized her breast size, seventy-three inches, as the basis of her promotional strategy, following on from the success of her prior film with Morgan, which bore a similar premise, *Deadly Weapons* (1974). In the latter film, Morgan's character seeks to avenge the death of her fiancé. Finding a criminal network who is responsible, she smothers each of the gang with her breasts, until she discovers that the leader of the ring is her father. Morgan, as Jane, "Double Agent 73," is a spy who has a camera implanted in her breast by her boss, as a way to identify the leader, Toplar, of a heroin-smuggling ring. Jane must infiltrate the ring and identify each member, which she does through subterfuge and seduction. One might object that Wishman's cinema is in fact disqualified from feminist attention, due to its trafficking in masculinist strategies of figuring the female body. However, this view is complicated if we consider how exploitation, *pace* Cook, was the available terrain for a woman like Wishman for making film in this historical moment and must be seen as the enabling ground for her circumvention of the codes of its formula. The gendered presupposition which literalizes the representational economy of women as commodified objects of exchange is destabilized by Wishman's lens.

Wishman's cinema at this moment had entered into the period of what Michael Bowen has called her "films of somatic betrayal," in which the body rebels or rejects its containment, or rejects the body's "owner." Writing about *Double Agent 73*, Bowen notes that in contrast to Wishman's earlier films of the 1960s, in which fetishization ensnares women as its object, here a model of sexual danger emerges in which "fetishization no longer kills its objects; it now kills its consumers, often with 'hysterical' results."[8] Wishman's reduplication of the mode's corporeal "attraction" acknowledges the fetishistic aspects of cinematic spectatorship and inverts them. The fetish of the breast is displaced from the breast itself to the fact of the presence of the camera and the photographic process. But the question is, what sort of fetish? I point to the dominance of a masochistic one, following on from the theorization of Gaylyn Studlar, in which, rather than the penis, the source of fetishism is in primary identification with the pre-Oedipal mother's body.[9]

Every revelation of Jane's breasts is a simultaneous acknowledgment of the masochistic spectator, a knowledge enacted by the reflective function of the *invisible* camera, signified by the eminent *visibility* of the breasts. Subsequently, there are actually three modes of referentiality to the woman "being seen" and "seeing": in the structure of exploitation cinema which presumes a sensational object, in the appearance of Morgan's body itself—a perceived "excess" which "calls attention to itself"—and in the knowledge of the fictional device, the presence of the camera, which redoubles the look of the audience.

Exploitation's identity as a genre which by economic necessity operates on a logic of attraction and the spectacular is dependent on the desire of the audience, a desire that must be produced before any films are actually shown, through marketing and promotion. Pam Cook notes that "much of the pleasure—and success—of exploitation films derives from the way they play on audience expectations of authorship and genre."[10] This manipulation of expectations is crucial to a feminist reading of Wishman's film, in that the institutional production of desire and acknowledgment of that production denaturalizes certain processes of gendered spectatorship.

Paul Watson terms this the "foreknowledge of spectacle," in which "the promotional drama itself provides a cultural text that invariably exceeds and outlives the movie it prefigures."[11] In the same sense, the gimmick of Morgan's body and optic breast, as an idea, as a *theoretical* object, has great potency as a springboard for feminist film theory's adjudication of sexual difference. The implicit critique of representation in *Double Agent 73* is inextricable from, and contingent on, Chesty Morgan's *oversignifying* body. Doane's call to consider the female body outside of divisive debates on essentialism is useful here; she incisively states:

> Both positions (essentialist and anti-essentialist) deny the necessity of posing a complex relation between the body and the psychic/signifying process, of using the body, in effect as a "prop." For Kristeva is right— the positing of a body *is* a condition of discursive practices . . . the stake does not simply concern an isolated image of the body. The attempt to "lean" on the body in order to formulate the woman's different relation to speech, to language, clarifies the fact that what is at stake is, rather, the syntax which constitutes the female body as a term.[12]

Doane stresses the importance of a syntax, which creates the body as a term within discourse and representation, in favor of focalization on a single image. Wishman's elaboration, in *Double Agent 73*, on the question of representational technology as an inclusion into the female body, in effect, creates a largely masochistic syntax. Although Wishman's place within a male-dominated field proscribes limitations on her films' structural and generic organization, *Double*

Agent 73, in its dizzying and insistent hand-held close-up shots, in its dulling, deracinating focus on Morgan's cleavage as subjective landscape—analogous to the facial close-up—provides a syntax which interrogates and threatens the spectatorial pleasure which it presumes to simultaneously appease. Morgan's body *as* apparatus, as screen, defines the parameters of the film's syntax. Wishman's film stages a conflict between Doane's position in which woman's acquisition of language is unclearly demarcated, and Studlar, who questions the validity of such a mystification.[13]

I would like to look more closely at the syntactical patterns through which Chesty Morgan's body, as Jane as "Double Agent 73," is presented to the spectator. Her excessive corporeality, marked by the size of her breasts which consistently erupt and destabilize the image, is a source for obsessive fixation by Wishman's camera, almost to the point of a reflexive disjunction. This excess is sanctioned by, conditional to, the masochistic context. The use of the close-up is obligatory, serving as a seizing, a punctuation of the film text, functioning to bring the spectator into a closer relation with Jane's body. The close-up is not reserved for Jane's body alone, however, but fixates on hands, phones, feet, and surfaces, seemingly a synesthetic, tactile rendering of the material environs of the diegesis.

The close-up is most striking when Jane's face is conflated or set in an associational relay with her breasts. The breasts attain a state of faciality, become subjectified through their visibility and the absent presence of the camera. In the hospital scene, Jane is lying down, having just gone through the surgery which has implanted the camera; a fast cut to a close-up of her exhausted face, which is heavily daubed with makeup, cuts again, to focus in on her post-operative bare breasts, on which a small bandage appears. This synecdochical relationship between the breasts and the face (and of the breasts and the body) has a number of implications. Within film criticism, the close-up has a history of phenomenological and epistemological articulations. The facial close-up, for a classic theorist such as Jean Epstein, was a prime example of *photogenie*, which has been interpreted by contemporary theorists such as Paul Willemen as a "lost object." Willemen writes,

> *Photogenie*, then refers to the unspeakable within the relation of looking and operates through the activation of a fantasy in the viewer which he or she refuses to verbalize. In this sense, it requires a viewer's complicity in refusing—as if refusal were sufficient to obliterate it—the fall into symbolic signification (language) and the corresponding privileging of a nostalgia for the pre-symbolic when "communication" was possible without language in a process of symbiosis with the mother. A trace of this nostalgia for the psychotic existence of pre-Oedipal childhood (that is for utopia) can be read from the way in which the term

"soul" is mobilized in these writings: the souls of the cinema and of the viewer are supposed to be able to "fuse" in a wordless interaction when divested of the inevitable material encumbrances inherent in any process of signification.[14]

Willemen's remarks are suggestive, despite his avoidance of the fact that the close-up is most often "embodied" by a woman's face. The effect of regression to the pre-Oedipal and the fusion of viewer and screen resemble the theorization of the "dream screen," elaborated by Robert Eberwein and taken up by Gaylyn Studlar, in which the cinematic apparatus produces a "cine-subject" that submits to the uncontrollable images on screen. I will resume a discussion of this notion of the dream screen in its relation to Jane's optic breasts later in this essay.

But, returning to the close-up and the effect of "reality" it induces, it is necessary to note Doane's analysis of the close-up; she comments that the face which appears as pure surface also belies a depth, and refers to Roland Barthes's "reading" of Garbo's face:

> Garbo still belongs to that moment in cinema . . . when one literally lost oneself in a human image as one would in a philtre, when the face represented a kind of absolute state of the flesh, which could neither be reached nor renounced.[15]

The conjunction of perception at the site of the flesh and the repetition of Willemen's observation of an impulse toward fusion returns us to the dialogic relation set up between Jane's face and breasts. The face as a site for the emotive and the performance of subjectivity enacts a series of exchanges with the breast. Getting "lost" in the close-up face seems literalized by the absolute presence of Jane's breasts. If anything, the breasts, implanted with the camera, further complicate the slippages between depth and surface that the facial close-up invokes.

If Doane's statement that "the face, more than any other bodily part, is *for* the other . . . mute without the other's reading" is applied to Jane's face, how does one account for the obsessive fetishization of the breasts? The subjectification of Jane's breasts through close-ups that ally them with the face, and the focus on Jane's breasts in reaction shots at key moments of tension, seems to imply an unreciprocated gaze, a cinematic body looking, activated by the knowledge of the interiorized camera. The implication is that the breast cannot be read, contained, fragmented, because it is also an agent of looking. The breast is usually not read at all as a face is but is an instrument of male erotic cathexis. The camera's assumption of a close-up, of closeness and proximity to the female body—as a way to access the body and appease the exploitation spectator—is too close for the spectator; it removes the "objectivity" of distance. For the closeness of the breast as representational technology implies its identification of the diegetic victim and the cinematic spectator. Morgan's body is not the object of an investigative epistemology, rather the breast is gathering evidence, and the look at the breasts is an inquiry into that invisible process, the impossible made possible through the mutability of the gimmick. In this way the breast *collects* the look. Thus, the status of Morgan's screen image as surface comes into question, as the materiality of her body and the aesthetic of close-ups forces a closeness onto the cinematic spectator which does not allow the spectator the agency of distance or objectification. The two cameras have performed it within the text for the spectator, presumptive of the desire for a "fusion" with the "ultimate flesh" of the female image, a flesh which exceeds the face.

Furthermore, it seems that such "closeness," denied by Doane as an untenable position for feminist film theory to assume, is a source of potency and imposition in *Double Agent 73*. In "Masquerade Reconsidered," Doane writes that

> to embrace and affirm the definition of femininity as closeness, immediacy, or proximity-to-self is to accept one's disempowerment in the cultural arena, to accept the idea that women are outside of language. To investigate this matter as an idea, with a certain cultural effectivity, is another matter altogether.[16]

Jane's body, in its closeness and enforced proximity to the spectator, is such an idea, and furthermore a *tactic*; not a positing of essence or a definition of femininity in a fixed position. The close-up, which imposes this closeness, is a representational strategy, in league with Studlar's delineation of masochistic spectatorship, which attempts to reclaim a fusion, a symbiosis with the abundant mother of the oral phase.[17] The figure of Jane, as maternal imago, manipulates the spectator, particularly via her fetishized implant, the invisible camera which can be seen as a disavowal of the father and of sexual difference via the attribution of a "phallic fetish" to the mother, "the child's attempt to create the mother as the ideal hermaphroditic parent."[18]

But what of this fusion? How do the notions of *photogenie*, the dream screen, and masochism coalesce at the site/sight of Chesty Morgan's photographing body? I would argue that Jane, as a cinematic mechanism, induces in her spectators/victims the effect of the apparatus, as instated by Jean Louis Baudry in his essay "The Apparatus": Baudry writes, "the cinematic apparatus brings about a state of artificial regression."[19] Studlar elaborates on Baudry's model of cinematic experience to promote the rendering of cinematic spectatorship as having masochistic qualities that challenge gendered viewing positions. The redeployment of the "dream screen," as a regression to "oral phase pleasures," aligns to the contractual structures by which the spectator submits to the film image. The originary site for desire is located at the state of unity with the mother's breast:

> The imaginary visual fusion with the cinematic dream screen results in a loss of ego boundaries analogous to the child's pre-sleep fusion with the breast . . . the spectatorial position duplicates the infant's passive, dependent position. The viewer like the masochist and the dreamer, adopts the "formless body image of the infant" and the feeling of animistic omnipotence that accompanies the infant's sense of oneness with the mother . . . The dream screen offers bliss but threatens obliteration of self as separate entity.[20]

Therefore, Jane can be seen as dream screen simultaneously for the actual audience, for the narrative victims, and for the audience identifying through the point of view of the victims. In a number of places in the film, Jane's breasts are rendered as surfaces through superimposition of other images onto her body. The first instance is when the surgery is being allegorically performed; the image of surgical implements and their tray is placed directly over her breasts, as her boss's voice indicates the assignment's demands. The overlayed image is incredibly suggestive in the relation between the dream screen and the speculatively sexuated status which the implanted camera affords for Jane. Jane's boss is also implicated as a masochistic spectator, the child who tries to create the mother as "hermaphroditic parent" in the psychoanalytic schema. The conflict between symbiosis and separation is staged through the employer as well; the camera in her breast simultaneously necessitates separation, via the assignment, and symbiosis, through the time ultimatum and her necessary return before the camera explodes.

Consequently, Jane's body and breasts are complicated by the inclusion of the camera in her body; on this level, she cannot be seen as a screen, a surface for projection, but must be acknowledged as a projective technology that arrests, and captures images, images that necessitate their own surface. Perhaps this is why the violence of her assaults is figured specifically in the figured loss of consciousness and even death for her victims. Jane enacts the "punishing mother" and the danger of separation. The imposition of a self, through the identifying practice of the photograph, brings Jane's body close to her victims and then necessitates the fatal separation. Death is signified through both symbiosis with and separation from Jane's maternal breast-camera.

Double Agent 73, and the seeing body at its center, literalizes the fishing joke put upon Jacques Lacan, recounted in his *Four Fundamental Concepts of Psychoanalysis*: out on a fishing expedition, young Lacan is hailed by one of the crew on his boat, who is pointing to an indistinguishable object in the water, "You see that? You see that can? Well it doesn't see you." Lacan concludes the opposite, that the sparkling reflection of the can did indeed see him, and that from its perspective, "I, at that moment . . . looked like nothing on earth. In short I was rather out of place in the picture."[21] The othered object is given the privilege of excluding and subjectifying Lacan only when the fact of his being sighted and seen is in question. Once the can sees, it must see the subject in order to put his existence and coherence into question. Similarly, the body of Jane is figured as the object that has been infused with a monstrous, troubling vision, given the power to dispel the epistemological certainty of the spectating self.

The term "victim" takes on an ironic tone within the context of a cinematic spectatorship that is masochistic; as Studlar indicates, "the cinematic dream screen defines the spectator through looking, just as the infant is defined by the mother's look."[22] The "owner" of the look, in Studlar's transposition from cinema to the oral phase, moves from the spectator's look to the mother's look; their relation is not one of gendered hierarchization but of mutual dependence, reciprocity tempered by the pleasurable punishment of the child/spectator.

Formally, Jane's assault of suspects operates within a consistent pattern of shots, in which the confrontation of the male subject with her corporeality effects a regressive move from the Oedipal to the pre-Oedipal. The initial implantation of the camera is contingent on Jane's sexual and bodily difference, both marked by her huge breasts; the implanted camera will work dependent on the seduction, Jane "using her own body as a disguise,"[23] the premise of the "Double Agent" moniker. A spy negotiates through modes of invisibility; yet here her role of spy depends on her being "seen" as sexed body, the seen objects, her breasts, luring her victim into a passive position in which she can trigger the camera. The camera passes as a woman, wearing the veil of her body in order to justify its function. Jane passes as a conventional exploitation actress. The pre-Oedipal supplants the Oedipal in a regressive shift away from sexuation.

The pre-Oedipal regression allows a momentary "forgetting" of Jane's sexual difference in favor of her image as an abundant, punishing mother. The passive position taken by her diegetic victims always involves a blurring of vision as if a hallucination or a falling into sleep; Jane drugs her victims through the application of poison or smoke, and on some occasions the method is choking. At these moments, we see Jane through the point of view of the victims; the actual cinematic spectator and the diegetic spectator to Jane are conflated in this point-of-view shot. *Double Agent 73* visualizes this condition of the masochistic spectator through formal devices which employ close-ups and zoom-ins, which assail the viewer with images of Jane's breasts as disembodied, floating forms, taking up the entire screen. In other scenes, however, where the spy is not in "terrorizing" photographic mode, the zoom-in on her breasts attempts to prescribe their stability and faciality. In these instances, the breasts appear unmoored, given an agency that seems to evade the frame itself.

The references to fusion with the image all imply a location in the pre-Oedipal, sexually undifferentiated position of infant nursing.

When Jane, standing with her breasts exposed, is ready to photograph her subjects, the cinematic audience sees her from below, as she looks down imperiously on the spectator. She lifts the left, activated breast to shoot; as the sound of the flash goes off, we see not a flash emanating from her direction, but a flash of the film itself, which registers the event with a blanking of the film screen, intermittently obliterating the image and the spectator's vision, puncturing the diegesis. The responsive quality of the framing cinema to the narrativized invisible camera in Jane's breast seems to acknowledge the assaultive power of such a technology and its threat to cinematic representation itself. This is frequently followed by a dematerializing blurring of the image from the victim's perspective staring at the hovering flesh of the breast that circulates over them. The point at which the victim, our point-of-view shot, loses consciousness or dies is the point at which the actual spectator is assailed and the framing apparatus that contains the narrative renders a fissure.

The collapse of the female body onto the cinematic apparatus can only be sustained for a limited time. The narrative's use of the deadline-producing explosive device, a precautionary measure, is employed by the boss, who cannot allow Jane's excessive body to incorporate the photographic technology. Or rather, he cannot allow the camera to replace him. At the climax, the boss states that "she is better off dead" than in the hands of Toplar, belied by the fact that Toplar in the film's narrative is revealed to be Jane's lover, to her dismay. As a reproductive device, the camera threatens to eliminate the child/spectator who has fantasized the impossible "hermaphroditic parent" of psychoanalytic models of pre-Oedipal desire. In *Double Agent 73*, how the *reproductive* mechanism serves in relation to the oral mother's body is ambivalent.

If the phallus is attributable to the camera inside the spy's breast, what of the penis? Feminist theory's contestation over the distanciation of the phallus from the penis in Lacanian psychoanalysis is crucial here, as it exposes the ambivalence between phallic power and the attributions of embodiment. This ambiguous function is also complicated by the terms of an exploitation cinema which makes such psycho-sexual investments overt rather than covert in the mode's narrative design. The instability of the phallus discussed by Mary Ann Doane, as referential to the figure of the masculine, explains the cohabitation of the camera as tool of phallic inscription and the breast, the dream screen on which the inscription and imprinting occurs. However, if the phallus, the camera, must be veiled, what of the veil itself? Following the logic of Doane's argument in "Veiling Over Desire," Wishman's film indicates that woman is not only the "substrate of representation,"[24] but that it is also possible that *representation is the substrate of woman*. If the veil is not a concealment of the female body, but the body itself, rendering itself more than visible, and gesturing to the photographic phallic fetish, the fetish of representation that resides within, then Wishman is orchestrating a radical critique of gendered spectatorship and the cinematic apparatus. The body has no essence beyond the ministrations of technology and epistemology upon it and through it.

The coalescence of two misplaced fetishes, Jane acquires the potency of mutable and split sexual morphologies. The role of sexual difference within the pre-Oedipal needs to be questioned further, for it seems to reach an impasse at the locus of Jane's body in relation to the child/spectator who seeks union. The necessary removal of the camera necessitated by the narrative would imply that within conventional social codes, the camera is attributed to and an instrument of phallic power, and must be wrested from its possible usurpation and incorporation by the woman. The camera must thus also be a bomb when a woman wields it. But the essentialism that undergirds this claim points to an impossible, if not false condition, in which gender characterizes the reproductive medium of photography. Wishman's cinema speaks to the limits of linking essence, representation, and gender in ascribing the photographic (and cinematic) apparatus. Yet if the "phallus is a fraud" and "can only take up its place by indicating the precariousness of any identity assumed by the subject,"[25] as Jacqueline Rose states, Wishman's film underscores this failure of the camera/phallus *tout court*. The camera will always explode.

Desire for the phallus which lies beyond Jane's flesh renders the transparency of power and subjection through spectatorship, a desire for the reproductive mechanism of power itself, beyond gender but ambiguously sexed. Wavering between the pre-Oedipal and the Oedipal, between the phantasmatic "hermaphroditic mother" and the uncertainty of having the phallus, the spectator of *Double Agent 73* registers the instability of pleasure around the site of sexual difference. It would seem that this is a belated process of regression, in which castration anxiety is effaced by the return to the undifferentiated, polymorphic sexuality of the pre-Oedipal parent, the *mother with a difference*, a place where nothing seems lost or separated. Desire and fetishization of the representational device seems patently naive, a dependence on fixity which is truly fictional, and always on the threshold of death.

In conclusion, the exploitation gimmick, in conjuncture with this bodily technology, embodied by Liliana Wilczkowska as Chesty Morgan as Jane as Double Agent 73, produces a heterocosm, which aligns itself with a reading of the text as masochistic in form. Studlar deploys the heterocosm as an emblematic space for the masochistic aesthetic of Joseph von Sternberg's films with Marlene Dietrich. Studlar quotes Harry Berger, Jr. on the heterocosmic painting to establish its terms: "the imaginary world is both disjunctive and hypothetical. It is not real life but art or artifice . . . a new and very different world created by the mind." Furthermore, Studlar claims that "verisimilitude is not the goal of the masochistic heterocosm."[26]

In *Double Agent 73*, the non-verisimilar masochistic heterocosm is a condition of possibility engendered by the preposterous, hothouse conventions of exploitation cinema, furthered by the reconfiguration of Jane's body by Wishman's narrative design. Her body, already hyperbolic in its appearance, her corporeality defined by the size of her breasts, and their ascription to a function which refracts the gaze, positions her in a place marked as fantastical. Jane is not "representative"; the specific materiality of her body and her corporeal difference counters her ability both to stand in for "all women" and to be idealized as perfect object. Although she "symbolizes" the pre-Oedipal maternal figure, it is not a universal motherhood but a specific version of the mother that is deployed strategically. Yet the heterocosm has its limits as an explanatory engine which contains the strategies of the film, and it can be critiqued as an unremittingly fantastic, utopian space sealed off from historical representation. Jane's body, in its specific embodiment, serves not only to maintain but to dispel the masochistic heterocosm; though not "representative" of the "average woman," her body becomes a representational technology, its materiality and multiple functions "convey[ing] more than it intends." As an instantiation of the real, her body both precedes and follows representation.[27] While the heterocosm violently disavows "reality," and the excessive real of the oversignifying returns us to materiality, both allow a space for a theoretical working out, a place to negotiate the conditions and technologies of representation and potentialities of the filmed female body.

Finally, the mention of strategies returns us to the notion of terrorism, which in the epigraph by Mary Ann Doane is used to point to a certain crisis in the representation of woman and of woman as representational subject for women filmmakers, and specifically feminist filmmakers. Terrorism explicitly presents as violence addressed inevitably toward women. In light of the "aggressive" and transgressive images of women so popular in exploitation, the question of "terrorism's" address becomes important. Doris Wishman's filming of the female body can be said to "terrorize," particularly within structures of masochistic spectatorship and codes of exploitation cinema. *Double Agent 73* complicates the position of women both in front of and behind the camera, and within the cinematic space itself. Doane herself comes to the conclusion that women cannot remain *unrepresentable*. In Wishman's cinema, women's representability is a material necessity but also a terrain for insurrection.

ACKNOWLEDGMENT

This is a slightly revised version of a chapter that originally appeared in *Unruly Pleasures: The Cult Film and Its Critics*, ed. Graeme Harper and Xavier Mendik (Godalming: FAB Press, 2000), 155–69.

NOTES

1. Sianne Ngai, *Theory of the Gimmick: Aesthetic Judgement and Capitalist Form* (Cambridge, MA: Harvard University Press, 2020).
2. Mary Ann Doane, "Woman's Stake: Filming the Female Body," in *Feminism and Film Theory*, ed. Constance Penley (New York: Routledge, 1988), 216.
3. Ibid., 221.
4. Gaylyn Studlar elaborates on the "masochistic heterocosm" of Joseph von Sternberg's films with Marlene Dietrich, in *In the Realm of Pleasure: Von Sternberg, Dietrich, and the Masochistic Aesthetic* (New York: Columbia University Press, 1988), 85–108.
5. Ibid., 192.
6. Pam Cook, "The Art of Exploitation, or How to Get into the Movies," *Monthly Film Bulletin* 52, no. 623 (December 1985): 367.
7. Paul Watson, "There's No Accounting for Taste: Exploitation Cinema and the Limits of Film Theory," in *Trash Aesthetics: Popular Culture and Its Audience*, ed. Deborah Cartmell (London: Pluto Press, 1997), 75.
8. Michael J. Bowen, "Embodiment and Realization: The Many Film-Bodies of Doris Wishman," *Wide Angle* 19, no. 3 (July 1997): 82.
9. Studlar, *In the Realm of Pleasure*, 42.
10. Cook, "The Art of Exploitation," 367.
11. Watson, "There's No Accounting for Taste," 79.
12. Doane, "Woman's Stake," 226.
13. Studlar, *In the Realm of Pleasure*, 32.
14. Paul Willemen, *Looks and Frictions: Essays in Cultural Studies and Film Theory* (Bloomington: Indiana University Press, 1994), 129.
15. Roland Barthes quoted in Mary Ann Doane, *Femmes Fatales: Feminism, Film Theory Psychoanalysis* (New York: Routledge, 1991), 47.
16. Doane, *Femmes Fatales*, 37.
17. Studlar, *In the Realm of Pleasure*, 43.
18. Ibid., 40.
19. Jean Louis Baudry, "The Apparatus: Metapsychological Approaches to the Impression of Reality in the Cinema," in *Film Theory and Criticism*, ed. Gerald Mast, Marshall Cohen, and Leo Braudy (New York: Oxford University Press, 1992), 703.
20. Studlar, *In the Realm of Pleasure*, 186, 187.
21. Jacques Lacan, *The Four Fundamental Concepts of Psycho-Analysis*, ed. Jacques-Alain Miller, trans. Alan Sheridan (London: Hogarth Press, 1977), 95–6.
22. Studlar, *In the Realm of Pleasure* , 188.
23. Michele Montrealy quoted in Doane, *Femmes Fatales*, 26.
24. Doane, *Femme Fatales*, 73.
25. Jacqueline Rose, "Introduction II," in *Feminine Sexuality: Jacques Lacan and the Ecole Freudienne*, ed. Juliet Mitchell and Jacqueline Rose, trans. Jacqueline Rose (New York: W. W. Norton, 1982), 40.
26. Studlar, *In the Realm of Pleasure*, 91, 93.
27. Peggy Phelan, *Unmarked: The Politics of Performance* (New York and London: Routledge, 1996), 2.

CHAPTER 2

The Girls in the Mirror: Women's Horror Filmmaking and Doris Wishman's *Each Time I Kill*

Alexandra Heller-Nicholas

Two years before Doris Wishman passed away from lymphoma at the age of ninety in 2002, *Spin Magazine*'s Joy Williams described in a feature article running around Florida's Coconut Grove from video store to video store with the filmmaker as they tried to access a machine to play a tape of Wishman's early film, *Hideout in the Sun* (1960). Clearly impressed with the octogenarian's energy, Williams implied some surprise that Wishman was "quite spry and seemingly indefatigable,"[1] words that describe with coincidental precision the sheer energy that drives Wishman's final film, *Each Time I Kill*. Completed and released posthumously in 2007, *Each Time I Kill* was Wishman's second horror film after 1983's *A Night to Dismember*, the last commercially distributed film in her lifetime despite making the later features *Satan Was a Lady* (2001) and *Dildo Heaven* (2002) before turning her attentions to her final film.[2] According to Christopher J. Jarmick, almost all of the principal photography for *Each Time I Kill*—shot in Miami and Coral Gables—ended in June 2002, just as the severity of Wishman's medical condition was becoming clear. In the two months between the end of filming and her death, she simultaneously endured chemotherapy and provided detailed feedback on how the film was to be finished after her passing, leaving notes when she lost the ability to speak for people including her biographer Michael Bowen, who also co-produced the final film.[3]

While Wishman has at times been considered as both an ally and an adversary to what is typically deemed to be "feminist" concerns, this chapter examines *Each Time I Kill* in specific relation to the similarities it shares with a number of other U.S. women-directed horror films that bookended it, *Mirror Mirror* (Marina Sargenti, 1990) and *The Dorm* (Rachel Talalay, 2014). These films are united by a striking central focus on female subjectivity, expressed in each case most powerfully through their outsider-girl protagonist's conversations with their own reflections, revealing the trauma and pressure each character faces in her respective film's narrative. Across these films, Wishman joins a community of women horror filmmakers whose concerns and relationship to genre manifest in *Each Time I Kill* specifically, regardless of whether these movies—or filmmakers—self-define as "feminist" or not. As I conclude, the shared focus in these films on identity, alienation, and femininity are powerful (although not wholly optimistic) interrogations on the pressures facing girls to live up to perceived expectations of what being an idealized young woman means, feels, and looks like.

Although *A Night to Dismember* and *Each Time I Kill* are technically Wishman's two most immediately recognizable horror features, monstrosity and violence permeated many of her earlier works. Most immediately are her roughies—*Bad Girls Go to Hell* (1964), *My Brother's Wife* (1966), and *Indecent Desires* (1968)—a grindhouse category defined by Mike Watt as "ill-tempered 'nudies,' with an equal amount of violence and sex throughout the running time."[4] Additionally, *The Amazing Transplant* (1970) foreshadowed the body-part swap horror that lies at the narrative core of *Each Time I Kill*. It follows protagonist Arthur Balen (Juan Fernandez) who blackmails a doctor to transplant the much-larger penis of his friend Felix to his own body after Felix's death, not knowing Felix's predilection for violence. Arthur is effectively possessed by Felix's manhood as it drives him to rape and murder women when triggered by the sight of gold earrings, Felix's personal kink. *The Amazing Transplant* and *Each Time I Kill* clearly differ in many ways, perhaps most notably in the striking centrality of female subjectivity in the latter. As Tania Modleski suggests, although there are some flashbacks to the rape survivor's experiences in *The Amazing Transplant*, the film as a whole is told from a male perspective.[5] And while a female character lies at the heart of Wishman's two collaborations with Chesty Morgan—*Deadly Weapons* (1974) and *Double Agent 73* (1974)—Morgan's seventy-three-inch bust is arguably presented less as a sexual spectacle as it is what Bowen more aptly describes as a "sexual monstrosity."[6]

However, *A Night to Dismember* is the most overt reference point in Wishman's filmography to her final movie, if simply only for the fact that *Each Time I Kill* includes actual footage from the director's earlier horror film: shown in a scene where the film's protagonist Ellie (Tiffany Paralta) goes on a movie date, with no less than John Waters also in attendance in a small, affectionate cameo. At first *A Night to Dismember* is striking for the almost overbearing dominance of a male voiceover that reduces its female characters to a near wholly object-like status, held formally and thus thematically at a consistent arm's length. Yet the version of the film that was released in 1983 (and later on video in 1989) was far from what Wishman had originally conceived for the project. Filmed in 1979, over half the negative was destroyed and it took Wishman eight months to cobble together the remaining footage with additional new footage in her attempt to create a rushed, coherent, releasable product. Up until this film, all of her movies were made either through her personal money or loans, so the financial stakes were higher than what she had worked with previously: for the first time, she was answerable to investors. While rough and barely intelligible (understandable, considering its history), few critics—even Wishman's most fervent admirers—can avoid acknowledging the overall clumsiness of the final released version of *A Night to Dismember*. There are, however, a number of striking, even beautiful, images in the film, particularly those recycled in *Each Time I Kill*. As Kier-La Janisse argues, "*A Night to Dismember*, while inept in every way, is odds-defyingly entertaining, and Wishman's bizarre, Dada-esque editing warrants a look."[7] Regardless, the experience of making her first official horror film was so traumatic that Wishman "considered this the film that nearly killed her,"[8] and she retired from movie making to live in Coral Gables with her sister, Pearl.

According to Rebekah McKendry, in Wishman's final years, "Wishman quietly advanced to the ripened age of eighty-eight and lived a relatively normal suburban life in Florida."[9] As McKendry tells it, Wishman's presence as a cult film legend had grown significantly by the end of the 1990s, and with her profile becoming more visible—everything from retrospectives at Harvard, to clips of her films shown in John Waters movies, and being interviewed by Conan O'Brien—she was returned firmly to the trash cinema auteurist canon. For McKendry, "Invigorated by the affirmation that her films were not lost to the exploitation dustbin, the now eighty-nine-year-old decided to make another movie."[10] That movie was *Each Time I Kill*. That Wishman's swansong should thematically align so closely to a number of other horror films made by women in the United States—*Mirror Mirror* and *The Dorm* in particular—provides tangible evidence of how vital a part of this community of women filmmakers she was, regardless of whether she viewed herself as particularly "feminist" or not. The focus in *Each Time I Kill* and these two films especially reveals a significant shared concern with questions surrounding femininity, identity, and peer pressure, all built around the shared iconography of the mirror and the subjectivity of being a young woman pressured to maintain stereotypical ideals of "beauty" and "normality."

DORIS WISHMAN, FEMINISM, AND WOMEN'S HORROR FILMMAKING

"Women have always been horror's lifeblood," wrote Evelyn Wang in 2017. "After all, one of our most iconic monsters was created one dark stormy night by a young woman who had (according to legend) grown weary of Lord Byron's threesomes."¹¹ There is a tidy poetic connection here between Wang's reframing Mary Shelley's *Frankenstein* as a kind of pressure release from the mundanity of sexual experimentation and Wishman's own turn from sexploitation to horror. With their shared focus on bodies in opened and hyper-elevated emotional and sensory states, Wishman's movement between these two genres is perhaps logical. As Linda Williams famously noted in her foundational 1991 article "Film Bodies: Gender, Genre, and Excess," pornography, low horror (such as slasher films), and women's weepies could all be conceptually conceived under the definitional umbrella of body genres.[12] For Williams, "the body spectacle is featured most sensationally in pornography's portrayal of orgasm, in horror's portrayal of violence and terror, and in melodrama's portrayal of weeping."[13] In terms of the relationship between horror and pornography specifically, as put bluntly by fellow filmmaker Roberta Findlay on her own move from sex films to horror movies and their respective emphasis on semen and blood, "You know the money shots in porn films? Well, this was just a different substance: it was red."[14]

As McKendry noted, in the case of *A Night to Dismember*, Wishman was attracted to making a horror movie simply because she felt there was money in it: *Halloween* (John Carpenter, 1978) had made impressively high returns for its originally low budget.[15] With *Each Time I Kill*, Wishman simply once again sought to cash in on a demonstrated money-maker, yet she had perhaps already learned with *A Night to Dismember* that this was not the easy win it might appear to be. Yet despite this—while not unique or specific to women's horror filmmaking either before or after *Each Time I Kill*—Wishman's final film presented in particularly fascinating ways shared fascinations that appear in horror films made by other women. *Mirror Mirror*, *Each Time I Kill*, and *The Dorm* do not suggest an essentialized singular female treatment of the thematic material at stake, but rather instead offer evidence of a steady fascination with the subjectivity of gendered performances of femininity that culminate around the object of the mirror in particular.

In part, the union of these three films is framed by the contemporary Women in Horror movement, triggered by feminist activist, zine maker, and filmmaker Hannah Neurotica with the publication of a manifesto in February 2010 declaring the first Women in Horror Recognition Month.[16] In 2014, filmmaker and critic Maude Michaud noted that this was a feminist grassroots movement that found its heritage in the 1990s Riot Grrrl punk movement and their DIY attitude and "girls to the front"[17] ethos. In the years since, women's horror filmmaking has found a mainstream audience with films like *American Mary* (Jen and Sylvia Soska, 2012), *The Babadook* (Jennifer Kent, 2014), *The Invitation* (Karyn Kusama, 2015), and *Raw* (Julia Ducournau, 2016).

As many women horror filmmakers have articulated in recent years,[18] concerns with their visibility in the industry reflect more widespread concerns such as those voiced by many across the industry, particularly in a the #MeToo era. In 2016, Karyn Kusama (director of 2009's *Jennifer's Body* and 2015's *The Invitation*) argued, "the problem with a lack of diversity in storytelling is our worldview narrows because of it . . . The stories that answer this call need to be made in order for us to understand how much we needed them."[19]

This recent Women in Horror movement also contains a historiographic component that has encouraged a looking back and rethinking of horror film history and canon formation. For horror director and producer Roxanne Benjamin,

> I don't think there's necessarily an uptick [in female horror creators] . . . but I would say there's probably more of an awareness of that now, mostly from the spotlight that's being shined on the disparity in the number of women directors versus male directors overall.[20]

While this rethinking of how women horror filmmakers have been historically important is clearly a key part of the contemporary women in horror movement, in the case of filmmakers like Roberta Findlay and Doris Wishman there lies the often casual exchange of "women's horror films" with "feminist horror films." In the case of Wishman, the so-called feminist question has been long debated. As Modleski asked in 2007,

> is the oeuvre of Wishman, as her very name suggests, the result of a straightforward case of penis envy in a woman who capitulated to the conventions of male pornography and "sexploitation" at its sleaziest? Or is it possible that a woman living in a prefeminist time and trafficking in genres that routinely dealt in violence against women may be said to have kept alive the right of women to sexuality even when it was killing them?[21]

While the questions Modleski ask are vital when considering Wishman's place in the history of women's horror filmmaking as well as sexploitation, it is perhaps important to emphasize that one answer that covers Wishman's entire filmography may not even be possible: while *Each Time I Kill* is certainly aligned with ideological leanings that can be interpreted as "feminist" from a contemporary perspective, this does not reduce the utility (even necessity) of assessing Wishman's films on a case by case basis. As Michaud notes, "even if a lot of femme-made films include a feminist message, the films directed by women do not automatically produce feminist content."[22]

Wishman herself explicitly rallied against "women's liberation" in an interview with Andrea Juno published in 1986.[23] Yet Juno herself rightly noted that "even though she says she's no feminist, Doris Wishman is definitely a positive women's role model, persisting as she has in a field saturated with men."[24] This has led more contemporary critics to comfortably label Wishman as a "proto-indie feminist auteur,"[25] McKendry embracing this term because "Wishman's wronged protagonists were always fighting against a male-driven, violent society. These women keep their emotional strength and use it as their weapon in the world of male violence. Despite being exploited, they emerge victors in the films."[26] Art theorist Peggy Phelan's deliberately loose definition of feminism may provide some utility when thinking through Wishman's work and practice from this perspective. For Phelan, "feminism is the conviction that gender has been, and continues to be, a fundamental category for the organization of culture. Moreover, the pattern of that organization usually favors men over women."[27] Through her signature spectacle of sexualized and/or traumatized bodies, time and time again Wishman's films demonstrate the relationship between gender and power: perhaps nowhere more immediately than in *Each Time I Kill*, where a young woman is driven to murder to become sexually attractive to men.

Even from this very broad definitional perspective, whether one deems Wishman herself—or even only specific films—to be "feminist" as such, it is not the sole or even primary basis upon which to consider her importance as a crucial figure in women's horror filmmaking. A useful point of comparison here is Roberta Findlay herself, who after making a number of roughies with her husband Michael (such as the iconic *Flesh* trilogy from 1967 to 1968) and the notorious *Snuff* in 1976, went on to make a number of highly successful hardcore pornography films. Her work here culminated in an exploitative "documentary" about the suicide of adult star Shauna Grant called *Shauna: Every Man's Fantasy* (1985), a film so tasteless it allegedly saw Findlay's reputation in the adult filmmaking industry destroyed.[28] Turning instead to horror, Findlay produced a number of low-budget films that have developed a cult audience in recent years, including *The Oracle* (1985), *Blood Sisters* (1987), *Prime Evil* (1988), and *Lurkers* (1988), before quitting filmmaking altogether after *Banned* (1989).[29] While it is essential to underscore the fact that Wishman's and Findlay's films and careers were strikingly different, aside from their movement between body genres and their work in roughies in particular, there are a number of curious intersections. Both were explicitly against the ideas of the women's liberation movement, and both were bewildered by later interest in their film work. "I don't know what is happening; the whole world's gone to pot," said Wishman of the rise in attention to her work in 1998.[30] Likewise, said Findlay in 2005, "people who like [my] . . . old movies seem to have deep psychological problems."[31]

Perhaps more optimistically, like contemporary genre filmmakers working with horror like Anna Biller (*The Love Witch*, 2016), both Wishman and Findlay were what we now call "slashies," taking on numerous jobs on their own films: Findlay directing, acting, producing, writing, editing, composing, and shooting many of her own films, while Wishman too directed, produced, edited, and casted her films, and location scouted. Wishman was an avid self-funder, a tradition revamped for many contemporary women genre filmmakers who find themselves excluded from more traditional funding pathways.[32] Even more poignantly, although the films in many ways could not be further apart, the way that French director Julia Ducournau talks about her hugely successful horror film *Raw* adheres with a near-striking precision to the thematic core that drives *Each Time I Kill* and its fascinations with genre, gender, and identity. For Ducournau in *Raw*, embracing the taboo "means complete freedom . . . but the freedom has a cost—freedom only exists with responsibility."[33] Elsewhere, she added "Horror [is] the expression of violence that you feel inside of you—and it's important we recognize that women feel violence and anger as well."[34] Whether we choose to define Doris Wishman and/or *Each Time I Kill* as "feminist" or not, there is no denying that this film at least overlaps in significant ways with many of the concerns of the contemporary Women in Horror movement, and directly with these very specific observations by Ducournau on *Raw*.

EACH TIME WE KILL: WOMEN'S HORROR FILMMAKING AND THE TRANSFORMING GIRL-OUTSIDER

In her 1998 feature on Wishman, Williams quotes the following observation by film student Blossom Lefcourt of her affection for the director's work:

> Why doesn't her work offend me? I think the answer to this lies partially in the idea that the themes in Wishman's work are so embedded in our cultural framework, so much a part of the mainstream, that one becomes immune to these images; they don't fully register after time.[35]

If this type of subjective experience of identity formation for young women is present in any of Wishman's films, it appears most compellingly and explicitly in *Each Time I Kill*. In the film a young woman named Ellie Saunders is so troubled by her perceived lack of physical attractiveness that she evokes an ancient curse to perform body-swap rituals with more attractive girls, killing them and gaining a new image (and a new sense of self) body part by body part. Body-swap films themselves have permeated the horror film genre with movies including but certainly not limited to *Mephisto Waltz* (Paul Wendkos, 1971), *Alison's Birthday* (Ian Coughlan, 1981), *The Skeleton Key* (Iain Softley, 2005), and most recently, *Get Out* (Jordan Peele, 2017). As films like *Ginger Snaps* (John Fawcett, 2000), *May* (Lucky McKee, 2002), and *Excision* (Richard Bates Jr., 2012) demonstrate, alienated young women who turn to violence are not rare in twenty-first-century horror, and *Each Time I Kill* shares narrative and thematic similarities with "ugly duckling" horror films including *Killer Bash* (David DeCoteau, 2005), Brian De Palma's *Carrie* (1974), its sequel *The Rage: Carrie 2* (Katt Shea, 1999), and most recently Kimberly Peirce's 2013 remake of the same name. Although unusually the final destiny does not arrive at the end of *Each Time I Kill*, the privileging of prom night in Wishman's film too evokes a strong connection to an enduring horror convention, typified again by *Carrie*, the classic slasher film *Prom Night* (Paul Lynch, 1980) and Nelson McCormick's 2008 remake of the same name, and—in terms of a woman-directed horror film focused explicitly on the subjectivity of female identity formation—Karen Skloss's *The Honor Farm* (2017).

The small amount of additional footage filmed for *Each Time I Kill* was by cult sexploitation director Joseph W. Sarno,[36] and one can speculate that Wishman and Sarno had known each other for many decades. Like Wishman, Sarno's *Veil of Blood* (1973) had experimented with horror filmmaking while establishing his name in sex films. According to his own interpretation of his filmography at least, Sarno's own words indicate an affinity for the precise female subjectivity that lies at the heart of *Each Time I Kill*. Said Sarno in a 1986 interview, "My point of view is more or less always from the woman's point of view; the fairy tales that my films are based on are from the woman's point of view. I stress the efficacy of women for themselves."[37] For V. Vale, Sarno's films "often portray people discovering their own true unconscious desires,"[38] an authorial trademark that can also be identified as running through *Each Time I Kill*.

Yet while Sarno and many other of Wishman's collaborators and friends may have been intuitively sympathetic to the thematic core of *Each Time I Kill*, as noted earlier and in Rebekah McKendry's conclusion to this volume, Wishman was giving detailed instructions on how the final film was to be put together from her literal deathbed. Despite its reunion of Wishman with her long-time cinematographer C. Davis Smith, it would be difficult to champion *Each Time I Kill* as Wishman's most polished, professional-looking film. However, it shares the palpable energy that marks some of her greatest work that in its own way too demonstrates what Bowen identified in her mid-1960s film work as "the operation of a unique and astonishing filmmaking intelligence."[39]

Set in Stanton, Florida, *Each Time I Kill* begins with a familiar horror cliché: a lightning storm erupts as a nervous man in a trench coat is stabbed by an unseen figure. His last words bookend the film's enigmatic core: to whom does he whisper with his dying breath, "I won't tell anyone"? Cutting in sharp tonal contrast to a high school classroom full of almost happy students, nerd-girl stereotype Ellie looks on sadly at Kate (Lisa Ferber) and her boyfriend Don (Rob Vidal) who chat excitedly about prom night. Looking for some small pleasure to console her for her clear sense of exclusion from such social rituals, she buys her regular drink from an ice cream parlor, befriending Angelo (Bill Perlach) who works behind the counter. Ellie has many friends (even popular ones) in the film, and Angelo is one of a number of characters who clearly like Ellie for who she is: outside of a group of punks who assault her on the street and a car-load of frat boys who sexually harass her, howling at her to imply she is a "dog," Ellie is harassed but is not a social outcast. Unlike the typical ugly duckling trope, Ellie has friends—some, like Tildi (Laudet Torres) are nerd-girls like her, but others, like Cindy (Melissa Perez), are attractive and popular, and similar girls like Kate are also friendly to her. Ellie is academically successful and when her mother Molly (Madelin Marchant) asks her why she is sad, her mother takes off the girl's glasses and says, "You're a nice-looking girl, dear, you must stop feeling sorry for yourself." Unlike Carrie White and so many other variations of this character, Ellie's flaws appear more strongly to her than they do to other people: her condition is closer to depression than being the victim of bullying. This is underscored by the kindness and attractiveness of her parents Molly and Tom (Fred Schneider from the band The B-52's), the unexpected death of whom deepens her depression even further.

Traumatized by grief and internalizing her negative feelings against herself—she screams the word "ugly" at the mirror and smashes it—Ellie considers suicide as she holds a razorblade close to her wrist. What stops her, however, is the sight of an "amulet" (in fact, a cheap dime-store locket) that she had discovered in the spooky, deserted former house of the Beetle family in her neighborhood. Earlier in the film, Tildi had explained (for the viewer's benefit rather than Ellie's, the latter dismissing it as nonsense) that fifty years ago a family lived there, the youngest of whom, Simon (David Frisch), was said to be possessed by the devil and was responsible for a series of mysterious disappearances. Curiously sneaking into the Beetle house after Tildi has left her, she discovers the amulet and takes it home with her. After cleaning it lovingly with a toothbrush, Ellie discovers inside a crudely burnt scrap of paper (designed, perhaps, to imply antiquity) which she reads through a voiceover:

> With this amulet, you can change your destiny
> Choose the person whose features you desire, this will be your victim
> After your victim is dead chant three times "I shall change my image and so change my destiny"

Dismissing it as rubbish, Ellie says, "As though a cheap piece of brass and a corny chant can make somebody beautiful." After the death of her parents, however, and driven to the brink of despair, she changes her mind and decides to give the ancient ritual a try.

Her first victim is Kate, who again, rather than being presented as a monstrous bully as is so typical of this trope, is instead kindly and supportive of her struggling single mother and younger brother. At a local beach, Kate and Don sunbathe and when Kate goes out in the water to swim by herself, Ellie strangles and drowns her and performs the ritual in order to gain Kate's clear, unblemished skin. Elsewhere, she enacts similar murders—her victims are Cindy in a house of mirrors at a funfair and the sickly Susan (Jaqueline Goldhagen) who lies seriously ill in hospital—in order to gain what Ellie has idealized as their beautiful teeth and hair respectively. Of interest here is that it is these three features alone that transform Ellie completely, all elements of her appearance that theoretically she could have changed on her own volition without a body count, be it through dental care, hair styling, diet, and/or introducing a new skincare regime. While perhaps the script was not created with such thought in mind, in the final film at least Ellie's psychologically damaging self-hatred is not rational. The film is concerned less with how "society" sees her as with how she sees herself.

Completely transformed, Ellie is a new girl and unrecognizable: she is confident and outgoing and (using the new alias Meg Townsend) she seduces Don and they begin dating. She tells everyone that Ellie has gone to live with her Aunt Belle (played by cult horror film legend Linnea Quigley) out of town. With Ellie/Meg's new destiny unfolding happily before her with only brief moments of guilt and regret at her murders, Aunt Belle's announcement that she is coming to visit sends Ellie/Meg into a wild panic and she murders her aunt at a train station before she arrives. Window shopping for wedding dresses and accepting the formal commitment of Don's class ring, Meg looks forward to prom night. Beforehand, however, her plan begins to come undone: suspecting he has discovered her secret, she murders Angelo (the scene at the film's opening) and her amulet is stolen. Having nightmares that her victims come back to haunt her, the film ends as she is herself murdered by Tildi who—now in possession of the amulet and the ritual instructions—seeks to change her destiny by stealing what she deems to be Meg's more attractive features.

While at times *Each Time I Kill* appears to be simply replaying the generic staples applicable to the ugly duckling horror film trope as it applies to high school girl outsiders, of particular note is the structural and narrative role of Ellie/Meg's bedroom mirror, which—for the bulk of the film—is cracked after Ellie had smashed it in a fit of depressed self-loathing. Scenes of Ellie deriding her reflected appearance with cruel language early in the film are replaced by a series of similar yet evolving moments when she preens, admiring each new "beautiful" feature as it appears after each murder. By the time she has fully transformed into Meg, she spends a significant amount of time posturing and posing in front of the mirror, giggling and telling herself how beautiful she is.

Similarly, mirrors also play central roles in both *The Dorm* and—as its very title suggests—*Mirror Mirror*. The latter follows goth girl Megan Gordon (Rainbow Harvest) who has recently moved to an elite private high school far from Los Angeles to help her and her mother Susan (Karen Black) recover from the death of Megan's father. The film begins with a flashback to the 1940s where the earlier inhabitants of the house are involved in a murder, later to be revealed as closely linked to the presence of a haunted full-length mirror that Megan discovers in her new bedroom and takes a liking to. After Megan discovers that the mirror is capable of fulfilling her wishes if it is "fed" (be it family dogs or sex partners), her rising attractiveness is reflected by a shift in her appearance from "freakish" goth girl to—much to the surprise of bitchy popular girls like Charleen Kane (Charlie Spradling)—a young woman who is considered attractive in a far more mainstream way, despite still wearing black clothes.

Like *Each Time I Kill*, *Mirror Mirror* is a woman-directed horror movie about a high school girl outsider whose physical transformation to what is coded within the film as broadly sexually attractive is punctuated by her close relationship to her bedroom mirror. As Kate Hagen noted in 2017,

> What *Mirror Mirror* lacks in performance and budget is made up for in terms of the universality of its themes: the teenage girl as pariah turned alpha predator is a classic story, but *Mirror Mirror*'s inclusion of Megan's recent grief on top of that outcast status gives her an adult awareness of pain that her peers cannot comprehend.[40]

For Hagen, "Most women struggle to love themselves from the moment they have a conception of a self, so when the mirror provides perfect love to Megan? She absolutely can't say no to its sinister bidding."[41]

How closely these films are thematically aligned in their ugly duckling horror transformation narratives warrants acknowledgment. Traumatized by the bullying she faces at her new school and her mother's decision to date the undertaker from the local pet cemetery, Megan walks sadly into her bedroom and utters her first wish, unaware of the effect it will have on her mirror: "I wish Daddy was here," screaming at her own reflection in the mirror before she collapses, miserable, on her bed. Megan and Ellie experience similar yet diverging experiences with self-hatred that is transformed by the mastery of new powers, closely linked to their relationships to their own reflections.

Likewise, the transformation of the protagonist in Rachel Talalay's *The Dorm* also plays out structurally through changes that are registered and privileged as appearing in a bedroom mirror, once more emphasizing the significance of how these outsider girls perceive themselves and how the corruption of that vision can have horrific results. The film was shot in Calgary as a television movie for MTV. By one account Talalay was drawn to the project "because of the themes of body image and self-esteem coursing beneath the Hitchcock and Polanski-inspired creepiness."[42] As Talalay noted in a 2014 interview,

What's remarkable about the project and what made me want to do it is that it has this very strong theme of female body image and questioning whether you would sell your soul for the perfect body. And in this new world of social media, the pressures on young people about body image are even worse than when I was a kid because it's everywhere. There's so much pressure on young people through advertising and it just seems to get worse. A horror film that examines the horror of what you would do for perfection and what that would do to you? What a great theme.[43]

In many ways updating the similar concerns of *Mirror Mirror* and *Each Time I Kill*, Talalay's movie highlights how technological changes have further complicated the already messy terrain young women must often navigate when wrestling with accepting their own identity and understanding their place in the world. The film follows Vivian (Alexis Knapp), who—recovering from a mental health collapse—decides to begin college away from home at Harker University, living in the suitably horror-sounding Usher House (the dorm of the film's title). Cautiously at first, Vivian accepts the welcoming friendship of her new dorm-mates who offer to provide her with a makeover. After wearing a clay facial mask at her friend's request, she has a nightmare in which she hears a cacophony of voices taunting her: "Ugly bitch," "Aren't you disgusted with yourself?," "Wouldn't you rather be beautiful?," "Let me give you what you need, Vivian." Awaking to find her face blistered and wounded, she peels away the damaged flesh to find underneath perfect skin. At first, Vivian is flattered by the attention, but as she develops a sexual relationship with Philip, one of the boys in the group (Max Lloyd-Jones), and on her friends' recommendations joins a class on ancient mythology, she begins to grow increasingly suspect of her newfound friends' motivations. As she becomes increasingly more beautiful, it is revealed that she is a human sacrifice, transformed so that her friends—members of an ancient cult—can bring their leader, the beautiful Violet Baker (also played by Knapp), back to life at Vivian's expense.

Like Megan and Ellie, Vivian narrates her emotional journey largely through one-way dialogue with her own reflection. This begins, again, in a continuing state of self-deprecation, and at different points throughout the early part of the film she says to her reflection, "I wish I was pretty," "It's OK, don't hate yourself, just be yourself . . . who am I kidding," "Oh you're hopeless." Mysteriously finding what is later revealed as Violet's favorite slinky red party dress in her cupboard, as Vivian transforms, so too does her reflection and her conversation with it: "Look how pretty we are!," says the glamourous Violet in the mirror as she stares out at Vivian. Crucially, all three films end with the deaths of their respective protagonists. On one hand, a surface reading might dismiss as misogynistic or moralistic the tendency here to kill off Ellie, Megan, and Vivian as punishment for their collective desires for transformation and to utilize the supernatural to derail what *Each Time I Kill* refers to as their "destiny" to remain outsiders in adulthood. Yet another—more positive—interpretation is not just possible, but more thematically in line with each of these three films. If each girl accepted herself for who she was while resisting temptation, her own beauty—articulated explicitly in each film as always there—may have come to the fore in less monstrous and violent ways. These girls are not punished for their vanity; rather, it is revealed that there is no shortcut to bypass the pain and alienation resulting from not fitting into the traditional templates of acceptable teenage girl femininity. These three films critique the social and cultural pressures placed on young women, not the young women themselves: that each girl either explicitly or implicitly struggles to live with mental health issues underscores the lack of support women face when they are not naturally cookie-cutter human Barbie dolls.

The final screen of *Each Time I Kill* notes it is "dedicated to the memory of Doris Wishman," and the film ends with moving footage of her showing Paralta how she wants Ellie to physically demonstrate her despair as she sits distraught on her bed. "I'm a frustrated actress, so that helps,"[44] Wishman told Andrea Juno in their 1986 interview, explaining her directorial style. There is much to ponder in this quote: as Judith Butler has so famously noted, "gender is always a doing . . . identity is performatively constituted by the very 'expressions' that are said to be its results."[45] What films like *Mirror Mirror*, *Each Time I Kill*, and *The Dorm* make almost explicit is that by being forced into a performance of idealized femininity, *many* women—especially young women yet to develop the psychological artillery to combat the dominant misogyny that riddles our culture—are in their own way "frustrated actresses" also. As Kate Hagen noted in the case of *Mirror Mirror* at least, "the specificity of the torment, triumph, and trauma endured by Megan shows the necessity of female authorship in horror: it takes a woman to truly convey the pain of femininity in lacerating, uncomfortable detail."[46] While the reduction of films by women horror directors to a unified, essentialized singularity is not just pointless but also arguably impossible, these three films share a vision of what the pressure to "perform" femininity is like for high school girls with distinct "insider" knowledge.

NOTES

1. Joy Williams, "Who's More Peculiar than Doris Wishman?," *Spin Magazine* (May 1998): 129.
2. Christopher J. Jarmick, "Doris Wishman" (Great Directors), *Senses of Cinema* 22 (October 2002), <http://sensesofcinema.com/2002/great-directors/wishman/> (last accessed November 3, 2020).
3. Ibid.

4. Mike Watt, *Fervid Filmmaking: 66 Cult Pictures of Vision, Verve and No Self-Restraint* (Jefferson, NC: McFarland, 2013), 24.
5. Tania Modleski, "Women's Cinema as Counterphobic Cinema: Doris Wishman as the Last Auteur," in *Sleaze Artists: Cinema at the Margins of Taste, Style, and Politics*, ed. Jeffrey Sconce (Durham, NC: Duke University Press, 2007), 56.
6. Michael J. Bowen, "Doris Wishman Meets the Avant-Garde," in *Underground U.S.A.: Filmmaking Beyond the Hollywood Canon*, ed. Xavier Mendik and Steven Jay Schneider (London and New York: Wallflower Press, 2002), 119.
7. Kier-La Janisse, *House of Psychotic Women: An Autobiographical Topography of Female Psychosis in Horror and Exploitation Films* (Godalming: FAB Press, 2012), 296.
8. Jarmick, "Doris Wishman."
9. Rebekah McKendry, "Fondling Your Eyeballs: Watching Doris Wishman," in *From the Arthouse to the Grindhouse: Highbrow and Lowbrow Transgression in Cinema's First Century*, ed. John Cline and Robert G. Weiner (Lanham, MD: Scarecrow Press, 2010), 62.
10. Ibid.
11. Evelyn Wang, "Welcome to the Golden Age of Women-Directed Horror," *Broadly*, last modified April 15, 2017, <https://broadly.vice.com/en_us/article/zmbnd5/welcome-to-the-golden-age-of-women-directed-horror> (last accessed November 3, 2020).
12. Linda Williams, "Film Bodies: Gender, Genre, and Excess," *Film Quarterly* 44.4 (Summer 1991): 2–13.
13. Ibid., 4.
14. Quote from the featurette *A Blood Sisters Reunion* on the 2004 Media Blasters home entertainment release of *Blood Sisters* (Roberta Findlay, 1987).
15. McKendry, "Fondling Your Eyeballs," 62.
16. Maude Michaud, "Horror Grrrls: Feminist Horror Filmmakers and Agency," *Offscreen* 18, no. 6–7 (July 2014), <offscreen.com/view/horror-grrrls> (last accessed November 3, 2020).
17. Ibid.
18. For example, see Samuel Fragoso, "Talking *Twilight* and the Difficulties of Being a Female Director with Catherine Hardwicke," *i-D Magazine*, last modified December 14, 2015, <https://i-d.vice.com/en_uk/article/evxqjm/talking-twilight-and-the-difficulties-of-being-a-female-director-with-catherine-hardwicke> (last accessed November 3, 2020); Christina Radish, "'XX' Directors Roxanne Benjamin & Annie Clark on Their All-Female Horror Anthology," *Collider*, last modified February 17, 2017, <collider.com/xx-roxanne-benjamin-annie-clark-interview/> (last accessed November 3, 2020); Rebecca Hawkes, "We Are the Weirdos: Meet the Women Changing the Face of Horror," *The Telegraph* (UK), last modified October 26, 2017, <https://www.telegraph.co.uk/films/0/weirdos-meet-women-changing-face-horror/> (last accessed November 3, 2020).
19. Quoted in Phoebe Reilly, "From 'Babadook' to 'Raw': The Rise of the Modern Female Horror Filmmaker," *Rolling Stone*, last modified October 26, 2016, <https://www.rollingstone.com/movies/features/the-rise-of-the-modern-female-horror-filmmaker-w446369> (last accessed November 3, 2020).
20. Quoted in Wang, "Welcome."
21. Modleski, "Women's Cinema," 48–9.
22. Michaud, "Horror Grrrls."
23. Andrea Juno, "Interview: Doris Wishman," in *Incredibly Strange Films*, ed. V. Vale and Andrea Juno (San Francisco: RE/Search Publications, 1986), 110.
24. Ibid.
25. Williams, "Who's More Peculiar," 127.
26. McKendry, "Fondling Your Eyeballs," 59.

27. Peggy Phelan, "Survey," in *Art and Feminism*, ed. Helena Reckitt (New York: Phaidon Press, 2012), 18.
28. Franklin Osanka and Sara Lee Johann, *Sourcebook on Pornography* (Lexington: Lexington Books, 1989), 87.
29. I write about Findlay's career at length in Alexandra Heller-Nicholas, "What's Inside a Girl?: Porn, Horror and the Films of Roberta Findlay," *Senses of Cinema* 80 (September 2016), <sensesofcinema.com/2016/american-extreme/porn-horror-roberta-findlay/> (last accessed November 3, 2020).
30. Quoted in Williams, "Who's More Peculiar," 128.
31. Quoted in J. R. Taylor, "The Curse of Her Filmography: Roberta Findlay's Grindhouse Legacy," *New York Press*, last modified July 20, 2005, <http://www.newyorkpress.com/18/29/film/JRTaylor.cfm> (last accessed March 30, 2008).
32. Juno, "Interview," 113. While again not unique to women's horror filmmaking, a number of key movies such as *The Babadook* and Ana Lily Amapour's *A Girl Walks Home Alone at Night* (2014) received significant financing through crowdfunding. See Reilly, "From 'Babadook' to 'Raw'"; Brendan Swift, "*The Babadook* Successfully Raises $30K Through Crowdfunding—Just," *Inside Film Magazine*, last modified September 27, 2012, <https://www.if.com.au/the-babadook-successfully-raises-30k-through-crowdfunding-just/> (last accessed November 3, 2020).
33. Alexandra Heller-Nicholas, *1000 Women in Horror, 1895–2018* (Orlando: BearManor Media, 2020), 164.
34. Reilly, "From 'Babadook' to 'Raw.'"
35. Quoted in Williams, "Who's More Peculiar," 130.
36. Jarmick, "Doris Wishman." He also notes that Sarno's wife, Peggy Steffans-Sarno, appeared in Wishman's *A Taste of Flesh* (1967).
37. V. Vale, "Interview: Joe Sarno," in *Incredibly Strange Films*, ed. V. Vale and Andrea Juno (San Francisco: RE/Search Publications, 1986), 93.
38. Ibid., 97.
39. Bowen, "Doris Wishman," 115.
40. Kate Hagen, "31 Days of Feminist Horror Films: *Mirror, Mirror*," *The Blacklist*, last modified October 16, 2017, <https://blog.blcklst.com/31-days-of-feminist-horror-films-mirror-mirror-579de6558242> (last accessed November 3, 2020).
41. Ibid.
42. Eric Volmers, "Q&A with Rachel Talalay, Director of the Calgary-Shot Horror Film, *The Dorm*," *Calgary Herald*, last modified November 5, 2014, <calgaryherald.com/entertainment/qa-with-rachel-talalay-director-of-the-calgary-shot-horror-film-the-dorm> (last accessed November 3, 2020).
43. Ibid.
44. Juno, "Interview," 110.
45. Judith Butler, *Gender Trouble: Feminism and the Subversion of Identity* (New York: Routledge, 1990), 25.
46. Hagen, "31 Days."

CHAPTER 3

Trans/sexual Negativity and the Ethics of (S)exploitation in *Let Me Die a Woman*

Harper Shalloe

A 1978 film relegated to the dustbin of trans media history and the aesthetic category of trash—Thomas Waugh supposing in his 2000 anthology *The Fruit Machine* that he is the only one to have seen the "sordid thing"—Doris Wishman's generically elusive and ethically suspect *Let Me Die a Woman* (*LMDW*) is ripe for critical return.[1] A film theorist's wet dream and a representational nightmare, *LMDW* makes not such strange bedfellows of documentary and softcore pornography, the afterglow that it generates always accompanied by a bad taste in one's mouth. Its sober discourse of transsexuality and its ethnographic tour of trans embodiment intoxicated by a number of bloody re-enactments, from castration via hammer and chisel to penetration too soon after vaginoplasty, *LMDW* is a film that one should be hard-pressed to like. Grabbing this grindhouse slime and running with it, picking up along the way a number of discarded objects and fishy interlocutors, I propose, perhaps provocatively, that *LMDW* contains the key to a psychoanalytic concept of transness, and even more provocatively, that a psychoanalytic concept of transness is something we should want.

Briefly, my argument is that *LMDW*'s intercutting of documentary and pornography can teach us something about sublimation, and that sublimation, in turn, can teach us something about transness. As I understand it, sublimation is a way of dealing with, by confronting and repeating, negativity: through sublimation, the subject confronts the world's fundamental incompletion by according an existing object the status and value of the one that is necessarily lost, thereby making that object (and, as we will see, that subject) into something new. Rather than forever bemoan the impossibility of fulfillment that this loss would seem to entail, sublimation allows the subject to find satisfaction in the very seat of negativity. If in the beginning is a hole, a hole that forecloses the possibility of a whole, sublimation gives shape and name to this lack by making something that exists in the world take the place of what cannot exist in the world, of the thing whose absence inaugurates the world, remaking the world in the process.

By "documentary" and "pornography," I want to signal assemblages of sound and image that evince commonly granted conventions, without filling out the content of those generic containers. That is, rather than try to determine what precisely documentary and pornography are, I proceed from the assumptions that most scenes in *LMDW* are likely to be recognized as one or the other, and that they are different, if not antithetical, forms, despite the affinities between them that Linda Williams and Bill Nichols, among others, have drawn.[2] If I maintain that pornography and documentary are contradictory, it is insofar as sex is the contradiction—the impossibility—of knowledge, though we will see why this analogy does not quite hold. It should be more or less obvious that we can glean the nexus of knowledge–power–pleasure in *LMDW*; my wager is that it is not only Foucault but Lacan whose thought the film usefully illuminates.

Doris Wishman's work in general, and *LMDW* in particular, is often located under the sign of (s)exploitation, one overburdened with ethical baggage. I am not interested in adjudicating claims regarding *LMDW*'s ethical failings but want to suggest that through its performance of sublimation, the film opens onto another valence of ethics. Instead of arguing that *LMDW*'s façade of sliminess gives way, upon closer reading, to subversiveness, I consider what the apparent etiology of that sliminess—not the intimacy, but rather the "extimacy" of documentary and pornography—might tell us about transness, desire, knowledge, and negativity.[3] If, for Lacan, the ethical act consists in grasping the negativity of being—and thus the non-totality of thought and the non-identicality of identity—through sublimation, which raises an object "to the dignity of the Thing," or makes something in the place of ontological nothing, then the film's sublimating montage might offer us a new way through Doris Wishman's ethical quagmire.[4]

Extending the psychoanalytic notion of negativity—central to what has been hailed the "antisocial thesis" in queer theory, and its critique of liberal sociality, stable identity, and the clamor for sexual redemption—to trans studies, I propose trans negativity as a concept of desire and an ethics of epistemic impossibility.[5] I discuss these dual valences of trans negativity in more detail below, but I want to briefly flag this concept's reliance on, and departure from, negativity as a queer theoretical tenet. Mine is a strong argument against the tendency to figure trans as the liberatory, the radical, and the new *par excellence*, which is to say as political futurity, and so I am very much with Lee Edelman and his critique of reproductive futurism as horizon of the political in *No Future: Queer Theory and the Death Drive*, a text paradigmatic of the antisocial turn.[6] But, *pace* Edelman, it seems to me that without the death drive, without the hole in the Symbolic and social order, and the desire that appears in its place, there would be nothing new, and dare I say, no future? In other words, I want to suggest that negativity might be not the negation of futurity, but rather its very condition of possibility. The drive that Edelman identifies with the figure of the queer, or the sublimation that I identify with transition, need not close down futurity, if we can disarticulate futurity from political fantasy, precisely because negativity propels the production of new ties; because sublimation, as the "destiny of the drive," re-bores the hole that holds opens, quite literally, space for new signifiers, novel relations, and as yet unthought ways of being.[7] It is precisely this negativity or lack that is, funnily enough, missing from extant scholarship on transness.

This chapter proceeds in two parts. In the first, I argue that recent theorizations of trans as a challenge to normative notions of ontology unwittingly repeat—albeit with crucial differences—Lacan's concept of sex. Reading trans and (Lacanian) sex together, I argue that transness as an experience of desire, and therefore of sublimation, opens onto the relationship between knowledge and pleasure that is the focus of the second part. While *LMDW* seems to engage in sublimation misunderstood as the substitution of a respectable object for a base, sexual one, or where knowledge pleasure periodically replaces sexual pleasure, it instead performs a sublimation *like* transition. Enacting this sublimation on a structural level, *LMDW* articulates—by not saying and not showing, and against what it seems to say and show—trans as an impasse of symbolic representation and epistemic capture. This is not to repeat the transphobic argument that trans people really do not know what they want, or the painfully skeptical question that every trans person has been asked at least once: *how can you really know?* The point is rather that there is something in trans that evades knowing, that ruins any attempt fully or finally to flesh its meaning out. Against unsurprising assertions that *LMDW* is exploitational because it makes trans bodies the objects of an epistephilic spectacle for prurient cis consumption, I argue that *LMDW* necessarily shelters something of transness from representation. The film undermines all of its attempts in this direction, from talking head interviews, to medical examinations, to simulated sex scenes, swerving sharply from its stated intention to "show, for the first time, [the] how and why" of transsexuality. What the film ultimately shows is that any knowledge of transness is indelibly rent by transness itself. We might understand this as *LMDW*'s ethical gesture.

THE SEXUAL RELATIONSHIP HAS GONE FISHING

In what I am tempted to call, though I am sure some would prefer that I did not, the new materialist strain of trans studies, trans is being understood as intimately entangled with the ontological indeterminacy ushered in by quantum field theory (it remains unclear precisely how);[8] as the movement that at once produces and unsettles ontology;[9] as what buzzes beside and in tension with ontology;[10] as what ungrounds the subject;[11] and as a capacity for embodied beings to differ from themselves.[12] What I find most significant about these claims is the sense that I have heard them all before, not only in old-timey theorizations of "queer," whose metonymic responsibility for the radical and resistive seems to have been lifted, but in Lacanian theorizations of sex. Indeed, Marquis Bey's assertion that "Trans* and Black [. . .] move in and through the abyss underlying ontology, rubbing up alongside it and causing it to fissure" reads remarkably like a description of the Real, of sex as ontological impediment, or being's internal exclusion.[13] What is new about these new materialist musings, then, is their replacement of sex with trans, in a tradition that more or less explicitly purports to offer a corrective to psychoanalysis, with its nagging insistence on language and its fixation on the highly suspect category of the subject; what is less new is the political potency that this ontological lack seems to brims with.

While the work summarized all too hastily above often insists that it is *definitely not doing this*, it venerates trans for precisely its purported fugitivity, its mad dash into the otherwise (and therefore the better), its capacity for un/becoming or messing up whatever *is*. We might describe this work as an odd mutation of identity politics, where trans is said to have nothing to do with either identity or politics, but is nevertheless conceived as necessarily antagonistic to the extant order of things—and I would note in passing that this is exactly how trans is figured in state surveillance and security imaginaries. As a "perpetual disruptive movement" or "the primordial force of unfixing openness,"[14] trans becomes one of the "Deleuzian positive predicates"—and of course "transsexualities"[15] actually was one—that Alenka Zupančič argues renders Deleuze's notion of negativity a politics that masquerades as an ontology.[16]

Contrasting Lacan's and Deleuze's conceptions of repetition, Zupančič argues that for their many similarities, an irreducible difference lies in Deleuze's refusal to really grapple with negativity. Reading *Difference and Repetition* and the concept of the "crack" in *The Logic of Sense*, Zupančič argues that whereas Lacan's understanding of repetition relies on a firm distinction between originary incompletion and the excess or surplus enjoyment that appears in its place, dragging this negativity onto the order of the signifier, such that the social becomes requisite to the repetition of difference or the production of the new, Deleuze collapses lack and excess, figuring negativity as productive in and of itself. For Deleuze, then, in the beginning is repetition, the crack or hole that immediately propels the production of difference, without the intervention of the subject or the social. This is, for Zupančič, a profoundly positive conception of negativity, and one that indeed slides into political-cum-ontological optimism, such that

> the triumph of "good"—that is, of the whole series of the Deleuzian positive predicates (horizontally rhizomatic versus vertically hierarchical, negativity as positive excess versus negativity as lack, multiplicity versus one, nomadic versus static [. . .])—is, so to speak, inscribed in the force of repetition itself.[17]

Zupančič argues that this paradoxical Deleuzian positivism—the underside of his concept of negativity as the primordial force of repetition, in which inhere the positive terms of the binary distinctions that pepper much of his work—renders his notion of negativity an ontology that looks an awful lot like a politics, "or, more precisely, like something that can do without politics, since it hands its task over to ontology."[18] While Deleuze conceives of negativity as the pure and positive force of the production of the new, as an ontological lack overflowing with political possibility, Lacan contends that it is only through sublimation, an operation of the subject that takes place on the level of the symbolic and the social, that we can re-bore the Real hole in reality and make room for something else, which is not to say something better.

While not as far from Lacan as they might seem, or might hope, the trans theorists cited above encounter some of the same pitfalls that Zupančič claims Deleuze does, inscribing epistemological and political resistance in the very category of transness by failing to see the subject as the necessary prerequisite for singularity. This overdetermination of negativity, or its *a priori* predication, negates precisely the radicality of the Lacanian concept: negativity's indeterminacy, contingency, and capacity to produce something new—for better or for worse. By fleshing negativity out, substantializing it with political positivity, these theorists figure transness as an ontological rend simply wont to upend the order of things. Instead, we might understand transition as a kind of sublimation, a creation of something out of nothing, a way of ushering something new into the world, about which nothing can be known in advance.[19]

Further, against the tendency to position trans as an originary swerve, a fugitive force, or a line of flight in discourses thoroughly saturated with the affects of Good Politics, it seems to me that trans need not name this problem for and of ontology anew, because psychoanalysis has already furnished us with such a name, not unironically, without such romantic intimations: sex. This is the meaning of Lacan's inflammatory "there's no such thing as a sexual relationship": sex is what is missing from the symbolic and the social, the negativity around which language and relationality incurve, the signifier that has always already gone fishing, as it were—indeed, in Lacan's reading of Freud's interpretation of the dream of the witty butcher's wife, a slice of smoked salmon becomes the missing object that kindles desire, the objectified impossibility of fishy fulfillment propelling repetition.[20] And while Grace Lavery has recently claimed, with reference to Joan Copjec's articulation of Lacan's formulas of sexuation as two ways in which sex splits thought, "that this particular strand of Lacanian theory will not easily lend itself to an explanation of trans phenomena," this notion of sex, and therefore of sublimation and the drives, in fact offers an apt analytic for transness: an analytic of negativity.[21] Reading trans and sex together can move us away from the question of what trans is, and toward the immanent impossibility of an answer, toward an ethics of epistemic impossibility.

Let us linger for a moment longer on the theorization of trans as a capacity for self-differentiation. For Jules Gill-Peterson, via Deleuze and Derrida, if the body is understood in its originary technicity, then transgender emerges as both a bodily capacity and a sign of the body's capacity, the way a body differs from itself and an "expression" of its immanent potential to do so.[22] In this account transition is one way, among others, of differing from oneself: "the body undergoing hormone therapy cannot be separated in kind from other living beings [. . .], for it is not a different kind of technicity than a cisgendered body, even if their respective becomings are radically distinct."[23] In a different theoretical lexicon, this self-differentiation is called sublimation.

In his seminar on ethics, where the concept receives its fullest treatment, Lacan defines sublimation as "satisfaction of the drive with a change of object, that is, without repression," emphasizing that this satisfaction derives not from an absolutely new object, nor an idealized imaginary one, but from an existing object's internal deviation, "a change of object *in itself*."[24] Sublimation works by wresting an object from itself, allowing the drive to circle around it incessantly, because it is never the same. This is not the whole story, and I will circle back to sublimation below, but for now I want to foreground that if, as Copjec convincingly claims, "it is not only the object of the drive that is split from itself; the subject, too is fractured through the drive's repetitions," such that "the ethics of psychoanalysis [. . .] is rather a matter of personal conversion, of the subjective necessity of going beyond oneself," then transition-cum-self-differentiation might be understood as a sublimation, an ethical act in no common sense of the word, a non-proprietary bodily capacity available to all subjects, material constraints notwithstanding, and crucially—we will see why in a minute—a repetition of the negativity in which desire nestles.[25]

This is not a matter of mere lexical preference: what even a promiscuous treatment of psychoanalysis can contribute to trans studies is long overdue attention to the indispensable roles that negativity and the desire that it inaugurates play. In the first place, thinking trans in terms of desire requires that we locate it firmly beyond the sphere of biology, since jouissance marks "the division between libido and nature," making desire unthinkable in terms of instinct or need, and rendering any efforts at essentializing etiologies vain.[26] But perhaps even more pressingly, psychoanalysis can offer an alternative to the gender identity model, a fairly recent invention in which gender is understood as a positive predicate of subjectivity, with some actual content, wholly disarticulated from any notion of desire. We can see this in the scramble to differentiate gender from sexual orientation in advocacy rhetorics, the hard and fast distinction littered across the Human Rights Campaign website, for example, as well as in other "progressive" educational materials, such as the egregious "genderbread person" that somatically segregates "identity" from "attraction."[27]

For these fervent insistences to the contrary, transness stubbornly asserts itself as desire. Andrea Long Chu tell us this in her instantly canonical "On Liking Women,"[28] but so does the much-maligned DSM-5,[29] which is at least one of the reasons why Chu's work has made such waves in what she recently characterized, in *Transgender Studies Quarterly*, as the stagnant pool that is the subfield.[30] Deborah Hartin, a trans activist prominent in the 1970s and one of *LMDW*'s interviewees, also says as much: "I'd like to fall in love, get married, and have children. Oh, I just want to be a woman!" Transness expresses not or not only an attribute of the conscious subject, but a desire that is structurally unfulfillable, and this not only because of the myriad conditions that continue to disallow possibilities for trans life, but simply because it is a desire, because the negativity that incites desire guarantees that it always desires more.

In Lacan's seminar on psychosis, he elaborates the revelation and reproduction of this negativity subtending the symbolic and social order with reference to "the hysteric's question."[31] This question is first posed, in the context of a case study about a Hungarian tram conductor, as: "Am I a man or a woman?" Lacan then swiftly restates it: "What is it to be a woman?"[32] This is the question, Lacan says, plaguing male and female hysterics alike. Rather than draw a facile analogy between the hysteric's question and the experience of transness (which obviously involves asking some version of it), understanding the hysteric's question as one about the negativity of sex can stress the relationship between transness and desire. Indeed, Lacan's contentious claim that "there's no such thing as a sexual relationship," that sex is the mark of symbolic incompletion, is related to his equally incendiary insistence that "*woman* does not exist," that woman is missing something.[33] Of course, everyone is missing something (i.e. is castrated), but only men are deluded enough to think that someone has it all (i.e. is not castrated), and that they could have it all too, prohibition notwithstanding. This is what makes women exemplary subjects, and, I would wager, what makes all hysterics ask after woman's ontological status.[34] In other words, the hysteric's question is one about the lack in being, about the negativity in which the subject, as a subject who desires, takes place. The hysteric's incessant interrogation, posed to the analyst, is never satisfied by any answer, precisely because the subject is irreducible to definition, is not identical to itself, and it therefore amounts to a repetition of that negativity, a ruination of totality.

To say that trans is a matter of sexuality, then, is not only to say that gender and sex are imbricated, but that if sex is the name psychoanalysis gives to the lack in language and in being, then trans is bound up with this hole that the drive re-bores, the hole that holds open, quite literally, the possibility of something new. The drive's circling around an object that ceaselessly differs from itself signals a suspension of the scene of desire, a desire for the repetition of excitation without the banality of release. In Zupančič's words, this object is "always and necessarily double: it is a surplus satisfaction as *sticking to the void* (to the gap in the order of being)."[35] The object of the drive is both a surplus and a deficit, a reification or congelation of negativity that cannot, for that reason, be self-identical.

This returns us to sublimation, to the satisfaction of the drive with a change of object: the double-ness of the object is its difference from itself, what allows the drive to keep turning, to repeat both the void and the extra enjoyment that is stuck to it, and to propel the production of the new. If it is a central lesson of psychoanalysis that desire is unsatisfied, because its object has always already skipped town, this is not, *pace* Chu, "the zero-order disappointment that structures all desire and makes it possible."[36] Desire's immanent unsatisfaction is not a guarantee of disappointment: sublimation allows for satisfaction without shutting down the machinations of selfhood, as the (impossible) fulfillment of desire would. Transition, as sublimation, is a way of sustaining one's desire, but getting something, some bit of enjoyment, a surplus of pleasure beyond simple satiation, nonetheless, because the object of the drive is not identical to itself. This ethical act cleaves space for new discourses and new relations to emerge from the lack in being that keeps us wanting. If trans is ontological, it is so as a negativity, a breach that holds open the possibility of something else. Not necessarily something better, but something else.

TRANS/SEXUALITY AND EDITING AS EDGING

"Let me tell you about an incident that occurred to a young male transsexual who went to Casablanca for the sex change operation." A balding man in a suit is seated behind a desk in a shag-carpeted, wood-paneled office. Dr. Leo Wollman, introduced to us earlier as "our guide through this strange new world," as "one of the pioneers who has devoted his career to exploring the frontiers of sexual identity," is espousing the importance of heeding the recovery period after sex reassignment surgery. The film, like the accompanying book sold in theater lobbies, written by Wishman under the pseudonym M. J. Lukas, "contains how-to information for prospective transsexuals," offering tips, tricks, and cautionary tales like this one.[37] Dr. Wollman explains that Rhoda, who had traveled to Casablanca for her surgery, was "extremely impatient to try out her new vagina," and thus seduced the cab driver taking her to the airport on her way back to the United States.

Foreboding piano music floods the scene, as we cut to a hallway down which a woman, presumably Rhoda, is leading a man. They enter a bedroom—which resembles a hotel about as much as Dr. Wollman's office does a medical facility—and begin to kiss, the scene growing more suspenseful as film noir-y violins stress the seduction's progression. As the pair undress, Rhoda is framed first from the waist up, and then in a mirror that narrowly excludes the crux of the cautionary tale. These shots suggest there is something to see, lingering just outside the frame, something that—if the violins are to be trusted—we will shortly be shown. But when Rhoda's vagina is finally revealed, there is nothing to see, or at least nothing to write home about. The music abruptly switches to the strains of old Hollywood romance as the couple gently caresses, the film cutting between the man's clenching cheeks and Rhoda's enraptured face. If they come together, and we cannot be sure that they do, the money shot seems to come later: as the taxi driver is leaving, the woman spreads her legs to reveal a pool of blood on the bed, punctuated by crashing cymbals. The grinning man closes the bedroom door, and we are back in Dr. Wollman's office, as the doctor, now framed in close-up, explains that "as a result of her sex impatience," Rhoda had to undergo a second surgery. "Of course, this is just an isolated instance. Most patients are more careful," he adds, lest we think this scene of softcore stupor turned bloody nightmare was trying to scare viewers cis.

My argument in this section proceeds from the claim that the content of this cautionary show-and-tell is not sex at all, and this not because of some soft/hardcore distinction, but because sex is the stumbling block of showing and telling. What the film really reveals here, in the cuts from Dr. Wollman's office to a hotel room in Casablanca and back again, is the cut of trans/sex, the desirous deadlock of all symbolic representation. *This* sex cannot be directly seen, but only appears in the seams between and beneath the film's scenes, in the negative space that conjoins and subtends its positive representations. If there is a contradiction here, it is not one between sexual spectacle and sober knowledge, but between sex as the negativity of thought and positive representation itself.

LMDW has been hailed a "pseudo-documentary,"[38] an "alleged documentary,"[39] a "semidocumentary,"[40] a "documentary-style grindhouse epic,"[41] and a "quasi documentary [. . .] surprisingly sympathetic to their subjects [sic] for what is basically an exploitative Mondo film at heart."[42] In these descriptions, from academic and popular sources alike, the category of documentary is always invoked, but never without qualification, as if the film had to be pulled back from its precipice at the last second, its sexual content precluding it from joining the genre's hallowed ranks. These descriptions therefore miss what I want to hazard is *LMDW*'s intervention: rather than that which disqualifies a film from the category of documentary, sex is the very condition of documentary's possibility, what propels the production of knowledge and guarantees its non-totality. The key to this intervention is not in the content of the *LMDW*'s erotic and/or educational images, but in their articulation, in the sublimating montage that I call editing as edging.

LMDW's intercutting of trans and sexuality—its trans/sexuality, perhaps—in the repeated emplacement of simulated sex scenes between transsexual talking heads, the doctor's dry discourse, and demonstrations of trans embodiment, performs the cut that is coextensive with social and symbolic space. Rather than analogize the cut vis-à-vis sex reassignment surgery, I want to take literally Lacan's claim that "the drive is precisely that *montage* by which sexuality participates in the psychical life, in a way that must conform to the gap-like structure that is the structure of the unconscious."[43] Editing is not only cutting but re-cutting, re-boring the constitutive lack in being that marks the failure of representation.[44] *LMDW*'s constant cutting between visual signs of pornography and documentary—and through this cutting, its avoidance of climax—makes and remakes sex as the rupture on which all representation is founded, a rupture that the drive must continually reproduce. But, as I have already suggested, it is not quite the juxtaposition of positive representational content that shows knowledge necessarily shot through with sex. To borrow Lacan's description of extimacy, sex "is at the center only in the sense that it is excluded."[45] Sex in the Lacanian sense is what is subtracted from both documentary and pornography, and it emerges in *LMDW* not in the contradiction between scenes of each, but between positive representation and negative space.[46] Sex as the stumbling block of documentary can only be gleaned from the sublimating rhythms of the film's montage, in the gaps between the only apparent co-presence of sex and sobriety. We never see sex in *LMDW*, but sex as the negativity structuring thought is made sensible through the film's performance of sublimation.

Lacan makes an interesting comment on this in his seventeenth seminar: discussing a study conducted at the University of Washington on the female orgasm, said to "emanat[e] from the total personality,"[47] that had been (misguidedly) taken up by some psychoanalysts as a testament to women's jouissance, Lacan writes,

> I do wonder how a movie camera that takes images in color, placed inside an appendage representing the penis, recording from the inside what takes place on the lining of what, on its being inserted, surrounds it, is capable of grasping the said total personality.[48]

While couched in humor, Lacan's point here is that whatever might be seen, it will not be jouissance. Pornography cannot be a positive representation of sex, because sex is what makes symbolic representation fail.

LMDW is crucially devoid of climaxes: we always cut to another scene of desire before we are ready. We will be watching a "true sex act," a scene of what we have been told to read as heterosexual sex, the film shuffling between shots of a woman's face, eyes closed and curly hair thrust into a pillow, of her breasts being sucked by her lover, and of the couple's caressing penises, when all of a sudden we cut to Dr. Wollman organizing medical supplies in an exam room. Or else we are in (another one of) Dr. Wollman's office(s), where he is describing silicone breast implants and reciting statistics about sex reassignment surgery, when we are unexpectedly confronted by a dark stage, an ominous drumroll, and a spot-lit figure with a chisel poised above her penis. These cuts are abrupt and clunky, the many threads of the film's motley texture not seamlessly but rather seam-fully strung together, miring the viewer in spatial and temporal dislocation. The film's construction is constantly on display, as we are drawn into the interstices between scenes, wondering what could possibly join one to another. In "Pornography and Documentary: Narrating the Alibi," one of very few pieces published about *LMDW*, Chuck Kleinhans even claims that for all of Dr. Wollman's futile attempts at suture, "the current version of the film is particularly disjointed, and I surmise from internal evidence that reels have been placed in the wrong order, increasing the film's disorientation."[49] I do not doubt that this is true, but want to suggest that the film's "inelegant juxtaposition of the MD's 'authoritative' calls for tolerance and understanding [. . .] with footage of cheap porn" works not or not only to "enhanc[e] its aura of sleaziness," but to give shape to the negativity subtending it, to attune us to trans/sexuality as the impossibility of representation.[50] This intercutting of documentary and pornography enacts a suspension of the scene of desire through the forestalling of release, a kind of cinematic edging. And while intercutting usually refers to movement between milieus within a single scene, the cinematic scene, like and as the scene of desire, might be drawn out, becoming coextensive with the film as (w)hole.

Describing courtly love, taken as the paradigmatic instance of sublimation, Lacan writes that "the techniques involved [. . .] are techniques of holding back, of suspension, of *amor interruptus*."[51] Identifying these with foreplay in the Freudian schema, with what runs counter to the pleasure principle, or the logic of the heightened tension followed by release, Lacan goes on to claim that "it is only insofar as the pleasure of desiring, or, more precisely, the pleasure of experiencing unpleasure, is sustained that we can speak of the sexual valorization of the preliminary stages of the act of love," of foreplay or, I submit, of edging.[52] As a practice of sublimation, edging allows for both satisfaction and the repetition of desire and its gap, because edging is not stopping before you get what you want, but not getting "it" as precisely what you want—unsatisfaction as the satisfying object of the drive. *LMDW*'s intercutting always jumps the gun, switching scenes before we are finished, and this editing as edging reveals and repeats the gap of trans/sex, allowing us to grasp this negativity that sustains it.

Indeed, if sublimation is the protocol of the drive, and the drive a montage that re-cuts the hole in being, the hole that prevents the closure of a whole, holding open space for something new, then sublimation aptly characterizes *LMDW*'s practice of editing as edging, its untimely cuts from sex to sobriety and back again. Holding together the most disparate of scenes, *LMDW*'s montage purports to show us everything, to offer a fullness of knowledge, but shows instead the impossibility of totality, and therefore of desire's fulfillment (which is not to say of satisfaction).

The prolongation of excitation and the repetition of desire—which is never fully or finally satisfied, lest the drive come screeching to a halt—is the shared structure of transness and of *LMDW*. The avoidance of climax makes *LMDW* profoundly disorienting: we have no idea when the film is going to end, and at the moment when it seems like it might—when we watch Debbie, who just wanted to be a woman, have sex "like any woman"—the film abruptly cuts to a shot of Steve, whose extended suicide story, containing not one but two sex scenes, conveys the futility of trying not to want to be a woman. In other words, *LMDW* refuses the narrative arc of transition: it does not finish with the fulfillment of Debbie's desire. The sustaining of the film's titular desire evinces the temporality of transness, a temporality belied by the model of gender identity. Conjuring again the specter of the medical definition of transness—a set of desires and a state of affective distress or dysphoria brought on by their unfulfillment—we can say that being trans is a lifelong condition, because if those desires could ever be fulfilled, at some point we would just become cis.

The structure of transness is one of suspension, of sustained spatial and temporal unmooring, of the prolonged in-between. Many have made this point, against popular narratives and work in trans studies that figure transition as a journey home, as a passage that is, at some definite point in time and space, concluded.[53] But the protracted temporality of transness is also the repetition of the scene of desire, and this not only because of the negativity that keeps the drive turning, and the surplus satisfaction that slips in to compensate, just a little, for the guarantee of unfulfillment, but because of the requirement—can we call it a compulsion?—to come out again, to change another document, to correct another hail, to bear another misrecognition that is really a recognition, a reminder of how one moves through the world in ways they did not choose and cannot do anything about. One is never done transitioning, because transition is a repetition of wanting without getting, but getting a little satisfaction anyway, even if that satisfaction is precisely the pleasure of not getting. And *LMDW* really never ends: through its montage, its extension of excitation, the film repeats its desire—*Let Me Die a Woman*—and its gap, the cut of trans/sex that is its—and, I would wager, all documentary's—condition of possibility.

For Kleinhans, documentary is nothing more than a flimsy façade for what he claims is *LMDW*'s core of undeniably exploitational content. "Documentary's 'gravity,' its 'discourse of sobriety,' provides the excuse that allows the naughty content to appear," Kleinhans argues, consigning the documentary features of the film to the realm of mere pretext.[54] Kleinhans labors to recuperate the narrator, cordoning off the doctor's "discourse of tolerance" from the film's "exploitation tactics of shock, cheap sensationalism, freakishness, and prurient voyeurism," reifying the apparent antagonism between documentary and pornography that I signaled above.[55] But by maintaining "sober realism" as documentary's baseline, Kleinhans installs an idealized norm purportedly uncontaminated by voyeurism, spectacle, or anything smacking of sex.[56]

I want to make an even stronger argument than those theorists unafraid to conjure documentary's sordid specters, those who aver the paucity of trying to delink serious knowledge and sober sight from prurient interest and leering looks. Elizabeth Cowie, for example, argues that "for all its seriousness, the documentary film nevertheless continues to involve more disreputable features of cinema [. . .], namely the pleasure and fascination of film as spectacle," of seeing the as-yet-unseen on screen.[57] Documentary always entails voyeurism, Cowie contends, but this pleasure in looking is only called voyeurism when the content of the images is salacious, rather than scientific. Bill Nichols similarly concurs that documentary knowledge is "a source of pleasure that is far from innocent," involving both "voyeurism and fetishism,"[58] if to a lesser degree than fiction film, and elsewhere Nichols, Christine Hansen, and Catherine Needham have likened the logics of pornography, ethnography, and documentary, claiming that they "share a discourse of domination" and "represent impulses born of desire: the desire to know and possess, to 'know' by possessing and possess by knowing."[59]

Nichols et al.'s problematic slippage between epistemo-visual and physical capture aside, I propose that the relationship between documentary and pornography is one not of intimacy, as Cowie and company would seem to suggest, but one of extimacy, where sex is what is subtracted from both. Sex is the stumbling block of documentary epistephilia: not the line it cannot cross, or the place it cannot go—I intend the sense of propriety implied here—but rather what (de)limits it. Sex is the impossibility that is documentary's condition of possibility, it is what cannot be represented and the stipulation of any symbolic representation.[60] Sex is not a boundary to be transgressed, but the constitutive absence of thought, the little lack around which the whole enterprise is built up.

Indeed, if sex is the name for what is missing from thought, a signifier for sex would (fore)close the space of knowledge production. Lacan puts it very plainly when he states that "what leads to knowledge is—allow me to justify this in the more or less long term—the hysteric's discourse."[61] If the hysteric's desire were ever fulfilled, if she ceased to call attention to the lack in being, knowledge would form the closed "sphere" that Lacan argues founds "political preaching."[62] Indeed, as he says of "this idea that knowledge can make a whole," "what is more beautiful, but also what is less open? What better resembles closure of satisfaction?"[63] Knowledge is incomplete, and it is incompleted by sex; it cannot form a whole, because of this hole. If academic knowledge production "ever did culminate in absolute knowledge, it would only be to mark the annulment, the failure, the disappearance at the conclusion of the only thing that motivates the function of knowledge—its dialectic with jouissance."[64] The hysteric reveals and repeats the incompletion of thought, forcing the production of new signifiers that will still not form a sphere.

But if *LMDW* offers a sense of sex as documentary's stumbling block in the seams supporting its representations, then what is the significance of the pornography, those scenes that look like, but cannot be, scenes of sex? I would venture that *LMDW* articulates trans as a matter of sexuality on two levels. On the one hand, the positive representations of what we recognize as sex attune us to the inextricability of transness and desire, on a more or less phenomenal level, offering a corrective to the gender identity model *avant la lettre*. *LMDW* shows and tells us that transness is less a category of being than a way of wanting. And relatedly, *LMDW* reveals—by not showing—sex as a problem of thought, undermining its own attempts at representation through the sublimating montage of trans/sexuality. What sublimation, as creation *ex nihilo*, produces, is precisely a sense of sex as the negativity around which thought incurves, a hold, however tentative, on "not just an impossibility of thought, but a void of Being."[65]

To tether trans to sex with a cut, without collapsing or rendering them analogous, is to situate trans in the hole of thought. In the popular clamor for etiologies (made-for-TV documentaries incessantly rely on visual signifiers of science to imply that the putatively biological cause of transness will soon be uncovered), in the incessant inquiring as to how one can know that they are trans (tellingly, the answer offered is always temporal, never substantive: *I just always knew*), and even in Lavery's intimation that if not psychoanalysis, then some kind of analysis ought to account for "trans phenomena," we can glimpse the desire for the knowledge about the thingness of transness, a desire that, like all desires, has no thing, or whose thing has always already gone fishing. Trans/sex is the site where the want to know is confronted by a gaping hole. Posing trans as an obstacle to thought need not be transphobic and might indeed be worked against reactionary arguments for transition's impossibility, without reversion to suspect rhetorics of essentialism. We have read enough Judith Butler to know that transness cannot express or confirm anything like an innate gender identity, and yet we want to be recognized otherwise anyway.

If we have a problem accounting for transness, avowing that gender is both a biopolitical category originating from outside of the subject, and something that many of us feel to be a fundamental, if not an outwardly indexed, part of ourselves, then one solution—perhaps the sole solution—is to understand transness as a problem for accounting, as a minus that does not lend itself to the arithmetic of positive symbolization. The only ethical concept of transness may be one of epistemic impossibility.

LMDW promises at its outset to tell us all about transness. Over a montage of anonymous bodies walking down a bustling city street, the narrator who will introduce Dr. Wollman to us begins a bait and switch: "We all know what sex we are. It is so obvious that it can be seen by the naked eye. We are male, or female." "But perhaps things are not so obvious," he proposes as the camera pans over a number of classical nudes, accompanied by anxious horns and cymbals. "Imagine, if you can, what it is like to be a woman imprisoned in the body of a man, or a man trapped in the body of a woman. Not male, not female, not homosexual." A collage of front pages fills the screen, corroborating the narrator's claim that "Recently, the world was shocked by the discovery of this third sex—the transsexual." Over close-ups of the newspapers, the narrator announces *LMDW*'s intentions: "We will meet real transsexuals. We will show, for the first time, how and why genetic men become real women, and genetic women become real men. We will take you behind these headlines." But behind these headlines, it turns out, lies no essential kernel. The "strange new world" of transsexuality, the "frontiers of sexual identity" that "pioneers" such as Dr. Wollman are at work exploring, appear indelibly incomplete, wrought by a gap or hole that the film constantly reproduces through its sublimating montage, (un)done by the seams, those bits of nothing, that hold together its positive representations. Knowing cannot follow from showing, because here showing marks the impossibility of knowing.

Recall that in the scene that began this section, when Rhoda's vagina is finally revealed, there is nothing—or rather, no Thing—to see. What is supposed to be the crux of the film's exploitation, its big top reveal, its slimy spectacle of transsexuality, looks like nothing in particular, indeed, like nothing at all. The film has already made explicit the limitations of visual knowledge: we cannot know sex, understood as a binarized biological reality, from seeing. But neither can we know trans/sex, it implies here, belying the narrator's early promises. The film can show as much fish as it likes, but all it reveals is the lack that ruins representational closure. *LMDW* performs its own failure, staging the impossibility of both documentary and pornography by making trans/sex, as that impossibility, sensible. The film is not identical to itself (literally, if Kleinhans is to be believed); it differs from itself as documentary, pornography, or (s)exploitation cinema, because those generic containers are incompleted by sex, by the lack that allows them to be otherwise. The film's sublimating montage, its giving shape to the trans/sexual negativity that subtends it, to the irreparable hole in the "big tent" of knowledge, might therefore offer another way to think the ethics of exploitation.[66]

NOTES

1. Thomas Waugh, *The Fruit Machine: Twenty Years of Writings on Queer Cinema* (Durham, NC: Duke University Press, 2000), 72.
2. Linda Williams, *Hard Core: Power, Pleasure, and the "Frenzy of the Visible"* (Berkeley: University of California Press, 1989), 34–57; Christine Hansen, Catherine Needham, and Bill Nichols, "Skin Flicks: Pornography, Ethnography, and the Discourses of Power," *Discourse* 11, no. 2 (Spring–Summer 1989): 64–79.
3. Jacques Lacan, *The Ethics of Psychoanalysis 1959–1960: The Seminar of Jacques Lacan Book VII*, ed. Jacques-Alain Miller, trans. Dennis Porter (New York: W. W. Norton, 1997), 139.
4. Ibid., 112.
5. For a useful summary of the negative or antisocial turn in queer theory see Robert L. Caserio, Lee Edelman, Judith Halberstam, José Esteban Muñoz, and Tim Dean, "The Antisocial Thesis in Queer Theory," *PMLA* 121, no. 3 (2006): 819–28. Notably, Edelman accuses Halberstam of almost the same positive conception of negativity that Alenka Zupančič does Deleuze, as I discuss below.
6. Lee Edelman, *No Future: Queer Theory and the Death Drive* (Durham, NC: Duke University Press, 2004).
7. "Contrary to vulgar understandings of it, then, sublimation is not something that happens to the drive under special circumstances; it is the proper destiny of the drive." Joan Copjec, *Imagine There's No Woman: Ethics and Sublimation* (Cambridge, MA: MIT Press, 2004), 30.
8. Karen Barad, "Transmaterialities: Trans*/Matter/Realities and Queer Political Imaginings," *GLQ: A Journal of Gay and Lesbian Studies* 21, no. 2–3 (2015): 387–422. I will grant that Barad is onto something with her insistence on the void and "self-birth," this something being, of course, a Lacanian something, something like sublimation as creation *ex nihilo* (see note 15).
9. Eva Hayward and Jami Weinstein, "Introduction: Tranimalities in the Age of Trans* Life," *TSQ: Transgender Studies Quarterly* 2, no. 2 (May 2015): 195–208.
10. Marquis Bey, "The Trans*-ness of Blackness, The Blackness of Trans*-ness," *TSQ: Transgender Studies Quarterly* 4, no. 2 (May 2017): 275–95.
11. Myra J. Hird, "Animal Trans," in *Queering the Non/human*, ed. Noreen Giffney and Myra J. Hird (New York: Routledge, 2008), 227–47.
12. Jules Gill-Peterson, "The Technical Capacities of the Body: Assembling Race, Technology, and Transgender," *TSQ: Transgender Studies Quarterly* 1, no. 3 (August 2014): 402–18.
13. Bey, "The Trans*-ness," 276.
14. Ibid., 287, 284.
15. Gilles Deleuze and Félix Guattari, *A Thousand Plateaus: Capitalism and Schizophrenia*, trans. Brian Massumi (Minneapolis: University of Minnesota Press, 2005), 147.
16. Alenka Zupančič, *What is Sex?* (Cambridge, MA: MIT Press, 2017), 124.
17. Ibid.
18. Ibid.

19. "Now if you consider the case from the point of view I first proposed, as an object made to represent the existence of the emptiness at the center of the real that is called the Thing, this emptiness as represented in the representation presents itself as a *nihil*, a nothing. And that is why the potter, just like you to whom I am speaking, creates the vase with his hands around this emptiness, creates it, just like the mythical creator, *ex nihilo*, starting with a hole." Lacan, *Ethics of Psychoanalysis*, 121.
20. Jacques Lacan, *On Feminine Sexuality, The Limits of Love and Knowledge, 1972–1973: Encore, The Seminar of Jacques Lacan Book XX*, ed. Jacques-Alain Miller, trans. Bruce Fink (New York: W. W. Norton, 1999), 12.
21. Grace Lavery, "The King's Two Anuses: Trans Feminism and Free Speech," *Differences* 30, no. 3 (2019): 141.
22. Gill-Peterson, "Technical Capacities," 406.
23. Ibid., 409.
24. Lacan, *Ethics of Psychoanalysis*, 293; my emphasis.
25. Copjec, *Imagine There's No Woman*, 44.
26. Jacques Lacan, *The Other Side of Psychoanalysis: The Seminar of Jacques Lacan, Book XVII*, ed. Jacques-Alain Miller, trans. Russell Grigg (New York: W. W. Norton, 2007), 78.
27. The Genderbread Person, <https://www.genderbread.org/> (last accessed November 3, 2020).
28. Andrea Long Chu, "On Liking Women," *n+1* 30 (Winter 2018), <https://nplusonemag.com/issue-30/essays/on-liking-women/> (last accessed November 3, 2020).
29. Of the six diagnostic criteria for "Gender Dysphoria in Adolescents and Adults," four are "desire[s]." "Gender Dysphoria" in *Diagnostic and Statistical Manual of Mental Disorders: DSM-5* (Arlington: American Psychiatric Association, 2013), <https://doi.org/10.1176/appi.books.9780890425596.dsm14> (last accessed November 3, 2020).
30. "Let's face it: Trans studies is over. If it isn't, it should be." Andrea Long Chu and Emmett Harsin Drager, "After Trans Studies," *Transgender Studies Quarterly* 6, no. 1 (February 2019): 103.
31. Jacques Lacan, *The Psychoses, 1955–1956: The Seminar of Jacques Lacan Book III*, ed. Jacques-Alain Miller, trans. Russell Grigg (New York: W. W. Norton, 1997), 161.
32. Ibid., 171.
33. Lacan, *On Feminine Sexuality*, 7.
34. "And yet if it is woman who is privileged in Lacan's analysis this is because she remains closer to the truth of being, while man obfuscates this truth through a nostalgic, secondary operation that allows him to maintain a belief in the plentitude of being to come." Copjec, *Imagine There's No Woman*, 7.
35. Zupančič, *What is Sex?*, 103.
36. Chu, "On Liking Women."
37. Susan Stryker, *Queer Pulp: Perverted Passions from the Golden Age of the Paperback* (San Francisco: Chronicle Books, 2001), 82.
38. Tania Modleski, "Women's Cinema as Counterphobic Cinema: Doris Wishman as the Last Auteur," in *Sleaze Artists: Cinema at the Margins of Taste, Style, and Politics*, ed. Jeffrey Sconce (Durham, NC: Duke University Press, 2007), 60.
39. Rebekah McKendry, "Fondling Your Eyeballs: Watching Doris Wishman," in *From the Arthouse to the Grindhouse: Highbrow and Lowbrow Transgression in Cinema's First Century*, ed. John Cline and Robert G. Weiner (Lanham, MD: Scarecrow Press, 2010), 60.
40. "*Let Me Die a Woman*," Wikipedia, <https://en.wikipedia.org/wiki/Let_Me_Die_a_Woman> (last accessed November 3, 2020).
41. "Let Me Die a Woman," Rotten Tomatoes, <https://www.rottentomatoes.com/m/let_me_die_a_woman_1974/> (last accessed November 3, 2020).

42. Ibid.
43. Jacques Lacan, *The Four Fundamental Concepts of Psychoanalysis: The Seminar of Jacques Lacan Book XI*, ed. Jacques-Alain Miller, trans. Alan Sheridan (New York: W. W. Norton, 1998), 176.
44. Kaja Silverman's work on suture is certainly not extraneous here, though a thorough engagement with it would take me too far afield of my argument. See Kaja Silverman, *The Subject of Semiotics* (Oxford: Oxford University Press, 1984).
45. Lacan, *Ethics of Psychoanalysis*, 71.
46. Pornography cannot be a positive representation of sex, because sex—if I have not sufficiently beaten you over the head with this point—is what makes representation fail. Knowing is not seeing, but rather seeing marks the impossibility of knowing.
47. Lacan, *Other Side of Psychoanalysis*, 71.
48. Ibid., 71–2.
49. Chuck Kleinhans, "Pornography and Documentary: Narrating the Alibi," in *Sleaze Artists: Cinema at the Margins of Taste, Style, and Politics*, ed. Jeffrey Sconce (Durham, NC: Duke University Press, 2007), 113.
50. Ibid., 114.
51. Lacan, *Ethics of Psychoanalysis*, 152.
52. Ibid.
53. See, for example, Lucas Cassidy Crawford, "Transgender Without Organs? Mobilizing a Geo-Affective Theory of Gender Modification," *WSQ: Women's Studies Quarterly* 36, no. 3–4 (Fall/Winter 2008): 127–43.
54. Kleinhans, "Pornography and Documentary," 97.
55. Ibid., 112, 114.
56. Ibid., 97.
57. Elizabeth Cowie, "The Spectacle of Reality and Documentary Film," *Documentary Box* 10 (1997), <https://www.yidff.jp/docbox/10/box10-1-e.html> (last accessed November 3, 2020).
58. Bill Nichols, *Representing Reality: Issues and Concepts in Documentary* (Bloomington: University of Indiana Press, 1991), 178. I want to note here that hasty recourse to the rhetorics of exploitation and domination not only elide the not so easily answered questions of precisely who is exploited, and by whom, but risks foreclosing in advance the possibility that those who participated in the film did so willingly, whether or not they found it enjoyable or empowering, which are not stipulations of participation in other kinds of moving images, but are often considered requirements to consent to appear in both documentary and pornography.
59. Hansen et al., "Skin Flicks," 67.
60. This is precisely Copjec's point in "Sex and the Euthanasia of Reason," the chapter that Lavery claims demonstrates psychoanalysis's failure before "trans phenomena." As Copjec argues, "Sex serves no other purpose than to limit reason," and to limit it from within, as the negativity that (un)grounds it. Copjec, *Read My Desire: Lacan against the Historicists* (Cambridge, MA: MIT Press, 1995), 207.
61. Lacan, *Other Side of Psychoanalysis*, 23.
62. Ibid., 30.
63. Ibid., 31.
64. Ibid., 35.
65. Copjec, *Imagine There's No Woman*, 36.
66. Ibid., 168.

PART II

Cultural History and Adult Film Studies

CHAPTER 4

Hardcore Wishman

Whitney Strub

"If you want to see a hardcore film, fine," Doris Wishman told Andrea Juno when interviewed for the pioneering exploitation history *Incredibly Strange Films* (1986), "but I couldn't make those films." She sounded uncertain, though; Juno had asked her if she would shoot hardcore, and after answering with a flat negative, she qualified it with something of a veiled confession: "not that I disapprove, but I don't think I'd be capable. Well, I *could*. At first I thought it was horrible, but it's not."[1]

In fact, she could and had. Wishman's two forays into hardcore, *Satan Was a Lady* and *Come with Me My Love* (both 1976), dropped unceremoniously into the second-tier mid-1970s theatrical pornography circuit, largely receding from memory once their initial runs completed their course. In being forgotten, they joined several other Wishman films that floated away from the historical archive. Early nudist works *Playgirls International* (1963) and *Behind the Nudist Curtain* (1964) remain currently lost, though with some hope of rediscovery, since only in 2017 did *The Prince and the Nature Girl* (1965) finally resurface. And her final films, *Dildo Heaven* (2002) and *Each Time I Kill* (completed posthumously in 2007), have yet to receive licensed distribution, though they circulate in bootleg form. What distinguishes the hardcore duo from these other semi-lost films, however, is that the films themselves were never lost; rather, their authorship was. Wishman successfully obscured her directorship for over two decades, and the small but robust body of Wishman scholarship has overlooked the films. Like other female exploitation filmmakers, Wishman's historical place has already been "reduced to parenthetical mentions, footnotes, and anecdotal asides," as Alicia Kozma writes of another important such figure, Stephanie Rothman; of her hardcore, we have only silence.[2]

What, then, do *Come with Me My Love* and *Satan Was a Lady* add to the Wishman canon? At one level, not much: these are minor works in an already marginal cinema, and begrudgingly shot, at that. They add one entry to the short list of female hardcore filmmakers in the 1970s, but production details, including precise dates, remain opaque, aside from those that step over Wishman's always-short fourth wall or bleed through her loose suture and declare themselves within the mise-en-scène itself—precisely the aspect of Wishman's work that has made her an iconic figure in the paracinematic milieu famously outlined by Jeffrey Sconce.[3]

Yet one of the defining features of Wishman's hardcore to any viewer attuned to her idiosyncratic style is the relative attenuation of precisely those features that most define her: the walking-feet shots, the abrupt cutaways to vases, paintings, or seemingly random objects (what Michael Bowen calls her "décor-body"[4]), the delirious montage of midtown Manhattan or South Florida landscapes, the cramped Queens apartment so obviously her own that something like *A Taste of Flesh* (1967) shares powerful affinities with Shirley Clarke's *Portrait of Jason*, released the same year into a different cultural world. In their altogether more pruned-down approach, *Come with Me* and *Satan* present a formal case study of a sexploitation filmmaker adjusting to hardcore, and some of the stylistic costs that shift demanded. While numerous continuities and sensibilities ultimately link Wishman's hardcore back to her other work, it inescapably reflects the challenge of adjusting to the new imperatives of a regime of maximum—and temporally sustained—visibility. It was meat shots *or* feet shots, and generic convention dictated which would prevail.

SEXPLOITATION GOES HARDCORE

Not every sexploitation filmmaker followed the drift to hardcore. Barry Mahon segued into children's films, then out of cinema; Russ Meyer went to Hollywood, and then returned to hardboiled but softcore sex films. But a great many did cross the penetrative Rubicon, navigating the transition in uneven ways. Radley Metzger became Henry Paris, and retained the stylized editing and debonair debauchery that had long marked his immediately recognizable work. Joe Sarno, too, added explicitness but continued at sex melodrama, even when masked under such crass titles as *The Trouble with Young Stuff* (1977). Meanwhile, others floundered: Michael Findlay, straight but ultimately stranded in gay hardcore, buried a grim, self-loathing, reflexive *cri de coeur* in a heterosexual loop-carrier, *Young and Wet* (1975), just before his untimely demise in a helicopter accident. In contrast, his former partner, Roberta Findlay, *found* her voice through hardcore, directing both bleak, surreal downers and anarchic comedies alike.

While most of these filmmakers shot under various pseudonyms, their directorial presence could still be felt and often identified, either through aesthetic continuities with their earlier work or, sometimes, public acknowledgment. Others of the era concealed their hardcore work. Herschell Gordon Lewis, best known as a gore pioneer for his *Blood Feast* (1963), also dabbled in sexploitation but denied crossing into hardcore all the way through restoration firm Vinegar Syndrome's 2013 recovery and distribution of his 1971 "white coater" *Black Love*. Gay softcore pioneer Pat Rocco has never acknowledged shooting explicit scenes, though on-the-record accounts have challenged his narrative.

Doris Wishman joined this group, insisting into the late 1990s that she had never made hardcore films. Clearly, the move into pornography was fraught for Wishman, evidenced in the disintegrating boundaries of sexploitation by the turn of the 1970s. When she returned to color after the run of black and white grindhouse roughies that occupied her for the second half of the 1960s, it was with two films anxious about the limits of sexual representation. *The Amazing Transplant* and *Love Toy* opened in quick succession, in late 1970 and early 1971 respectively, and grappled with the place of softcore in the age of the "white coater" featuring unsimulated (if often cold and clinical) sex. Their solution was to hedge: full-frontal male nudity in both, with future hardcore cameraman João (billed as Juan) Fernandes not entirely flaccid at times in *Amazing Transplant*, and realistic-looking oral sex in *Love Toy*. If the Chesty Morgan films of 1974 suggested a retrenchment to gentler R-rated territory, an anxious need to hold hardcore at bay reverberated through a rare newspaper article about a Wishman production in 1975. As she geared up to shoot *Daughters of Mata Hari*, a sequel of sorts to the Chesty Morgan duo, the *Miami News* ran a brief piece, "Moviemakers Seek Buxom Miamians." It concluded with associate producer Sharon Lee emphasizing that this was *definitely* "not a porno film." Indeed, *The Immoral Three*, as it was eventually titled for release, was arguably Wishman's most conventionally ambitious film, featuring location shooting in Miami, New York, and Las Vegas, and containing plentiful nudity but only moderately graphic sex.[5]

Yet the ineluctable market drift toward hardcore carried Wishman along as it had the other sexploitation filmmakers of her era. Her films fit seamlessly into the grind of the lower-budget hardcore features that hovered below the marquee titles of the porno chic era. Lacking the budget or wit of Metzger's *The Opening of Misty Beethoven* or even the darkly propulsive crude energy of Shaun Costello's *Midnight Desires*, both from the same year, *Satan* and *Come with Me* instead joined the spate of perfunctory sexual potboilers that primarily strung together straightforward fucking with nominal narrative stitching.

Satan Was a Lady arrived first, playing in Los Angeles and Danville, Virginia, in February 1976, before entering a distributional circuit that ran from New Jersey to Florida and even into Utah (where the film was seized by police in May).[6] Meanwhile, *Come with Me My Love* appeared in Charleston, West Virginia, in late July 1976, and seems to have had a more limited release, reaching Detroit in October, Minneapolis in November, and Los Angeles only in December.[7] The first film hinges on intrafamilial tensions, with sex-driven conspiracies between and among two sisters, their mother, and the fiancé of one of them. The other tells a lowbrow-Gothic ghost story, beginning with a jealous husband who murders his cheating wife before killing himself, only to reappear decades later haunting, assaulting, and romancing a new inhabitant of the same apartment who resembles the dead wife, killing her various lovers while attempting to woo her into the afterlife alongside him.

HARDCORE RELUCTANCE

Satan Was a Lady wastes no time ushering Wishman (producing and directing as "Kenyon Wintel") into the hardcore era, opening on star Bree Anthony receiving manual stimulation, oral sex, and penetrative sex from her male partner Tony Richards. Tiny shards of narrative drop in, among meat shots that sometimes require quick focus-pulling after unwieldy zooms. Midway through the sex scene, Annie Sprinkle arrives, in what is presumably the same room, though a resolute absence of spatial coordinates gives the cutting a Kuleshov-degree-zero effect; "my little sister," Sprinkle declares to herself, with a sort of bemused approximation of shock, departing before the scene arrives at its money shot. Finished, Anthony laughs to Richards, "Imagine if mother could see us now!"

Until its final three minutes, when a doctor retroactively expounds 90 percent of the film's plot, that set-up lays out the basic narrative contours of *Satan*, a tale of voyeurism, romantic tension, and betrayal. Its coital requirements leave little room for subplot refinement; in a brief seventy minutes, it includes seven sex scenes. While the more sophisticated hardcore filmmakers integrated character development and plot-advancing dialogue into their sex scenes, for the most part Wishman pauses the narrative, shooting stand-alone sexual interludes. *Come with Me My Love* is even more sex-heavy, cramming ten sex scenes into its seventy-four minutes. While its supernatural story is woven through some of those encounters, for the most part this again results in a near-loop experience of brief dialogue scenes as framing for borderline-decontextualized sex.

The weight of this sex emphasis tips the cinematic scale away from Wishman's defining tropes, a banalization that helped preserve Wishman's anonymity but also resulted in rather rote hardcore. Her first New York City roughie, *The Sex Perils of Paulette* (1964), had begun with nearly ten minutes of star Anna Karol strolling the city, embedding the film in a concrete urban setting whose very historicity provides much of its spectatorial pleasure, as Elena Gorfinkel has shown of the classic Times Square grindhouse canon.[8] Structurally, the footage served as filler, but stylistically it defined Wishman's mark, sometimes adding seasonal affective resonance, as when the stark autumnal barrenness of the Queens trees in *Indecent Desires* (1968) mirrored and underscored the emotional landscape of its lonely, alienated characters. Hardcore afforded a diminished platform for these touches. Though set in fictional Kenmare City, with an opening flashback to 1925, *Come with Me* offers almost no sense of place aside from a brief exterior shot of an apartment building and a short scene in a park, both clearly New York. Likewise, when a character in *Satan* sets up a meeting at "4th and Barlow," instead of the expected street corner, we cut directly into the inside of an apartment, skipping over the establishing shot that might develop tone by situating these characters in a social world.

At the center, then, lies the sex. Wishman's approach to sex is a fairly indifferent one, haphazard in its rhythm and devoid of any apparent commitment to generating erotic heat. Characters fornicate without undue enthusiasm, and instead of a "frenzy of the visible" as per Linda Williams, Wishman offers a more routinized factory of the visible, working through the various sexual permutations as if crossing off a checklist.[9] A brief scene between C.J. Laing and Tony Richards in *Satan* most bluntly articulates the sexual ethos at play: Richards we know already from his wooing of Bree Anthony, but mid-70s mainstay Laing simply enters the picture unannounced; they drunkenly stumble into an apartment and almost immediately commence penetrative sex without foreplay, which ends without even the money shot that had become a staple of the genre by this point. When an impatient Sprinkle calls, Richards simply swats Laing on the ass and sends her out, allowing for incremental plot advancement as Sprinkle warns, "I wouldn't want to have to go to the district attorney" with incriminating records she holds, and he blurts, "You bitch," before hanging up on her.

Come with Me My Love as well opens with a perfunctory sex scene, with the slight frisson of a voyeur spying on a couple balanced against somewhat underlit meat-shot close-ups. It ends poorly, with the snoop muttering, "My wife and my best friend," before shooting both of them, and then himself, thus setting up the haunting that animates the film's nominal plot, as a woman resembling the wife later moves into the building and receives sexual night visits from the husband's ghost.

In a sense, it is this sexual nonchalance, more than any spectral presence, that most drives the film's woozy ambience. In the second sex scene, shortly following the first, porno chic-era star Vanessa del Rio walks into a room with a man and woman fucking on a bed with pink sheets. "Mind if I join you?," she casually asks, leading to a threesome that culminates in a calmly desultory ejaculation and a sudden zoom into the man's cock, a belated (and unsuccessful) attempt to interject excitement through a sort of lens-thrusting formal maneuver. Only Annie Sprinkle brings unfettered carnality to either film, and often in spite of Wishman's general erotic disinvestment. Her solitary masturbation scene in *Satan Was a Lady*, rolling and writhing on a couch in corset and stockings, constitutes a rare break from the otherwise pervasive erotic doldrums—and also points to Sprinkle's membership in the cohort of female performers who claimed their own forms of authorship by shaping pornographic representation through their erotic labor, as Heather Butler has noted of Sprinkle's 1970s peer Georgina Spelvin, who like Sprinkle often queered heterosexual depictions with her own insistent versions of pleasure and desire.[10]

Still, in the end Wishman assumed the officially sanctioned author function of the films, and her construction of hardcore sex showed that maximum visibility did not ultimately resolve the tensions contained within sexploitation's softcore anxiety. Elena Gorfinkel has most thoroughly explored the ambivalent looking relations bound within 1960s sexploitation's softcore strictures. She finds "the guilty expenditure" central to sexploitation's "diegetic structure of prohibition and ellipsis," with the anxiety over the desired but deferred sexual release of ultimate visibility resulting in "pessimistic, frequently shame-drenched" narratives that both express and release that tension.[11] Certainly that captures the flow of Wishman's roughies, with their downbeat, despairing endings. But the advent of hardcore did not deliver the utopian liberation it promised; while newfound explicitness strained to reach an unmediated "real" sex that scholars in the wake of Michel Foucault's pioneering *History of Sexuality, Volume 1* would begin to doubt existed at all outside the discursive arena, Wishman's hardcore lapsed into precisely the grim prognoses of her softcore. *Satan Was a Lady* ends with Bree Anthony frozen in what might be a permanent "state of shock" after her lover and family conspire against her, faking his death only to trigger her heart condition by having his ostensible corpse come to life in the coffin when she bows down for a final kiss goodbye. *Come with Me My Love* sends its passive protagonist, played by Ursula Austin, into an afterlife with the possessive husband who had murdered his cheating wife in 1925 and stalked her as the reincarnated version. "In death, you're mine," his final words to her as they wander into their ghostly conjoining, reasserts the same violent patriarchal control that ensnared the female leads of such earlier films as *Bad Girls Go to Hell* and *Indecent Desires*.

Indeed, it was in part this recursive highlighting of male sexual violence, fulfilling generic requirements for presumptively male grindhouse patrons even while offering glimpses of a proto-feminist critique, that informed some scholarly efforts to recuperate Wishman into feminist film history (though she herself repudiated the word). Thus, Moya Luckett locates an assertion of "the primacy of feminine spectatorship" in her films, while Tania Modleski finds women's bodies "less isolated as a site of fragmentation," or, "at the very least, the films seem to suggest that there are more things of interest to look at in the world than women's butts.'"[12] To the extent that the hardcore duo intervenes here, it is to recycle certain of these themes. The bed as a site of particular vulnerability for women, as portrayed in *Bad Girls*, finds echo in *Come with Me*, in which the spirit of the jealous dead husband assaults Austin's character Abby in her sleep (in typical hetero-porn logic, she quickly comes to welcome these attacks); likewise, the supernatural theme of *Indecent Desires*, which links a doll to a real woman's sensations, reverberates in the ghostly narrative of the hardcore film. Women remained menaced in Wishman's hardcore, and yet without the snarling vicious edge of the roughies—a sign that explicitness repaid *some*, though not all, of the guilty expenditure. When *Satan Was a Lady* moves into a BDSM scene between Annie Sprinkle and Bobby Astyr, it is with good cheer that she submits to his bondage gear, shrugging, "I'll try anything once." As he chains her spread-eagled to the bed, she laughs, smiles, and offers affirmative consent, with an "Okay, let's go!"

Authorship of this sexual enthusiasm surely once more goes to Sprinkle rather than Wishman. Sprinkle adopted the same giddy exuberance in nearly every role she played, and mocked her own dramatic range, claiming it was not the sex, but "the acting that's embarrassing."[13] Indeed, some question remains as to how involved Wishman actually was in shooting the sex, with cinematographer C. Davis Smith later suggesting that she would simply instruct him to "Go ahead and do what you have to," leaving the room for the actual sex.[14] All of this complicates any reductively auteurist readings of Wishman's hardcore (along with much of her earlier work), and yet the fact remains that she was the driving force in creating these works. Abby in *Come with Me* serves as something of her avatar, drifting impassively through the film's perfunctory sexual combinations. If one pivotal moment in *Bad Girls Go to Hell* had involved lesbian desire thwarted by internalized shame ("I love you too," protagonist Meg tells the woman who provides the only solace she knows, "that's why I must go"), *Come with Me* plays as something of the jaundiced rejoinder, a decade later and after the purported liberation of hardcore's sex utopias. Abby blankly submits to Annie Sprinkle's advances, but a cursory lesbian hardcore scene offers no more escape than the coiled constraints of softcore sexploitation. The ghost-husband stabs Sprinkle while she makes postcoital coffee, and Abby simply wanders home to bed. Lesbianism, held in abeyance in the roughies but at least full of promise and potential, deflates here to the same tedium as heterosexuality. In some ways, Wishman's hardcore vision of sex and its relation to freedom is even more dismal than that of her roughies—if anything marks her authorship, it is this. Porn scholars have paid insufficient attention to the efforts at negation and refusal by reluctant pornographers, from the gay Zebedy Colt's attempts to smuggle queer eros into his straight hardcore, to the active hostility of Roger Watkins, unhappily stuck in a porno rut as Richard Mahler and committed to making his sex films as joyless and grim as possible.[15] This group was Doris Wishman's hardcore cohort.

THE ABSENT AUTEUR

Despite the time crunch imposed by the sex, several Wishman motifs reverberated across the films, as when Bree Anthony takes an outdoor stroll in *Satan was a Lady* replete with cutaways to random plants and water; back at home, she looks out the window to a high-rise view of a highway adorned with storefront lights coming into focus from an initial blur, a shot reused from *Love Toy*. Wishman frequently recycled footage, and her nudist film *The Prince and the Nature Girl*, for instance, links to both hardcore films: a shot of a New York sunset with flaring color saturating the cloudy sky recurs in both, while even a brief shot of water lapping over a pair of rocks is transplanted from its original nudist colony into Bree Anthony's Central Park stroll in *Satan* (suggesting the dense organic web of re-presented footage that binds Wishman's films together, the same shot can be seen in black and white in another Central Park scene, in 1966's *Another Day, Another Man*). Christopher Jarmick also finds filler footage from *Double Agent 73* recurring in *Come with Me*.[16]

Wishman's stylistic tics recur in her hardcore, too. Beyond the decor shots, Central Park strolls that culminate in upward camera pans to tree-branch-entangled skies appear in both—again, linking her nudist work to the roughies and extending into the porn. The belabored avoidance of speaking faces to conceal (but inadvertently highlight) the MOS shooting is another staple. And after a quick opening negative image in *Come with Me*, the film's first actual scene begins with a shot of feet walking up stairs, something of a directorial signature. For that matter, cast carryover on *Come with Me* suggests possible shooting continuities with *The Immoral Three*, with which it shares actors Roger Caine, Ed Marshall, and Levi Richards—with almost no documentary evidence of the production, such insinuating glimpses are the closest one can currently come to excavating the history of Wishman's working practices.[17] Her uniquely loopy approach to filmmaking also results in some striking images: in *Come with Me*, one wonderfully composed shot of a dead man's torso in a bathtub, with a sink basin's corner occupying the foreground and nearly half the frame, as a bar of soap and the man's penis seem to float toward one another, multiple visual echoes running through the lopsided arrangement; in *Satan*, an entire sex scene in negative image, calling to mind both the infamous solarized ejaculations of porno chic classic *Behind the Green Door* (1972) and Barbara Rubin's phantasmagoric underground sex film *Christmas on Earth* (1963). Perhaps most revealing, Wishman's own distinct voice briefly enters both hardcore films for short voiceover narration of internal thoughts by the female leads.[18]

Still, these tells are muted, and credited director Kenyon Wintel's name is no reveal, even if it faintly echoes the "Dawn Whitman" screenplay attribution she often used. No known record suggests anyone at the time identified it as the work of Wishman. Indeed, her male pseudonyms preserved her anonymity at the cost of potentially better box office. As Laura Helen Marks notes, male directors such as Shaun Costello and Anthony Spinelli often relied on female pseudonyms as deliberate marketing tools.[19] Wishman's peer Roberta Findlay, meanwhile, drew press interest for her anomalous role as a female hardcore filmmaker. When her *Angel No. 9* came out in 1975, she played the iconoclast to the hilt, telling the Camden, New Jersey, *Courier-Post* that she had no sympathy for feminism, since "maybe I hate both men and women." Reporter Bill Wine called her "the only female pornographer working in 35mm film."[20] Concealed behind her male pseudonyms, Wishman could draw no such publicity.

And so, in these anonymous hour-long slabs of sexual filler, Wishman crossed over from softcore, losing much of what had made her work distinct. Without the hook of a female pornographer, neither drew much attention in the way of reviews, and then into obscurity they sank. A 1982 *Variety* ad from Leisure Time Booking included *Satan* as a third-tier title for international sales.[21] In the 1990s *Come with Me* circulated on VHS as *The Haunted Pussy*, as part of Something Weird Video's "Sexy Shocker Hardcore Horrors" series. By 2017 they had both come into the ownership of Vinegar Syndrome, the premier adult-film restoration and distribution outfit, though as of this writing they have not been reissued, circulating primarily on streaming-site bootlegs of an unlicensed Alpha Blue Archives DVD put out in 2005.[22]

When a *Spin* reporter called Wishman for an article about female pornographers in 1995, Wishman curtly declared, "I know nothing about pornography" and hung up. An unnamed "ex-porn star" was quoted noting, "Doris was the worst! She had no sensibility about sex. I never understood why this little old lady was making dirty movies."[23] Still, as late as 1997, when Michael Bowen's *Wide Angle* article introduced Wishman into scholarly film studies literature, her narrative prevailed, as Bowen noted her "distrust of hardcore" (surely true) and attributed its advent to "a different generation with new desires."[24] Another *Spin* article the next year, as she was rediscovered by a cult audience and catapulted into a relative limelight that included appearing on *Late Night with Conan O'Brien*, again described her career as "eschewing true porn."[25]

Only after performer Annie Sprinkle—clearly the aforementioned ex-porn source—offhandedly mentioned her work with Wishman in her late-90s performance piece (later released on DVD) *Annie Sprinkle's Herstory of Porn: Reel to Real* was Wishman's hardcore authorship officially established, with a 1998 article in *Paper Mag* that verified her authorship of *Come with Me*.[26] Before Wishman's 2002 passing, Bowen managed to get her on the record about the films, albeit quite tersely; she recalled that they were not shot back to back, but could not establish a timeline vis-à-vis the Chesty Morgan films, *Deadly Weapons* and *Double Agent 73* (both 1974).[27] When Wishman broke nearly two decades of retirement to make another film called *Satan Was a Lady* in 2001, it was no acknowledgment of the earlier version, sharing nothing but a title—with its opening flogging scene and blackmailing hustler, it was much closer to a remake of her 1968 roughie *Too Much Too Often!*.

And so we are left with two films of imprecisely known origin and deliberately hidden authorship, notable less for their content than the sheer fact of their existence. *Satan Was a Lady* and *Come with Me My Love* are hardly the Rosetta Stones of Wishmanography. Rather, they represent case studies of a sexploitation filmmaker shifting uncomfortably into hardcore, leaving residual traces of her ambivalence smeared across their mundane sex scenes.

NOTES

1. Andrea Juno, "Interview: Doris Wishman," *Incredibly Strange Films*, ed. V. Vale and Andrea Juno (San Francisco: RE/Search Publications, 1986), 112.
2. Alicia Kozma, "Stephanie Rothman Does Not Exist: Narrating a Lost History of Women in Film," *Camera Obscura* 32, no. 1 (2017): 179.
3. Jeffrey Sconce, "'Trashing' the Academy: Taste, Excess, and an Emerging Politics of Cinematic Style," *Screen* 36, no. 4 (Winter 1995): 371–93. Michael Bowen describes this quality of Wishman's work as a form of realism, one that "tends to expose the conditions of its actuality not so much by preserving the attributes of time and space as they are experienced in the so-called 'real world' as by exposing the processes of manufacture which bring the film-vision into being." Michael J. Bowen, "Embodiment and Realization: The Many Film-Bodies of Doris Wishman," *Wide Angle* 19, no. 3 (July 1997): 73.
4. Bowen, "Embodiment and Realization," 76.
5. Herb Rau, "Moviemakers Seek Buxom Miamians," *Miami News*, July 10, 1975.
6. "Seize X-Rated Films," *Salt Lake Tribune*, May 14, 1976.
7. All of these dates are based on Newspaper.com searches, which is an imperfect method but, in the absence of reliable archival sources, this is the most comprehensive database available for this kind of research.
8. Elena Gorfinkel, "Tales of Times Square: Sexploitation's Secret History of Place," in *Taking Place: Location and the Moving Image*, ed. John David Rhodes and Elena Gorfinkel (Minneapolis: University of Minnesota Press, 2011), 55–76.
9. Linda Williams, *Hard Core: Power, Pleasure, and the "Frenzy of the Visible"* (Berkeley: University of California Press, 1989).
10. Heather Butler, "What Do You Call a Lesbian with Long Fingers? The Development of Lesbian and Dyke Pornography," in *Porn Studies*, ed. Linda Williams (Durham, NC: Duke University Press, 2004), 167–97.
11. Elena Gorfinkel, *Lewd Looks: American Sexploitation Cinema in the 1960s* (Minneapolis and London: University of Minnesota Press, 2017), 99, 9.
12. Moya Luckett, "Sexploitation as Feminine Territory: The Films of Doris Wishman," in *Defining Cult Movies: The Cultural Politics of Oppositional Taste*, ed. Mark Jancovich, Antonio Lázaro Reboll, Julian Stringer, and Andy Willis (Manchester: Manchester University Press, 2003), 149; Tania Modleski, "Women's Cinema as Counterphobic Cinema: Doris Wishman as the Last Auteur," in *Sleaze Artists: Cinema at the Margins of Taste, Style, and Politics*, ed. Jeffrey Sconce (Durham, NC: Duke University Press, 2007), 55.
13. Annie Sprinkle, *Hardcore from the Heart: The Pleasures, Profits, and Politics of Sex in Performance*, ed. Gabrielle Cody (London: Continuum, 2001), 48.

14. Quoted in Christopher J. Jarmick, "Doris Wishman" (Great Directors), *Senses of Cinema* 22 (October 2002), <http://sensesofcinema.com/2002/great-directors/wishman/> (last accessed November 3, 2020).
15. On Colt see Whitney Strub, "Sex Wishes and Virgin Dreams: Zebedy Colt's Reactionary Queer Heterosmut and the Elusive Porn Archive," *GLQ: A Journal of Lesbian and Gay Studies* 23, no. 3 (2017): 359–90. Mahler's key run of *Her Name Was Lisa* (1979), *Corruption* (1983), *Midnight Heat* (1983), and *American Babylon* (1985) has received virtually no scholarly attention, but comprises a powerful quartet of deliberate heterosexual failure.
16. Jarmick, "Doris Wishman."
17. For a masterful example of this sort of undertaking (what Peter Alilunas, in his own archaeological study of early adult video, calls "trace historiography") see Michael Bowen's liner notes to the 2005 Synapse DVD release of *Let Me Die a Woman*. Peter Alilunas, *Smutty Little Movies: The Creation and Regulation of Adult Video* (Berkeley: University of California Press, 2016).
18. I am indebted to Michael Bowen for this observation.
19. Laura Helen Marks, "Re-sexualizing Scrooge: Gender, Spectatorship, and the Subversion of Genre in Shaun Costello's *The Passions of Carol*," in *Porno Chic and the Sex Wars: American Sexual Representation in the 1970s*, ed. Carolyn Bronstein and Whitney Strub (Amherst: University of Massachusetts Press, 2016), 58.
20. Bill Wine, "Robert Findlay's Love of Films is Hardcore," *Courier-Post*, February 8, 1975.
21. Leisure Time 1982 releases ad, *Variety*, May 12, 1982, 153.
22. Vinegar Syndrome cofounder Joe Rubin explains the chain of rights: "The films were owned by Gail, which was taken over by Coastline. We bought all of Coastline's rights. ABA release was unlicensed but the films are PD [public domain]." Email to author, November 5, 2017.
23. Elizabeth Gilbert, "Pussy Galore," *Spin*, April 1, 1995, 152.
24. Bowen, "Embodiment and Realization," 80.
25. Joy Williams, "More Peculiar than Doris Wishman," *Spin*, May 1, 1998, 128.
26. "The Mother of Exploitation: Doris Wishman," *Paper Mag*, February 28, 1998, <http://www.papermag.com/the-mother-of-exploitation-doris-wishman-1425142961.html> (last accessed November 3, 2020). See also the transcript in Sprinkle, *Hardcore from the Heart*, 48.
27. Doris Wishman interview with Michael Bowen, August 19, 2001, shared with author by Bowen.

CHAPTER 5

Bad Bis Go to Hell: Bisexuality as Transgressive and Lucrative in Doris Wishman's Roughies

Finley Freibert

> "Sara . . . This man, this Mike, I don't even know how to describe him . . . If you marry him that will be your finish . . . This man is a fiend. When I have the courage, I'll explain why I keep him in my employ."
>
> —Gordon Dite to his daughter, Sara, in *Too Much Too Often!* (1967)

Although the post-dubbed dialogue is not perfect, and the delivery is rather stilted, the above quote conveys that there is something different yet difficult to articulate about Mike, a mysterious figure in Doris Wishman's late 1960s roughie. According to Gordon, marrying Mike will result in ruin for Sara, and there is some reason—in this instance, blackmail—why her father cannot fire him. Mike's unspeakable quality becomes apparent long before this exchange between Sara and her father. His sexual experiences are not exclusively with women or with men: Mike is bisexual. Depictions of bisexual masculinity were extremely rare in the 1960s and remain relatively infrequent in both film and television today.[1] This chapter will examine Doris Wishman's recurrent experimentation with bisexual content during a short span of her 1960s filmography.

Doris Wishman's directorial career can be loosely partitioned into four periods: nudist films and "nudie cuties" shot in color (1960–5), black and white "roughies" (1965–8), post-1969 genre bricolages, and films reflecting her newfound cult status released after 2000.[2] Within sexploitation historiography, the "roughie" trend of the 1960s is typically defined as a sexploitation subgenre in which sexual themes are juxtaposed against violent imagery, ensconced within a melodramatic narrative, and usually filmed in black and white.[3] The inclusion of sex and violence in the form of rape or sadomasochism marked the roughie genre's divergence from the perceived innocence of previous nudist exposés and nudie cutie cycles. An underacknowledged observation regarding the roughies' negative take on all matters sexual is that their violent and sexually "deviant" content was often mediated through depictions of non-normative sexual identities. This chapter focuses on Wishman's roughie period to examine the specific methods she employed to push the limits of the genre's representations of "deviant" sexual behaviors and identities.

Here, several of Doris Wishman's bisexual roughies are surveyed to counter a dominant historical tendency to erase bisexuality before the 1970s. Since queer content was not a roughie prerequisite and because the sexploitation market was increasingly competitive, this chapter argues that the repetition of the bisexual-as-transgressive theme within Wishman's roughies evinces the market value of bisexuality during the sexual revolution of the 1960s. This market value is indexed not only by the crossover appeal of non-normative sexual content as generally transgressive, but also by these films' specific appeals to niche audiences composed of individuals that are curious of, harbor contempt for, are attracted to, or identify with bisexual desires and practices.

To forward this argument, the chapter proceeds in three segments. In the first section, I draw on bisexual studies and queer histories to show that queer audiences and urban spaces of sexual media formed a significant and overlooked social context for the sexploitation films that emerged on the brink of the gay liberation movement. Second, several films are analyzed to trace Wishman's bisexual representational practices, most commonly through narrative and formal techniques that centralize a female character. Finally, *Too Much Too Often!* is examined for its unprecedented representation of a young and attractive bisexual man. The advertising of this film reveals not only that bisexuality was a publicly visible identity by the late 1960s, but also that sexploitation marketing specifically addressed queer consumers at this moment.

BISEXUALITY BEFORE GAY LIBERATION

Before analyzing Wishman's bisexual roughies it is imperative to underscore the links among urban sexual marketplaces, queer constituencies, and the sexploitation film industry. Drawing the connections among these histories not only contributes to an overlooked aspect of sexploitation historiography that queer audiences frequented adult theaters, but it also provides the contextual frame wherein Doris Wishman developed her bisexual narratives.[4] As we will see in the third section, this context explains why the marketing for one of Wishman's roughies embraced noticeably queer tactics.

Like homosexuality, bisexuality was a publicly visible phenomenon before gay liberation. While the definition of bisexuality remains a contested subject, during the 1960s it signified either attraction to men and women or a form of "sexual inversion."[5] These understandings of bisexuality, like that of homosexuality in the 1960s, derive from the pathologizing discourses of psychoanalysis and sexology.[6] There is a tendency in histories of sexuality to cast bisexuality as a byproduct of gay liberation: either by historicizing "bisexual chic" to the 1970s or by attributing the advent of the bisexual movement and its conjoined visibility politics to the 1980s.[7] Yet public forms of bisexual visibility predate gay liberation and affirm the existence of bisexuality beside (not as product of) homosexuality. To demonstrate how bisexuals became discernable in the motion picture media, it is necessary to map one of the primary sites of bisexual public visibility, the adult media marketplace, wherein Doris Wishman's films existed. By locating a form of bisexual visibility before the gay liberation moment this chapter asserts that the bisexual identity was not a secondary byproduct of gay and lesbian identities but stood alone as a distinct constellation of desires and ways of being. Historians of American gay and lesbian movements have noted an inclination in LGBTQ+ cultural memory for pre-1970s gay and lesbian identities, practices, and desires to be forgotten or overlooked. For instance, George Chauncey and John D'Emilio have attributed this tendency to mythmaking practices that enshrine the Stonewall uprising of June 28, 1969 as the breaking point away from the isolation and invisibility of the era of "the closet."[8] Thus, to counter the historical erasures of such mythmaking practices several queer historians have produced work that traces the rich histories of gay and lesbian practices and identities before Stonewall.[9] Historians of bisexuality have faced a different set of obstacles when historicizing pre-Stonewall bisexuality. First, there is a tendency within histories of sexuality to perceive bisexuality as a byproduct of the formation of homosexuality and heterosexuality as categories.[10] Second, since national networks of bisexual organizing were forged in the late 1980s and through the 1990s, there is a perception that bisexual consciousness and visibility did not exist before this time.[11] Finally, historical figures or fictional representations of bisexuality often go unnoticed because bisexuality is both difficult to represent and often imperceptible to persons not identifying as bisexual.[12] In the analysis of a particular set of Doris Wishman films that follows, this chapter addresses all three of these historical problems by tracing how bisexuality was made to be legible in the 1960s.

The adult media marketplace was a sector of public culture where bisexuality became visible before gay liberation of the 1970s. In particular, adult media began to incorporate bisexual representations throughout the 60s, I argue, to appeal to those curious of, having contempt for, attracted to, or possibly identifying as bisexuals. Before analyzing how bisexuality was depicted, it is necessary to understand the context through which queer sexualities became lucrative subjects in postwar sexual media.

Queer history links to the adult media industries because one of the few places that sustained queer visibility in public through the 1960s was the sexual marketplace. This marketplace included bars, adult bookstores, grindhouse theaters, and cruising sites typically located in urban areas within a close proximity. It was in venues like these that the anonymous stroller could view sexual media or obtain sexual experiences, often for a price. Before gay liberation, the urban sexual marketplace provided one of the few places in which queers could exist in public, cultivate shared culture, and communicate with one another.[13] Intentionally or not, the media commodities present within the sexual marketplace interpellated queer consumers by representing queer practices and identities. During the postwar period, the formations of gay enclaves in urban centers across the U.S. resulted in businesses' eventual awareness of the possibility of profiting from the queer dollar. This realization, along with the emergence of gay-owned businesses, facilitated a pre-liberation form of marketing toward queer consumers.[14] In this period, adult media commodities (including magazines, mass market paperbacks, mail order media, and publicly exhibited adult films) that represented queer desires, practices, and identities were present in the sexual marketplace and increasingly catered to queer consumers through their advertising.

There are several examples where adult media commodities targeted not only heterosexuals, but also gay and lesbian audiences. Beginning in the 1930s, the beefcake photography industry spawned several periodicals and mail order services that targeted gay men.[15] Pulp novels of the 1950s and 1960s depicting lesbians typically targeted straight male readers, but had a crossover audience of queer women.[16] Jeffrey Escoffier has discussed the significance of adult mass-oriented sociological texts (or pulp non-fiction) for gay male audiences, stating that "closeted gay men used the popular sociology, literary, and psychoanalytic discourses to name themselves, describe themselves, judge themselves—and, by these means, to homosexualize themselves."[17] Indeed, by 1967 it could be stated that producers of sexualized print media were obliged to incorporated queer content to attract gay consumers: "it is now de rigeur [sic] for the novels sold in sex-oriented bookstalls to contain passages of appeal to homosexuals."[18]

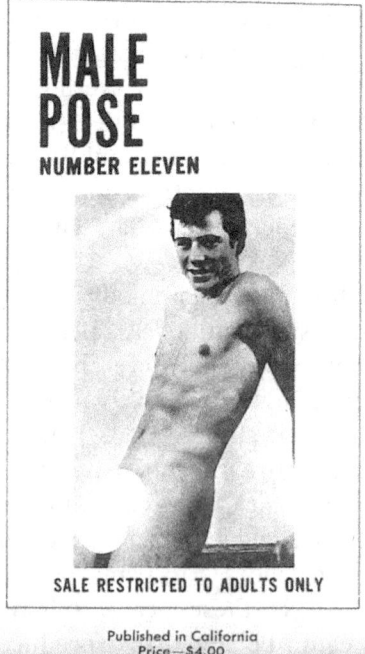

Figure 5.1 Examples of 1960s print commodities that marketed sexual identities and practices. Thomas C. Lynch and Charles A. O'Brien, "A Report to the California Legislature on Obscenity (Sacramento: Dept. of Justice, 1967)." Courtesy Government Information Collection, Henry Madden Library, Fresno, CA

While much attention has been afforded to appeals to homosexual consumers in the adult media marketplace, the existence of and appeals to bisexual consumers have been all but overlooked.[19] By the late 1960s, bisexual content was consistently employed in at least four formats circulating in the adult media marketplace: pulp non-fiction (such as mass market paperback sociology texts), pulp fiction, "arthouse" cinema, and exploitation film. While several authors have examined the queer appeals of adult-oriented print media during the 1960s, exploitation cinema has not substantially been examined as a site of queer audience formations.

During this period, bisexual consumers were equally, yet often unintentionally, hailed by advertising practices and content juxtapositions within adult media markets. However, the proliferation of bisexual representation in the 1960s was not solely or even primarily due to a niche appeal to bisexual consumers. Bisexuality became a lucrative subject for mass market exploitation following the popularity of Alfred Kinsey's reports on male and female sexuality, respectively published in 1948 and 1953. In general, these reports facilitated public conversations about sexual practices and expanded Americans' sexual vocabularies. More specifically, Kinsey's report on male sexuality emphasized a controversial and often contested conclusion that approximately half the population of white American men had experienced same-sex sexual contact at some point in their lives.[20] An effect of the widespread distribution and popularity of Kinsey's reports was the projection of non-normative sexual identities and practices into the public spotlight, particularly bisexuality. Following the Kinsey reports, one of the primary locations for bisexual representation in the 1960s was the mass market non-fiction paperback. Non-fiction print exposés of bisexuality took a variety of tones ranging from bitterly biphobic accounts to well-intentioned sympathetic portraits of individual bisexuals.[21] Pulp fiction also engaged bisexual representation, and this often occurred implicitly through the inclusion of gay erotic couplings within otherwise "straight" narratives.[22]

Media containing bisexual subject matter proliferated through crossover appeals to at least four market sectors. These market segments are not strictly defined and can overlap in certain cases. First, particularly when spun in a negative light, the topic of bisexuality appealed to a dominant homophobic and biphobic sensibility. This bigoted sensibility enjoyed a voyeuristic look into the lives of "deviants" and reflected contempt for bisexuals and queers in general. Second, bisexual representational strategies could garner a mass appeal to folks curious about or possibly open to bisexuals. This was true of those aware of the rise of "free love" and "swinger" culture during the sexual revolution wherein bisexuality came to denote a new and exciting form of sexual experimentation. Third, the depictions of bisexual practices appealed to those (regardless of sexual orientation) attracted to bisexuals as creatures who complicate the sexual binary of gay or straight sexual inclination. For instance, early bisexual activist

Stephen Donaldson has noted how his bisexual identity was seen as a desirable quality by some of his gay male sexual partners.[23] Finally, bisexual representation constituted a niche appeal to those whose experiences or desires aligned with bisexuality, whether monosexual-identifying or bisexual-identifying.

Doris Wishman primarily focused her 1960s film narratives on the downfalls of queer women living in New York City. As we will see in the next section, within these narratives her protagonists often navigated the crisis of bisexuality as they negotiated sexual experiences with partners of more than one gender. Since these films mainly targeted and were attended by a male audience,[24] they likely catered to the two voyeuristic appeals of those phobic of or curious about bisexual women. However, as discussed below, the advertising for a particular film reveals a unique example of crossover marketing to both heterosexual and queer audiences. Ultimately, Wishman's commitment to mining non-normative sexual representations reveals her to be one of the earliest adopters of bisexual content in the commercial film industry of the 1960s.

BI-SPLOITATION: DORIS WISHMAN'S QUEER REPRESENTATIONAL STRATEGIES

As one of several media consumed at semi-public venues in urban sexual marketplaces, sexploitation films increasingly turned to queer content during and especially by the end of the 1960s. European imports, sometimes doctored with added sexual content for the American market, often involved queer female characters; representative films include *The Twilight Girls* (1961) and *Wild Roots of Love* (1962). In a *Los Angeles Times* review of *Wild Roots of Love*, the author alleges that the combination of queer content with inserted nudity is what creates an exploitation film: "It's the homosexual angle, hypoed by a couple of crudely inserted nudie shots, that puts the picture in the exploitation market."[25] Later American-produced sexploitation films, particularly those directed by Joe Sarno and Nick Millard, would exploit lesbian content as a prime marketable component of their features. Nick Millard's non-sync sound travelogues, such as *Nympho* (1965) and *Chantal* (1968), typically focused on a young woman's sexual awakening. Joe Sarno was known for directing urban and suburban sexualized melodramas. His notable examples that drew on lesbian content include *Sin in the Suburbs* (1964) and *All the Sins of Sodom* (1968). According to trade press accounts, by the end of the 1960s a lesbian sequence was considered obligatory in sexploitation film.[26] Queer content, however, was not a prerequisite for the roughie subgenre; thus Doris Wishman's selective employment of bisexual content can be seen as a significant development within the constraints of that subgenre.

Wishman's idiosyncratic intervention in sexploitation's roughie trend is primarily one of narrativizing queer content in a manner that situates bisexuality as a tendency facilitated by individuals' choices, surroundings, and interactions with urban sexual cultures of the time. While the exact frequency is not known, within the sexual marketplace discussed above, fictional print media often narrativized bisexuality with both male and female characters. On the other hand, until 1968 sexploitation motion pictures almost exclusively delivered queer representation via female characters, and in this sense Wishman's more frequent association of bisexuality with women was aligned with other sexploitation films from that time.[27] However, Wishman's depictions of bisexuality diverged from more typical employments of queer content in sexploitation that either associated queerness with "sophisticated" European culture or that framed same-sex practices between women as experimentation and a function of the desires of men.[28] Instead, Wishman includes queer practices as components of (often female) character histories, and in so doing produces queer representations that extend beyond connotations of arthouse sophistication or hetero-patriarchal male experimentation.

The difficulty of conveying bisexuality visually, particularly with the medium of film, stems from three components: its durative element, its frequent dependence on unspoken desires, and its denigration by cultural attitudes that depend on bisexuality's erasure. First, unlike monosexual identities, bisexuality is extremely difficult to visualize in a synchronic snapshot.[29] Whereas a picture of same-sex or opposite-sex embrace can immediately connote homosexuality or heterosexuality, it takes the knowledge of an individual's self-identification or past to convey their bisexuality.[30] Second, in filmic invocations of monosexual subjectivities, one's sexual identity is determined by the gender of the person they are sexually attracted to, so only a single depiction of desire is necessary to visualize a monosexual identity. This is not the case with bisexuals, and thus one method of representing bisexuality (especially in print media) is to include a self-reflection or other indication of the individual's attraction to more than one gender. Third, because monosexual identities are so culturally pervasive and because monosexual readers can be ignorant of—or actively deny—the existence of bisexuality, there is a tendency for bisexual characters' sexual identities to be erased or reinterpreted as monosexual. Film is a particularly apt medium for representing bisexuality due to its durative format. Further, sexploitation film's reliance on numerous sequences of sexual activity and frequent use of voiceover to convey individual character desires allows the form to address the previously described visibility constraints on bisexual representation, particularly the first two.

As other authors have observed, a constitutive structure of 1960s sexploitation is the runtime's partition into narrative and spectacle. Essentially, the sexploitation narrative exists solely to provide a framework holding together numerous instances of sexual spectacle. Following Linda Williams's discussion of a parallel phenomenon in hardcore pornography, David Andrews has described this dichotomous structure of sexploitation as a division into narrative and "number."[31] David Church has addressed these interspersed sequences of spectacle as sexploitation's "modular attractions" and emphasizes the manner in which these sequences could be repurposed in later films or transmediated into adult magazine spreads for further profit.[32]

Wishman's solution to this partition challenge doubles as a lucrative method for displaying sexual transgressivity, usually in the form of bisexuality. During her roughie period, Wishman consistently depicted deviations from monogamous heterosexual norms in order to provide the transgressive appeal that the roughie necessitated. By stitching these moments of sexual transgressivity together in a narrative form and by sustaining a focus on a small group of characters, Wishman frequently solidified sexual practices (the scenes of spectacle), culturally perceived to deviate from the status quo, onto non-normative identities including bisexuals, lesbians, sadists, sex workers, or sex addicts. Visual depictions of non-normative practices or identities had simultaneous niche and crossover appeals. The niche was the specific target audience that sought a certain type of content, for example scenes of sadism. The crossover audience comprised audiences who were curious about "deviant" practices in general and could be satisfied in seeing any of the sequences of spectacle.

Recollections from Wishman and her associates confirm this tactic of narrating sexual histories to represent identities. An actress in Wishman's later films recalls a quip from Wishman in response to the actress's well wishes: "you're only saying that because you want to play a lesbian."[33] In an earlier interview, Wishman describes her method of developing character histories as actor-oriented and functioning to differentiate her characterization strategy from other sexploitation screenwriters: "I give my characters a case history, I mean, they don't just suddenly appear. They have to have lives, they don't just appear on the screen. By giving them a case history I think they can act better."[34]

Wishman's method was particularly apt at representing bisexuality because she focused on sexual histories through the use of flashback and through sustained focus on individual characters for the length of a film. Wishman primarily employed two (sometimes overlapping) formal techniques in her 1960s films in order to convey bisexuality as a radically disruptive practice and identity category. These techniques are deployed almost exclusively in conjunction with a sustained narrative focus on one female character, the contemporaneous archetype of the "single girl," a young female protagonist depicted as seeking self-actualization and having mobility in an urban area.[35] The first formal technique is an implication of bisexual tendencies through dialogue that is usually off-screen. When in the form of an internal monologue, this technique is particularly successful in conveying bisexuality because it allows for the statement or suggestion of an individual character's desires. The second technique is the creation of intimate spatial or narrative proximity between a lesbian and a woman who is initially perceived to be heterosexual. The effect of this technique is to queer the female protagonist who was originally coded as heterosexual, through an association with a character implied to be lesbian. This second technique is the most frequently employed by Wishman and is a structure that makes bisexuality visible since the character's actions and implied relationships do not correlate to a single gender.

Wishman's technique for representing bisexual subjectivities through off-screen dialogue is a component of her more general cost-saving strategy of shooting without sync sound. This strategy was so frequently employed by Wishman that its associated effects on sequencing and framing have come to connote a kind of directorial signature contributing to her films' disjointed qualities.[36] When inner monologue is engaged to further the narrative it can convey an individual character's commentary on the action at hand, can progress the narrative by indicating the character's intentions, and can often heighten the film's sexual elements through the expression of inner desires or anxieties.

This internal monologue technique spans a major portion of Wishman's first roughie, *The Sex Perils of Paulette* (1965).[37] The film portrays a typical "single girl" narrative: a young woman from a small town, Paulette (Anna Karol), attempts to make it in the city as an actress. After moving in with a sex worker named Tracy (Darlene Bennett), Paulette has difficulty maintaining steady employment. Sam (played by handsome hunk and Wishman regular Sam Stewart), a man posing as a theatrical agent, pushes Paulette into prostitution. Unable to cope with the secrecy and shameful associations of her occupation, Paulette ultimately refuses a marriage proposal from her small-town boyfriend. The cinematography and voiceover impart Paulette's anxieties over her bisexual desires in an early sequence when Tracy and Sam introduce her to swinger culture at a house party. Reflected by her monologue and the leering camera that connotes her gaze, Paulette is overwhelmed by the sexual couplings occurring at the party. A point-of-view shot from Paulette's perspective emphasizes Paulette's discomfort over her queer encounter with an unnamed black woman at the party. A low-angle point-of-view shot is accompanied by Paulette's inner monologue wherein she states her cautious attraction toward the woman: "I suppose she was pretty good, but I had only one thought in mind, I had to get away." As evinced by the subjective camera and the internalized dialogue, this bisexual encounter fosters Paulette's uneasy yet attentive desire as the woman meets her gaze, begins to strip, and discards her clothes into Paulette's face.

The second technique for depicting non-monosexual queer content occurs with the tight framing that constructs the physical proximity between Paulette and the unnamed black dancer. Wishman utilizes spatial or narrative proximity between queer figures to convey bisexuality through the frequently used narrative structure of cohabitation between women, which leads to or exists as an effect of the breakdown of an already established heterosexual marriage. For instance, in *Another Day, Another Man* (1966), Tess, a sex worker whose husky voice and masculine outfit code her as implicitly queer, is further portrayed as debasing her roommate's heterosexuality when she jokes about her roommate's husband: "He'd probably think I might contaminate you."

An exemplary deployment of this second technique occurs in *Bad Girls Go to Hell* (1965). This film follows newlywed Meg Kelton (Gigi Darlene), who flees from her marriage after killing a janitor who sexually assaulted her. Upon arriving in New York City, Meg attempts cohabitation with various strangers, but faces numerous problems involving her newfound roommates' ill intentions ranging from physical abuse to blackmail. The film concludes in a circular manner, wherein it is revealed that the opening sequence was a premonition.

One of Meg's more successful attempts at rooming with a stranger occurs with a lesbian named Della (Dawn Bennett). After escaping from the abusive clutches of a rough and muscular alcoholic (Sam Stewart), Meg meanders through the city streets with her suitcases until she is approached by the friendly, leather jacket-clad Tracy (Dawn Bennett's twin sister Darlene Bennett). Once Meg divulges that she does not have a place to stay, Tracy encourages Meg to room with her sister Della. Lounging on the couch in a revealing lace body stocking, Della welcomes Meg to her apartment. That night she joins Meg in bed, and although Meg is welcoming toward Della's embrace after initial reservations, she ultimately decides she cannot continue in the relationship and leaves.

Meg's bisexuality is revealed by her spatial and narrative proximity to these two women. Both Tracy and Della are coded as lesbians, but in different ways. Initially, Tracy is introduced wearing a black leather jacket and pants, a look Wishman used more than once to signify a butch lesbian.[38] Additionally, Tracy's butchness is emphasized through masculine attire, the pickup of Meg on the street, and her reference to saving a "damsel in distress." Della's queerness, on the other hand, is left an open question until she joins Meg in bed. A tight medium shot of Della and Meg lying together initially conveys Meg's reticence when she responds to Della's caresses by inching out of the frame. However, a cut to a full shot first highlights the distance Della leaves between the two women, which is subsequently closed by Meg as she decides to consent to the encounter. In Wishman's signature style of cutting away to mundane objects, the sequence concludes with close-ups of the two women's feet and items around the bedroom.

The encounter between Meg and Della serves both to evoke the queerness of the two women and to code Meg's bisexuality specifically as a fleeting identity-inflection point. Meg's ambiguous reservation about staying with Della, although they both profess their love to one another, can be read either as portraying a homophobic rejection of the social stigma involved in taking a same-sex partner or as Meg's attempt at protecting Della from the baggage of her past. Regardless of the interpretation, Meg's bisexuality exists in the film as an unstated element of sexual "deviation" that links with the for-profit boundary pushing embraced by sexploitation of this period. Importantly, this bisexual-by-proxy technique is evident on a condensed level in two capsule summaries that informed *Bad Girls Go to Hell*'s marketing and later industrial categorization. The first of these summaries appears in the film's pressbook where Della is explicitly identified as a lesbian.[39] The second appears in the American Film Institute's summary that refers to Della's seduction of Meg as "lesbian advances."[40] Unlike lesbian sexuality, bisexuality is not mentioned specifically, yet as in the film, it appears in the print synopsis through narrative condensation that centralizes the character history of Meg and the emphasis on a sequence of lesbian proximity.

As discussed in this section, Doris Wishman often visualized bisexuality through at least two methods of formal and narrative signification. While the marketing of these films did not usually imply the presence of bisexuality in each film, bisexual content was selectively employed by Wishman as one of several transgressive and lucrative components incorporated into the general form of the 1960s roughie. As we will see in the next section, in the late 1960s Wishman took a risky move when she expanded her gendered depiction of bisexuality with the story of a male hustler.

"THE 'ANIMALS' ARE HERE!" THE MARKETABILITY OF MALE BISEXUAL CONTENT

Unlike the frequency of queer female figures described in the above section, Wishman's engagements with queer male content were not as commonplace in her roughie period. However, in a rare move to market to non-straight audiences, Wishman experimented with male-on-male sadomasochism in the film *Too Much Too Often!*. While differing from full-fledged "all male" films that exclusively featured sexual contact between men, this movie had a unique bisexual appeal that cannot be fully understood as aligning with either a straight or gay target audience. This content was exploited by the marketing campaign of *Too Much Too Often!*, both in print advertisements and in the trailer.

In general, exploitation filmmakers were slow to adopt content that did not appeal to an idealized straight male gaze. However, several sexploitation films of the mid-1960s did begin to engage in queer male representation, yet they almost exclusively sidelined such characters or stereotypically coded them as psychotic queer villains.[41] In the 1960s, underground cinema was the primary film venue that engaged overt and commercially exploitable queer male content and encoded the male body as a site of visual pleasure. Yet one of the significant precursors that informed 1960s underground film was the marginal film industry sector of exploitation cinema.[42]

Exploitation and underground film formed a kind of feedback loop, in which one borrowed from another's content and audiences in the hopes of turning a greater profit. As Janet Staiger has described, underground films of the early 1960s embraced exploitation cinema's sexual content, niche targeting practices, and marginal consumption sites.[43] Underground film went on to employ sexual (usually gay male) content to target socially and sexually marginalized audiences at venues separate from mainstream motion picture exhibition.[44] Yet by the late 1960s, seeing that this non-heterosexual niche was commercially viable, exploitation producers, exhibitors, and distributors began to reappropriate from gay underground cinema.[45] In particular, in mid-1967, New York's Cameo Theatre screened the gay-oriented Andy Milligan film *Vapors* (1965) alongside two typical sexploitation features and employed an advertising campaign that targeted different sexual demographics depending on the newspaper.[46] California-based exhibitor Shan Sayles is often cited as the first to develop a continuous exhibition policy that openly embraced and explicitly marketed gay pornographic films. This policy began at Sayles's Los Angeles Park Theatre with the June 1968 "World's First Homosexual Film Festival."[47] By 1969, prominent sexploitation distributor Stanley Borden, competitor to Wishman's distributors Jerry Balsam and Phil Levine, began distributing the gay softcore movie *Stud Farm* (1969).[48] Borden entered the gay male market at this time because although he claimed to have observed the market's emergence earlier in the decade, he was hesitant to be among the first to test it.[49]

It was in this context that Wishman's *Too Much Too Often!* was produced and then released in December of 1967.[50] Significantly, this feature exploited queer male content in a manner very different from sexploitation of this period. The film follows a young bisexual man who is not only unabashedly villainous, but also framed in a sexually appealing manner.[51] Further, rather than embrace an exclusively heterosexual or homosexual audience address, *Too Much Too Often!* facilitates a kind of bisexual address. As we will see, both the film's trailer and print advertising exploited this ambiguous bisexual appeal.

Too Much Too Often! tells the story of a bisexual hustler named Mike Torson who exploits both men and women for his sadistic pleasure and as a means to acquire financial power. Mike blackmails a masochistic customer, Gordon Dite, into hiring Mike at his advertising firm. Gordon's daughter, Sara, then falls in love with Mike, who subsequently manipulates the agency's secretary in order to steal Gordon's clients. Desperate to stop Mike from marrying his daughter and disrupting his business, Gordon hires Sam, a detective and previous victim of Mike, to disrupt Mike and Sara's relationship. The movie ends when Sam and Gordon show up at Mike's apartment, pummel the hustler, and then extricate Sara from his clutches.

Mike's bisexuality is introduced both overtly and sensationally through an opening sequence of queer sadomasochism. In a dimly lit room with bare walls and a lone desk, the diegetic sounds of whip cracks and male grunts accompany a soundtrack comprised of frenzied trumpets and the percussive tremolo of stringed instruments. Gordon Dite, a bald advertising executive bent over the desk with hands bound, is shirtless and perspires as Mike whips him. Mike, wearing menacing sunglasses indoors, makes Gordon's back bleed with each lash. After several lashes, framed through over-the-shoulder and point-of-view shots from Mike's perspective, Mike winds up the whip, places it in his back pocket, and fixes up his hair with a comb. The sequence concludes with a climactic grunt by Gordon, after which Mike exits to meet up with his female lover. In a kind of reversal of the bisexual-by-proxy method described previously, Mike's queerness is underscored first with the sequence of same-sex sexual practice, and it is not until we observe he has a female lover that his bisexuality becomes evident.

Mike's characterization as bisexual is reinforced through narrative elements that associate his persona with two queer signifiers: sadism and narcissism. Additionally, a brief reference to queer urban codes for sadomasochistic subcultural practices solidifies the characterization. First, Mike is construed as a bisexual sadist. This is obvious from the opening sequence wherein Mike flogs Gordon, and Mike's queer sadistic tendencies are underscored by his cruelty toward and physical abuse of the numerous women he encounters. This conflation of sadism with queer identities depends on both general anti-gay sentiments and the phobic popular discourse that gay men were pathological sadists. Cold War homophobia was undergirded by the belief that gay men were open to blackmail and other forms of manipulation by communists.[52] One facet of this anti-gay ideology sutured queer masculinity to pathological sadomasochism. This conflation was legitimized through psychoanalytic discourses that both pathologized homosexuality and diagnosed sadism as linking to the homosexual's (or bisexual's) ailment.[53] By 1952, the pathological association of homosexuality was solidified when the Diagnostic and Statistical Manual of the American Psychiatric Association categorized homosexuality as a disorder. During the Cold War, popular discourse often conflated these homophobic discourses to portray homosexual and sadistic tendencies as threats to vulnerable youth.[54]

Second, Mike's narcissism is reinforced by several sequences in which he admires his own reflection. Narcissism has long been mythically associated with homosexuality due to self-love's implication of same-sex attraction.[55] On multiple occasions throughout the film, Mike perfects his pompadour, delighting in his appearance in the mirror. At the film's conclusion, Mike is combing his hair once again directly before Sam permanently damages his face by grinding it under the heel of his shoe. While the available cut of the film concludes with

Mike moaning on the floor after recalling his past crimes, the film's pressbook and the *AFI Catalog*'s summary both point to a possible alternate ending or previously intended ending that more explicitly play on Mike's queer vanity by referencing a mirror. In the concluding paragraph in the pressbook summary, Mike's narcissism and shock at his disfigured face is described as the reason he faints in the film's final shot: "Torson comes out of the flashback, and feels his bloody face. He had always thought of himself as handsome and was constantly looking in the mirror. As he realizes what has happened, he falls back unconscious."[56] The summary in the *AFI Catalog* further states, "Torson, alone, looks into the mirror at his ruined face and falls unconscious," which again ties together the angle of vanity that is reiterated in the rest of the film to signify Torson's non-normative sexuality.[57]

Since *Too Much Too Often!* employs bisexual male content in a manner underexplored by previous sexploitation films, its analysis prompts the questions of why this content was being engaged and who was being targeted. At the time this film was made, the imagined audiences of sexploitation were straight working-class men, a perception that remained in American popular consciousness as the figure of the dirty old man in a raincoat.[58] Yet as discussed above, by the mid-1960s the sexploitation market was beginning to take notice of the viability of male same-sex content for targeting queer audiences. By drawing on phobic discourses that collocate "deviant" sexuality with pathologized sadism and narcissism, the film appears to cater somewhat to a heteronormative gaze. However, besides these phobic appeals, the film and its advertising evince more specific tactics for targeting non-straight audiences.

Too Much Too Often! internally encodes at least three references to specific signifiers of male same-sex sexual culture of the 1960s. One reference is to underground signifiers of dominant and submissive roles in gay bondage subculture. The second is an illusion to "the closet," in its pre-Stonewall sense, as a gay subcultural term for an incognito homosexual identity. The third reference is to codes of urban gay sexual invitation.

Following the opening bondage and whipping sequence, Mike returns to his apartment where his girlfriend greets him. She then asks about a whip that is rolled up and sticking out of his back-right pocket. During the 1960s, participants in queer sadomasochistic subcultures used codes such as this to signify dominant and submissive roles to potential sexual partners. As stated in a contemporaneous issue of the San Francisco based gay magazine *Vector*, an item in the back-right pocket would have signified a dominant sexual preference in New York: "The signs and symbols of S&M are a language all their own. A chain, earring, belt buckle or keys worn on the left is S, on the right it means M. On the East coast it is the opposite so be careful when traveling."[59]

Halfway through the film Gordon shows up at Mike's apartment in order to intimidate him into not seeing Sara anymore. After Gordon enters, Mike seductively reclines across a couch as he smokes a cigarette. As Gordon approaches Mike and assertively inquires about the whereabouts of his daughter, Mike crosses his legs and then touches Gordon with his free hand quipping, "How should I know?" Gordon then accuses Mike of lying to which Mike replies, "Why should I? Go on, search the place. Look in all the closets." Via a point-of-view shot, Mike blows smoke into Gordon's face, "Take it easy. How about a drink? . . . I could give you the beating of your life, but then you'd enjoy it." Finally, Mike gets up to check his hair in the mirror and suggests to Gordon that he might marry Sara. To this Gordon angrily threatens, "If you don't leave my daughter alone I'll tell her what you're really like." Mike cracks his whip and replies, "Then you'll have to tell her what you're like too."

Other than this obvious reference to each character's queer essence implied in the repeated phrase "what you're really like," this sequence displays two direct references to gay male subculture of the 1960s. The first reference is Mike's line suggesting a search of "the closets." As George Chauncey has discussed, before Stonewall "the closet" was a shorthand for a covert existence as gay in public that did not emerge as a subcultural signifier until the 1960s.[60] The usage of the term by Mike as an innuendo for "closeted" homosexuality is supported by the fact that at the end of the sequence both Gordon and Mike threaten outing one another to Sara. The second reference to gay male subculture, specifically urban pickup codes that involved the sharing of a cigarette or beverage, occurs when Mike offers a drink to Gordon while blowing smoke in his face. During the pre-Stonewall period of the twentieth century, smoking, and especially a request for a light, was an implicit form of sexual invitation between men.[61] The invitational ambiguity of Mike's actions is further emphasized in the cinematography. The shift of the camera's position from a full shot showing the profiles of the two to a point-of-view shot of Mike from Gordon's perspective advances the impression that Mike's dialogue and posture are relaxed and open toward Gordon. This perspective conveys to the viewer, more directly than the previous profile shot, the sexual and flirtatious engagement that Mike advances. In sum, the fact that Mike blows smoke at Gordon, tells him to get more comfortable, offers him a drink, and engages open body language all signal that Mike is offering more than a drink or a smoke.

The marketing of *Too Much Too Often!*, as well as the film's overt references to actual gay and bisexual male subcultural codes from the period evince its inscription to audiences other than straight men. The film's trailer exploits footage from the opening same-sex sadomasochism sequence and includes over-the-top voiceover ballyhooing the angle that the anti-hero of the film "goes both ways": "See what happens when man turns animal for the erotic pleasures of women [pause] and men!" While most of the trailer's runtime focuses on displaying sequences of nude women as the narrator lists all the women that Mike "ruins," it concludes by returning to the issue of Mike's bisexuality as a crisis of existence: "Many have said that a man so evil, so full of naked passion and wild desires, could not really be, but you will see that he does exist in *Too Much Too Often!*"[62] This final line invites the spectator to come observe how bisexuality is visually brought into being, and prefigures a later bisexual activist goal of refuting the biphobic position that bisexuals do not exist. This goal is often addressed through visibility tactics like referring to historical bisexual figures or presenting ideal "good" bisexuals as representative of bisexual existence in general. Obviously, the trailer's only function is to draw an audience, and thus the trailer's exclamation that bisexuality exists entails its coding as exotic, transgressive, and even evil.

Other than the trailer, the film's pressbook includes potential newspaper ad mats displaying four images from the film interspersed with exclamatory text.[63] For the most part these potential ads are typical of sexploitation advertising of the time in their descriptive ad copy, display of scantily clad female bodies, reliance on heterosexual coupling, and implication of misogynist violence.[64] For example, one frame with the tagline "THE LOVE-INS!" depicts a woman's naked back as she embraces the torso of a reclining shirtless man. Another frame implies opposite-sex sexualized violence with a lingerie-clad woman lying flat on her back between the silhouettes of an aggressor's legs, the tag reading "THE SAVAGE ATTACK!" Although the majority of these potential ads indicate standard sexploitation appeals, one stands out for its overt advertising of the film's queer male sexual content. This image shows Mike striking a whip across the shirtless backside of a man in trousers. The ad positions its viewer over-the-shoulder of Mike's silhouette, aligning the viewer with his perspective as he thrashes his bent-over partner's rear. Unlike the typical sexploitation ads that code their target consumer as a voyeuristic onlooker, through its over-the-shoulder framing this ad formally encourages the consumer to align with the position of the bisexual hustler. To further distinguish this advertising mode, rather than a descriptive declaration as in the above taglines, this ad's copy invites queer-identified consumers to imagine themselves in the dominant position encoded by the imperative mode of the exclamation directed toward the reader: "WHIP ME WHIP ME!"

While the consumer reception of the queer-oriented "WHIP ME!" ad for *Too Much Too Often!* is unclear, the fact that certain exhibitors specifically chose this image to advertise the film shows that it was perceived to have some potential for attracting audiences to theaters. Further, during a period of strict newspaper ad censorship, this advertisement's communication of same-sex male sadomasochism without the invocation of illicit words evinces a method of bypassing censorship with the use of pictorial allusion.[65] While most of the newspaper ads I have come across do not make use of this queer ad, there are select occurrences I have found in Gettysburg, Pennsylvania and Lubbock, Texas for the Cross Keys Drive-in and the Fine Arts Drive-in Theatre, respectively.[66] In particular, the Fine Arts advertisement facilitates a kind of bisexual appeal by featuring a dual illustration: on the left is a bikini-clad woman cranking a noisemaker, and on the right is the still of Mike whipping Gordon with the caption "IT'S A CRAZY, MIXED UP **DIRTY WORLD** THEY LIVE IN!"[67] Amazingly, the relatively benign title of the film is censored in this advertisement, and yet the image and tagline exert such signifying force that the implication of an outré "dirty world" of male-on-male sex and sadomasochism becomes surprisingly obvious. A survey of contemporaneous ads from the Fine Arts reveals that the practice of title excision was frequent enough to be the theater's general policy (perhaps to generate consumer curiosity). Yet this ad was exceptional since the theater seldom, if ever again, employed such queer imagery in advertising a softcore film.

CONCLUSION

Doris Wishman's career has garnered much attention by feminist film scholars. Although she famously did not identify as a feminist, her films have been read from a feminist perspective with both redemptive and ambivalent appraisals.[68] While these perspectives are productive in highlighting Wishman's formal and representational techniques that confronted dominant and masculinist modes employed by Hollywood, they tend to overlook the numerous bisexual strategies employed both in Wishman's films and in her films' advertising toward audiences that were not uniformly heterosexual.

While feminist political readings of Wishman's films are generative, I have attempted here to reconstruct the significance of her 1960s roughies to queer film history. Understanding the roughie as a fluctuating trend, rather than coherent genre, underscores Wishman's choice to engage bisexuality as a capitalization on lucrative timely content. Tracing the intersection of queer consumers with venues of sexual media explains the overlooked queer audience targeted by this capitalization as well as the crossover appeals of bisexual content to those not identifying as bisexual. Wishman's representations of bisexual women diverged notably from other queer representations in sexploitation, since she was committed to recording the sexual histories of these figures (often for the full duration of the film). By excavating bisexuality from the films' narratives and advertising artifacts, myths that relegate bisexuality to the post-Stonewall era can be shattered. Finally, Wishman's depiction of male bisexuality evinces that the subject was viable and visible at least four years prior to one of the most frequently cited films to first centralize male bisexuality, *Sunday Bloody Sunday* (1971). In observing the bisexual history of Doris Wishman's roughies we can glimpse a sliver of the occluded place of bisexuality in the 1960s.

ACKNOWLEDGMENTS

I am extremely grateful to Lisa Petrucci for providing access to the *Too Much Too Often! Campaign Manual* from the collection of Something Weird Video. Something Weird Video is an invaluable resource and continues to provide access to many of Doris Wishman's films through its website. Thanks also to Jimmy Maslon and the librarians of the Henry Madden Library.

NOTES

1. For a recent analysis of contemporary representations of bisexuality see Maria San Filippo, *The B Word: Bisexuality in Contemporary Film and Television* (Bloomington: Indiana University Press, 2013).
2. For the essential history of American sexploitation's formation, trends, reception, and regulation see Elena Gorfinkel, *Lewd Looks: American Sexploitation Cinema in the 1960s* (Minneapolis and London: University of Minnesota Press, 2017).
3. An early discussion of sexploitation roughies as a genre occurs in Kenneth Turan and Stephen Zito, "Blood Lust: Ghoulies, Roughies, and Kinkies," in *Sinema: American Pornographic Films and the People Who Make Them* (New York: Praeger, 1974), 19–25.
4. For a brief mention in the popular press of queer patrons of sexploitation theaters see John Hallowell, "Making Movies for the Goon Trade—Sex! Money! Monotony!," *New York World Journal Tribune*, January 8, 1967, 4. In interviews, Wishman has discussed her role in both directing and writing her films; see, for instance, Mike Watt, "When I Die I'll Make Films in Hell: Doris Wishman, the Queen of Exploitation Cinema Speaks!!," *Femme Fatales* 11, no. 2 (February 2002): 16–23.
5. "Inversion" here meant an innate incorporation of both male and female traits. For more on the historical usage see George Chauncey, "From Sexual Inversion to Homosexuality: Medicine and the Changing Conceptualization of Female Deviance," *Salmagundi*, no. 58/59 (1982): 114–46. For this concept's relation to bisexuality see Steven Angelides, *A History of Bisexuality* (Chicago: University of Chicago Press, 2001).
6. Bisexual activists and academics have done much work to intervene in and shed the pathological connotation of these definitions. Following these interventions, my personal preference for its definition is: bisexuality is the sexual identity in which one's sexual object choice is determined by factors other than gender. This definition allows us as bisexuals to counter the phobic accusation that "bisexuals affirm the gender binary." For an excellent survey of bisexual theory see Donald Eugene Hall and Maria Pramaggiore (eds.), *RePresenting Bisexualities* (New York: New York University Press, 1996).
7. For example, Vicki Lynn Eaklor, *Queer America: A GLBT History of the 20th Century* (Westport, CT: Greenwood Press, 2008), 181; David A. Gerstner (ed.), *Routledge International Encyclopedia of Queer Culture* (London: Routledge, 2006), 79–80.
8. John D'Emilio, "Capitalism and Gay Identity," in *Making Trouble: Essays on Gay History, Politics, and the University* (New York: Routledge, 1992), 4; George Chauncey, *Gay New York:*

Gender, Urban Culture, and the Makings of the Gay Male World, 1890–1940 (New York: Basic Books, 1994), 1–2.
9. Representative books include Chauncey, *Gay New York*; Lillian Faderman, *Odd Girls and Twilight Lovers: A History of Lesbian Life in Twentieth-Century America* (New York: Columbia University Press, 1991).
10. This misperception is addressed in Angelides's *History of Bisexuality*.
11. Eaklor, *Queer America*, 181; Gerstner, *Queer Culture*, 79–80.
12. For a thorough discussion of viewers' abilities to perceive bisexuality as part of its visibility and invisibility see San Filippo, *B Word*, 1–45.
13. Jeffrey Escoffier, *American Homo: Community and Perversity* (Berkeley: University of California Press, 1998), 71–5.
14. Blaine J. Branchik, "Out in the Market: A History of the Gay Market Segment in the United States," *Journal of Macromarketing* 22, no. 1 (June 1, 2002): 86–97.
15. For sources on this history see Jeffrey Escoffier, *Bigger than Life: The History of Gay Porn Cinema from Beefcake to Hardcore* (Philadelphia: Running Press, 2009); Thomas Waugh, *Hard to Imagine: Gay Male Eroticism in Photography and Film from Their Beginnings to Stonewall* (New York: Columbia University Press, 1996).
16. Whitney Strub, "Queer Smut, Queer Rights," in *New Views on Pornography: Sexuality, Politics, and the Law*, ed. Lynn Comella and Shira Tarrant (Santa Barbara: Praeger, 2015), 148–50.
17. Jeffrey Escoffier, *American Homo*, 93.
18. "More Homo Pix For N.Y. Following B.O. Success of 'Deathwatch', 'Hustler,'" *Variety*, August 9, 1967, 16.
19. A notable exception is the chapter on bisexual pulp novels in Susan Stryker, "Twisted Paths and Tangled Webs," in *Queer Pulp: Perverted Passions from the Golden Age of the Paperback* (San Francisco: Chronicle Books, 2001), 27–48.
20. Alfred C. Kinsey, Wardell B. Pomeroy, and Clyde E. Martin, *Sexual Behavior in the Human Male* (Philadelphia: W.B. Saunders, 1948).
21. Examples include Patricia Durant and Keith Nelson, *The Bisexual Revolution* (Cleveland: Classics Library, 1968); Preston Harriman, *Bi-Sexuality, Normal or Not?* (North Hollywood: Dominion, 1969).
22. Stryker, "Twisted."
23. Stephen Donaldson, "The Bisexual Movement's Beginnings in the 70s: A Personal Retrospective," in *Bisexual Politics: Theories, Queries, and Visions*, ed. Naomi Tucker (New York: Haworth Press, 1995), 38.
24. Popular press articles from across the country in the 1960s reported that men were the dominant audience for adult theaters at this time; for example, see Hallowell, "Making Movies," 4, 7. However, women were increasingly targeted as a viable audience by the end of the decade and into the 1970s, usually as part of the emergent "couples" audience for hardcore movies.
25. Kevin Thomas, "'Wild Roots of Love' Short of Development," *Los Angeles Times*, November 10, 1965, D14.
26. For a proposed formulaic list of necessary sequences see Kent E. Carroll, "Porno-Hypo Showmanship," *Variety*, August 13, 1969, 7. Justin Wyatt has historicized the relation of increasing sexual permissiveness in exploitation and adult film with the rise of the studio ratings system; see Justin Wyatt, "Selling 'Atrocious Sexual Behavior': Revising Sexualities in the Marketplace for Adult Film of the 1960s," in *Swinging Single: Representing Sexuality in the 1960s*, ed. Hilary Radner and Moya Luckett (Minneapolis: University of Minnesota Press, 1999), 105–31.

27. June of 1968 is when the Park Theatre in Los Angeles began its policy of targeting a gay (and bisexual) male demographic. Although it consisted of both gay underground films and softcore erotica, this event is generally considered the beginning of publicly exhibited gay pornography; see Escoffier, *Bigger than Life*, 47.
28. Examples of the former include Radley Metzger's films of the 1960s. The latter include, for instance, Joe Sarno's *All the Sins of Sodom*.
29. Several authors have noted the necessity of a temporal component for representing bisexuality. See, for instance, San Filippo, *B Word*, 34–40.
30. An orgiastic depiction of polyamory is an obvious exception, yet it conforms to a narrow notion of bisexuality steeped in stereotypes linking bisexual promiscuity to recreational swinger culture.
31. David Andrews, *Soft in the Middle: The Contemporary Softcore Feature in Its Contexts* (Columbus: Ohio State University Press, 2006), 2, 47–59.
32. David Church, "Between Fantasy and Reality: Sexploitation, Fan Magazines, and William Rotsler's 'Adults-Only' Career," *Film History* 26, no. 3 (2014): 124–30.
33. Lisa Ferber, "A Tiny Little Mae West or Something," *Cult Movies*, no. 37 (2002): 74.
34. Bill Orcutt, "Doris Wishman Interview," *Muckraker*, no. 8 (1997): 30.
35. For a book-length study of the archetype of the "single girl" see Katherine J. Lehman, *Those Girls: Single Women in Sixties and Seventies Popular Culture* (Lawrence: University Press of Kansas, 2011).
36. A typical example is the inversion of shot-reverse-shot editing for character dialogue wherein the listener is shown and the speaker obscured. Some sources attribute this stylistic tendency to C. Davis Smith, the cinematographer who most often worked with Wishman.
37. Other 1960s sexploitation filmmakers such as Nick Millard and Ron Sullivan also commonly produced non-sync sound features with narratives constructed by (usually female) post-dubbed internal monologue.
38. To convey a lesbian identity a similar costuming choice is chosen for Tess in *Another Day, Another Man* and Della in *My Brother's Wife*.
39. *Bad Girls Go to Hell Pressbook* (New York: Juri Pictures, c. 1965). My analysis of this pressbook is dependent on the portion of it published in the DVD slideshow produced by Something Weird Video: "Doris Wishman Gallery of Exploitation Art," in *Bad Girls Go to Hell/Another Day, Another Man* (Chatsworth: Image Entertainment, 2000), DVD.
40. "Bad Girls Go to Hell," *American Film Institute Catalog of Feature Films*, <https://www.afi.com/members/catalog/DetailView.aspx?s=&Movie=21790> (last accessed April 27, 2017). Hereafter cited as *AFI Catalog*.
41. For examples of queer male supporting characters in 1960s sexploitation see *Olga's House of Shame* (1964) and *Take Me Naked* (1965). For a notable early example of a pathologically coded gay villain see *Watch the Birdie* (1965).
42. For a discussion of the triangulation of underground cinema, exploitation influences, and queer context see Janet Staiger, "Finding Community in the Early 1960s: Underground Cinema and Sexual Politics," in *Swinging Single*, ed. Radner and Luckett, 45.
43. Ibid., 41.
44. Ibid., 41–5.
45. For instance, Louis Sher's Sherpix distributed Andy Warhol's *Flesh* (1968) and *Lonesome Cowboys* (1968).
46. "More Homo Pix For N.Y.," 7.
47. Ad copy from Park Cinema ad, *Los Angeles Free Press*, June 21, 1968, 37. Escoffier traces a history of this theater and its policy in *Bigger than Life*.

48. Balsam and Levine were the two primary distributors of Wishman's films during the 1960s. Balsam ran J.E.R. Pictures Inc. and Levine was president of Jerand Film Distributors.
49. "Rise of Gotham Cinemas for Sex and Homo Biz," *Variety*, July 9, 1969, 61.
50. The *AFI Catalog* lists the premiere as June of 1968 in Champaign, IL. There was an earlier premiere at two Philadelphia theaters, the Walton Art and Abbe Art Cinema, on December 15, 1967. The premiere of *Too Much Too Often!* in Philadelphia featured the full ad copy: "THE 'ANIMALS' ARE HERE . . . The two-legged variety, male and female!! It's a crazy mixed-up dirty world they live in. It has no boundaries, no limits and no inhibitions of any kind!! See it all shamelessly exposed in TOO MUCH . . . TOO OFTEN." Movie Listings, *Philadelphia Inquirer*, December 15, 1967, 16.
51. This is a significant divergence from the precedents mentioned above, for instance from *Watch the Birdie* (1965) whose gay villain is coded both as shameful and unattractive.
52. See John D'Emilio, "The Homosexual Menace: The Politics of Sexuality in Cold War America," in *Making Trouble*, 57–73.
53. For example, see Wilhelm Stekel, "Relation of Sadomasochism to Homosexuality," in *Sadism and Masochism: The Psychology of Hatred and Cruelty* (London: Vision Press, [1929] 1953), 137–201. For further discussion see Angelides, *History of Bisexuality*, 71–103.
54. Representative examples include Charles Grutzner, "One Boy May Stir Gang to Violence," *New York Times*, 1955, 83; "Youthful Crimes Laid to Society," *New York Times*, 1954, 14. For a filmic example see *The Detective* (1968).
55. Like sadism, psychoanalysis has similarly sutured narcissism to homosexuality, as discussed in Steven Bruhm, *Reflecting Narcissus: A Queer Aesthetic* (Minneapolis: University of Minnesota Press, 2001), 1–19. A common point of reference is the depiction of narcissism in Oscar Wilde's *The Picture of Dorian Gray*.
56. *Too Much Too Often! Campaign Manual* (New York: Jerand Film Distributors, c. 1967), 2, Something Weird Video Collection, Seattle, WA. Access courtesy Lisa Petrucci.
57. "Too Much Too Often!" *AFI Catalog* (last accessed April 27, 2017).
58. For discussions of the presumed "lowbrow" working-class and straight male address of 1960s sexploitation see David Andrews, "The Disorderly Feminization of Classical Sexploitation," in *Soft in the Middle*, 45–76; Elena Gorfinkel, "Tales of Times Square: Sexploitation's Secret History of Place," in *Taking Place: Location and the Moving Image*, ed. John David Rhodes and Elena Gorfinkel (Minneapolis: University of Minnesota Press, 2011), 57; Eric Schaefer, "Pandering to the 'Goon Trade': Framing the Sexploitation Audience through Advertising," in *Sleaze Artists: Cinema at the Margins of Taste, Style, and Politics*, ed. Jeffrey Sconce (Durham, NC: Duke University Press, 2007), 19–46.
59. L. Whipplasch, "Why Leather? Or 'What's a nice boy like me doing tied to a stake like this?'" *Vector*, 4, no. 7 (June 1968): 5.
60. Chauncey, *Gay New York*, 374–75, n.7.
61. Chris Cagle, "Rough Trade: Sexual Taxonomy in Postwar America," in *RePresenting Bisexualities*, ed. Hall and Pramaggiore, 234–52.
62. Collection of Doris Wishman trailers in *Bad Girls Go to Hell/Another Day, Another Man*, DVD.
63. *Too Much Too Often! Campaign Manual*, 4.
64. For a discussions of typical 1960s sexploitation advertising see Schaefer, "Pandering," 19–46; Mark Betz, "Art, Exploitation, Underground," in *Defining Cult Movies: The Cultural Politics of Oppositional Taste*, ed. Mark Jancovich, Antonio Lázaro Reboll, Julian Stringer, and Andy Willis (Manchester: Manchester University Press, 2003), 202–22.
65. By 1965 several newspapers across the U.S. had adopted similar policies governing advertisements. In addition to sensationalistic words, this newspaper code specifically

outlawed words that at that time implied same-sex sexuality such as "homosexual," "lesbian," "third sex," and "pervert." See "L.A. Times Tightens Pix Ad Code," *Daily Variety*, January 19, 1965, 1, 4; "Throw Rocks at Sexpot Copy: Hearst Joins War on Leer," *Variety*, February 24, 1965, 5; "Chi Sun Times & Daily News Set Stiff Standards on Pix Ads Papers Will Accept," *Daily Variety*, March 3, 1965, 3.
66. Cross Keys Drive-in, advertisement, *The Gettysburg Times*, May 16, 1970, 4; Fine Arts, advertisement, *Lubbock Avalanche Journal*, March 26, 1969, A-7.
67. Capitals and boldface as in the original ad.
68. For a redemptive take on Wishman's films see Moya Luckett, "Sexploitation as Feminine Territory: The Films of Doris Wishman," in *Defining Cult Movies*, ed. Jancovich et al., 142–56. For a more ambivalent appraisal see Tania Modleski, "Women's Cinema as Counterphobic Cinema: Doris Wishman as the Last Auteur," in *Sleaze Artists*, ed. Sconce, 47–70.

CHAPTER 6

"It's strange, but it's wonderful": Doris Wishman's *Nude on the Moon*

Karen Joan Kohoutek

In Doris Wishman's space fantasy *Nude on the Moon* (1960), a pair of astronauts discover an Edenic natural environment on the moon, its pools and gardens populated by telepathic nudists. This chapter will discuss the ways in which the film's narrative subverts the conventions of genre and the expectation of verisimilitude, in order to serve its concern with male emotional development and the possibility of transcending the gender roles that limit both men and women. In doing so, the chapter will provide a starting point for re-evaluating the film, a relatively obscure and unremarked production which is nonetheless sui generis. It is significant as both an example of and a departure from the space travel and nudist genres, and an important entry in Wishman's body of work in exploitation cinema.

To this end, this chapter discusses *Nude on the Moon* in the context of the space travel and nudist genres, as well as how it relates to the gender norms of its time. There is little available criticism on *Nude on the Moon*, in the context of either contemporaneous science fiction or Wishman's larger oeuvre, where attention has focused primarily on the more extreme aspects of her career, particularly the roughies.[1] Given the lack of existing in-depth analysis on the film, this chapter will probe the text in some detail, highlighting the way specific scenes and dialogue contribute to an understanding of the larger themes. It will also provide information about the film's production for the benefit of future Wishman scholars.

Nude on the Moon has been called the "*Plan 9 from Outer Space* of nudist movies,"[2] hinting at both its science fiction ambition and the technical limitations of its obvious low budget. Despite the latter, this light-hearted fantasy remains a uniquely imaginative project, diverging from the limits of a specific genre to provide a perhaps surprising depth of commentary about social attitudes and romantic negotiations at the time of its filming, in the historic moment when the United States stood on the verge of conquering space travel.

Filmed eight years before people would walk on the lunar surface, and seven before *2001: A Space Odyssey* (Stanley Kubrick, 1968) would bring a new level of realism and sophistication to the cinema of space travel, the film utilizes familiar conventions of the outer space genre, with a plot reflective of the real-life contemporary space race. When it veers into the genre of the nudist film, *Nude on the Moon* diverges from the generic expectations of either category, becoming stylistically fluid within the liberating space of an overtly non-realistic narrative. In doing so, what could appear to be a simple utopia designed for male spectators ends up as more of an emotional utopia, an environment in which men are free to respond to women, emotionally and sexually, without the baggage of social constraints.

THE PRODUCTION

Doris Wishman began her career in the early 1960s with a series of nudist films, later expanding into other styles, all of which have led to her classification as a director of cult, exploitation, or sexploitation films.[3] She became perhaps best known for her work in the "roughies": harder-edge dramas containing nudity and overt sexual activity, violence, and rape, which comprise "the largest chunks of Wishman's career, as well as most of her well-known works."[4] These films, with their often harsh views of gender relations, have garnered more attention than *Nude on the Moon*, which, with its depiction of a more innocent sexuality and ultimately optimistic view of male–female romantic interactions, presents a different facet of Wishman's work.

Wishman made eight films in the nudist genre between 1960 and 1965, shooting and releasing them so close together that the order is not always clear.[5] Regardless of the exact date, *Nude on the Moon* was one of her earliest efforts; it fits into "the late period of nudist exploitation films," which "lasted only from 1960 to 1968."[6] The larger nudist genre had existed for decades, with films that purported to express nudist philosophy, while also exploiting the desire of (presumed male) audiences to view attractive naked women. Typically, the nudist films of this era attempted to portray "a nonsexual atmosphere," with a "continued nudist line of sexual innocence."[7] With the presentation of nudity no longer strictly limited to (purported) non-fiction and educational productions, this era's films included the genre of "nudie cuties," which featured minimalist, even cursory storylines, frequently still embedded in documentary-style footage of sunbathing and sports activities at nudist camps.

In context, Wishman's first entries were more narratively ambitious than the genre required. *Hideout in the Sun* (c. 1960) contains a bank robbery, and

Nude on the Moon, generally credited as her second feature, has been called a "single-film science fiction subgenre,"[8] a combination of the nudist and space exploration genres which remains unique both in her career and in the history of exploitation cinema.

As her outer space location, Wishman made use of the real-life tourist attraction of Coral Castle, in Homestead, Florida.[9] The site still operates as a museum, and multiple books and documentaries discuss the mystery of how its founder single-handedly erected the stone monuments that stood in for alien architecture.[10] Most of this material avoids mentioning the attraction's prominent role in a nudist film,[11] but Coral Castle's own advertising, starting in the 1950s, featured the sex appeal of "bathing-suited beauties" and the promise of romance, elements that are also found in Wishman's film.

Apart from its value as an exotic found location, the Coral Castle setting allowed Wishman to circumvent some of the restrictions put on filmmakers by real nudist camps; the film's seal of approval from the fictional "American Moonbathing Association" is an inside jab at the sometimes uncooperative American Sunbathing Association.[12] The cast was no more seasoned than its director: *Nude on the Moon* is the only film credit for the top-billed Marietta, in the dual role of the Moon Queen and the earthbound Cathy, and for Lester Brown, the co-lead playing young scientist Jeff Huntley. The career of the second male lead, avuncular William Mayer playing Professor Nichols, consists solely of parts in Wishman's nudist films.[13]

Figure 6.1 Moon residents at the real-life Coral Castle. Courtesy of Something Weird Video

Like many low-budget filmmakers of her time, Wishman utilized various techniques to cut down on the need to synchronize dialogue in her films, including voiceover narration and off-screen dialogue. She sometimes "put together her story line in the editing room," and avoiding shots of the actors' mouths "allowed her to dub in any dialogue she believed could work for the story."[14] In *Nude on the Moon*, for instance, the astronauts' life support systems consist of snorkel-like oxygen tubes, which block a direct view of their lips. Wishman also extends this tendency by utilizing telepathy. None of the moon people speak, but their queen's thoughts are heard in whispery, disembodied voiceovers; when she makes a decree, she ironically concludes: "I have spoken."[15] In this case, as with many of Wishman's films, the budgetary constraints probably helped inspire the "wealth of imagination" on display.[16]

THE TRIP TO THE MOON

Released the same year that the Soviet Union and the United States put their first men into orbit, *Nude on the Moon* has been considered an artifact from a time "when the whole country watched as NASA built the moon program, entranced by images of men walking in space."[17] The design of the ship, a very slim, tapering cylinder, is reminiscent of that in the influential film *Destination Moon* (1950) and other popular science fiction of the time. It also has a resemblance to the real-life Mercury Redstone rocket in use by NASA in 1961, a detail that grounds the film in the contemporary world.[18]

The film's veneer of verisimilitude aligns it with the kind of imaginative mise-en-scène found in other science fiction films of its time, just as, for example, the voyage itself follows a familiar process: radio contact with some kind of mission control, men inside the capsule flipping switches and reciting technical processes. The film's first thirty minutes contain a surprisingly straight-faced, if implausible, drama about a journey to the moon. In contrast to the nudist element presented up front, the length of time devoted to introducing the characters and the situation shows a restraint and concern for narrative not always seen in the genre.

These astronauts are independent scientists who have built their own rocket while waiting for government funding, and when the film begins, Jeff learns of a three-million-dollar inheritance, which will allow them to fully finance their trip to the moon. This plot point may have been motivated by the film's obvious low budget, a means of freeing Wishman from the obligation to be true in any way to the realities of the contemporary space program, but it also introduces elements that will later have a thematic payoff.

In this early section, the scientists work in montages at the lab and engage in a lengthy technical discussion on the problem of taking off again to return from the moon, stressing the extremes and rapid changes of temperature known to exist there. Additional problems are addressed, including the moon's surface of rocky rubble and the likelihood of encountering volcanic ash. All of this is in line with the kind of scientific dialogue that provided a sense of realism to the science fiction of the time.[19]

In these conversations, the Professor, immediately established as a mentor to his younger colleague, points out that they have been working theoretically and lack practical experience, saying, "there's much we don't know about the moon." While this is true on a simple plot level, the foregrounding of a lack of experience foreshadows a developing theme about sexual awakening and emotional maturation that will carry through the rest of the film.

The men have a single employee at their laboratory facility, Cathy, who is dedicated and efficient, as well as attractive, and even sensual. In clear cues to the audience, she is introduced in a red dress, and in a scene revealing her love for Jeff, sultry saxophone music plays on the soundtrack as she stares longingly at his picture.[20] At the same time, she strives to maintain a professional persona throughout the film, and to prevent her feelings from interfering with her job. Cathy's late hours are noted by the Professor. He sees through her excuses about improving her work, appreciating her professional competence, but also suggests, "your interest in your job is a little extraordinary." His attitude reinforces the underlying implication that romantic feelings for her employer are a woman's only motive to take a real interest in her job. The film shows he has an accurate perception of her romantic aspirations, which is probably no surprise, since this idea about working women was not uncommon in its time.

Lynn Peril, a cultural critic specializing in women's roles during this period, quotes various sources on women's place in the workforce into the 1960s, which generally assume that women with jobs "would prefer home and marriage," but will dedicate themselves to career when "a normal life is denied them." Mirroring Cathy's position in the office, Peril adds that "the excessive devotion with which the super-secretary was supposed to treat her boss" led to the stereotype of a "spinster who sacrificed a life outside the office in favor of her love (often unrequited) for her charismatic boss."[21] The ground-breaking book *Sex and the Single Girl* (1962) rejects the notion that a woman with a job is necessarily pining for marriage, but it does state that "a girl in love with her boss will knock herself out seven days a week and wish there were more days," exactly the kind of behavior Cathy displays.[22] It stands to reason that Cathy's position was likely familiar to audiences of the time.

When the Professor presses Cathy on her feelings, she replies, "He's so involved with this project . . . he doesn't know I exist." The Professor largely agrees with Cathy's assessment, saying, "Jeff is completely absorbed in his work . . . all I've ever heard him talk about is rocket propellants, the laws of gravity." This idea is contextualized by a minor complication: an off-screen red herring of a romantic rival, who is almost immediately established as someone that Jeff considers only a childhood friend. The introduction of this never-seen character helps establish Jeff's dedication to bachelorhood, as he remains oblivious to the romantic potential of all the women in his life.

The situation presented here illustrates a distinction in how men and women can be unequally perceived within the same workplace, affected by the assumptions of the larger society. Cathy and Jeff are dedicated to their careers, willing to make sacrifices in their personal lives, but their motives for doing so are judged very differently. Jeff's colleagues are concerned that he works more than is good for him, but no one assumes that his single-minded focus on science springs from a romantic attachment. However, that is exactly the assumption made about Cathy.

The film does not, however, ignore the fact that relationships, even leading to marriage, play a part in men's emotional lives, as well. The male leads have two significant conversations that specifically address Jeff's future and the possibility of romance having a place in his life. First, at the prospect of Jeff spending his entire inheritance on a single trip to space, the Professor reminds him that the money could enable him to settle down, marry, and live happily, to which he emphatically responds with, "Marriage? Me? No sir!" As the voyage nears, the Professor presses Jeff again, telling him outright, "I'd like to see you happy with a wife, with a family." This time, Jeff's response is almost angry, insisting, "I'm not interested in marriage, or settling down. Science is my life, and nothing else." He adamantly tells the Professor that his view is fixed and unchangeable: he does not want to have to say this "ever again."

It is not common in either the science fiction or the nudist films of the era to develop the interest in a man's emotional life as *Nude on the Moon* does in this part of the film. While Wishman was operating within a genre with established conventions, there is little doubt that she was personally responsible for the work's thematic elements, emphasizing in an interview the degree to which she was in control of her productions: "I write them myself. Then I direct them, choose the casting, crew location—almost everything . . . I know what I want."[23]

ON THE MOON

At the point when the astronauts set off on their voyage, the film's realistic elements begin to give way. First they enter a wooded area and climb a large scaffolding to enter the rocket. When the camera pulls back to show the entire craft in a belated establishing shot, the rocket stands alone in what appears to be a desert plain, with no trees or scaffolding near it: a background that in no way matches the previous shots.

Similarly, after the rocket lands, the establishing shot presents a landscape aligned with realistic expectations of the moon's surface and the astronauts'

Figure 6.2 Establishing shot of the bleak lunar surface. Courtesy of Something Weird Video

earlier descriptions. It is barren, rocky, and bleak, full of craters and bathed in green light, the kind of lifeless lunar environment familiar from other science fiction films.[24] The moment they open the door, however, they marvel at what they are seeing off-screen: "It doesn't look anything like what we had imagined." When the audience is shown what the characters see, the men are standing on green grass, amid clusters of palm fronds. No attempt is made to reconcile the shot of the rocket landing, shown a few moments earlier, with the shot of the characters walking out its door.

It is impossible to say how much Wishman's inexperience, the limitations of her budget, or the speed of production played into the style of the film.[25] Other critics have argued that, like her "bizarre cutaways," "her more brazen continuity violations appear intentional," as stylistic choices.[26] The unabashed juxtaposition of incongruous landscapes—and the lack of continuity between the environments experienced within and without the spacecraft—creates a disorienting effect. The pretense of straightforward science fiction and space exploration begins to give way to an overtly fantastical environment, more a land of enchantment—or setting from a fairy tale—than a subject of scientific inquiry.

At this point, all the information presented about the moon's environment—the rubble and the volcanic ash—is abandoned. The astronauts discuss how all the existing telescopic evidence has shown the moon to be barren rock,

Figure 6.3 Astronauts surrounded by palm trees. Courtesy of Something Weird Video

and Jeff asks pointedly, "How do we know it is the moon?" Adding to the element of space fantasy, the Professor immediately discovers some rocks, which he recognizes as pure gold. They worry that its composition may be altered by radiation on the return trip: "Suppose it turns to worthless dust?" The Professor wants to take as much as possible to finance a second trip, but Jeff, concerned about the danger of adding extra weight to the rocket, wants to focus on the original mission, saying, "We came here for science. Why are we looking for gold?"

Although this initially seems to be a digression, the conflict, with one man wanting to abandon the scientific mission for a perceived treasure, recurs almost immediately in a different form, with the roles shifted; now Jeff is the one to forget about science. The detail also ties into the film's ongoing themes. The fear that the gold will just weigh them down resonates metaphorically with Jeff's feelings about love and marriage, which at this point are still hostile. Like the gold, the possibility of romance is there for the taking, with a woman who loves him right under his nose, but he views the idea as merely a distraction from his intellectual goals.

Their surprising discoveries about the lunar environment take a truly unexpected turn when the astronauts discover a group of moon residents in a lush garden, the women topless and the men wearing only almost-nude shorts. Later, a few toddlers will be seen, providing some evidence of a reproductive cycle and aging process, but otherwise the people seen in the film are all young and attractive. A few men will be seen performing physical tasks, but the lunar society otherwise appears to be a leisurely, uneventful Eden, where time is passed with "all the stock nudist camp clichés ... volleyball, sunbathing, standing in front of strategically-placed shrubs."[27] Back on Earth the astronauts had earnestly discussed the moon's dangerous environment, but its residents instead appear acclimated to a warm, pleasant climate.

In one of the film's endearingly naive touches, the moon people wear headband antennas, which look exactly like toy ones; this seems the least amount of effort that could go into making the moon people appear alien.[28] Similarly, the queen will be seen wielding a scepter that looks much like a child's magic wand. Again, these elements may be primarily the result of the film's low budget, but they also work to symbolically position the moon kingdom as an unreal environment, in contrast to the earlier, fairly realistic settings, and also a site of playful, childlike innocence.

The leader of the moon people is a woman on a stone throne, one of Coral Castle's attractions. Apart from a more confident posture and cheerful expression, she is an exact doppelganger of Cathy, although neither of the men ever notes the resemblance until they are back on Earth. When Jeff meets the queen, they seem to share an immediate rapport. She touches his arm and chest, and his smile, along with the obvious catch in his voice, suggests he is not as indifferent to women as he had earlier insisted. In a sudden reversal, the Professor is the one focused on the mission; while he seems amused by the curious, half-naked women who swarm around him, he continues to collect scientific samples while Jeff lingers at the queen's side. "Now Jeff, really, remember what we came here for ... we've got to do some work ... you're acting like a schoolboy!" the Professor admonishes him, but Jeff is unembarrassed. "I feel like a schoolboy. I've never felt like this in my life." When the Professor voices Jeff's previous priorities, saying, "don't forget, we're scientists," Jeff says he would rather "speak" to the queen.

It seems significant that the couple is unable to communicate verbally. The language barrier seems to add to their attraction rather than detract from it, in an interaction that is primarily physical, although chaste. Freed from intellectual activity and his dominant identity as a rational, scientific person, Jeff visibly softens. The relationship that develops between Jeff and the Moon Queen is unburdened by pre-existing societal roles or the baggage of earthly expectations mentioned by the Professor, such as marriage and family. The removed, even dream-like setting appears to offer an emotional utopia, where a man and woman can meet as individuals and be naturally, mutually drawn to one another. While this work of gentle titillation is far from hardcore pornography on a spectrum of cinematic eroticism, the latter has been described as "a profoundly 'escapist' genre," one which "distracts audiences from the deeper social or political causes of the disturbed relations between the sexes; and yet paradoxically . . . must address some of the real experiences and needs of its audience."[29]

In a fantastic lunar environment, contrasted with the workaday Earth world, Jeff's long-term resistance to romantic love is abruptly circumvented. The situation contains an element of light satire: the character so resolutely established as a man of science, disdainful of marriage and female attention, does a complete turn-around, calling himself a lovesick "schoolboy" as soon as he sees a woman's naked breasts. While Wishman's film shows the emphasis on "nonerotic nudism" common to the nudist genre,[30] it seems improbable that his sudden romantic interest would not follow from sexual attraction, even as his removal from his ordinary environment frees him to embrace this change.

Although nothing is overtly sexual in their interaction, the Moon Queen is open about her interest in Jeff, which differentiates her from her earthly look-alike, who has kept her emotions hidden. While Jeff could not imagine his co-worker as a sexual being or potential partner, he cannot avoid seeing the Moon Queen's nudity and reacting to it with attraction. By exposing her breasts, the Moon Queen reveals a confident sexual maturation, in a context where doing so appears innocent and natural; this element fits with the established tropes of nudist cinema, which was often concerned with the depiction of the nudist lifestyle as "healthy and innocent."[31]

When the men do temporarily return to their mission collecting "highly useful data," this takes the form of photographing the moon residents as they engage in various games and activities, lounge by the pool, and perform interpretive dance. "Now there's some lovely creatures. They're going to pose for us," the Professor says, while light, whimsical music plays in the background. This lengthy sequence, over fifteen minutes long, offers viewers what they would expect from a more traditional nudist film: the observation of attractive, half-naked women engaging in leisure activities divorced from any narrative function.

Throughout, the behavior of the astronauts is utterly deadpan, accepting the act of observing topless sunbathers as part of their legitimate scientific research. The nudity is so at odds with the characters' deadpan behavior that the contradiction foregrounds the absurdity of the idyll, which has been described as a "humorous commentary" on the theoretical "educational value" of similar sequences in nudist cinema.[32] This scene of men, fully clothed in spacesuits, photographing half-naked women as they go about their lives contains a voyeuristic element, even a literalized depiction of the male gaze. This may provide evidence of Wishman as a woman fitting into a man's world by incorporating the biases of the male gaze, literalized here by a scientist's camera: "Women directors work with the codes and conventions of patriarchal ideologies and genres."[33] However, as both a woman and a cult filmmaker, existing by definition in an oppositional position to mainstream cinema, Wishman can potentially operate as an exemplar of an "alternative cinema," which "provides a space for the birth of a cinema which . . . challenges the basic assumptions of the mainstream film."[34] Behind the fictional camera held by men, the locus of control remains a woman who is filming them, dictating their behavior, which lends a subversive edge to a scenario that might otherwise seem straightforwardly dominated by the male gaze.

As the astronauts' oxygen supply eventually dwindles, Jeff has been fully converted into a romantic, insisting on staying behind, even if that means his death: "Maybe I'm mad, but I cannot leave here." He suggests they bring the Moon Queen back to Earth, and the Professor turns his previous attitudes against him, questioning, "have you forgotten your plans, your projects?" But Jeff is now as vehement as he was in their previous arguments, but from the opposite side: "Don't you understand? I'm in love. For the first time in my life, I care for someone." The queen, however, refuses to allow his sacrifice, using her magic wand to hypnotize him so he can be brought to the spacecraft in time. Once they are back in the rocket and preparing for the transition back to Earth, the craft is again presented in a green-lit, barren moonscape, from which Wishman cuts to the blue skies and green foliage of the Coral Castle grounds, where the lunar nudists are waving goodbye. The lack of visual continuity marks the boundaries between the film's narrative elements that exist within the science fiction genre and the ones that place it in the nudist genre, as well as a liminal space between realism and fantasy.

THE RESOLUTION

The act of coming "back to Earth" after this idyll takes on an overtly symbolic quality. Both men lost consciousness during the voyage and, having lost their camera and samples, return without evidence of having gone anywhere at all. Without that evidence, their experiences on the moon become colored with the connotations of a dream. With the scientific community skeptical about their achievement, the film's resolution re-emphasizes the idea that they cannot be sure of where they went, placing the film's events in a space separate from rational causality.

Wherever he went in spatial and scientific terms, on some level Jeff encountered a world with such different social organization and open expressions of sexuality that it has changed his entire view of love and relationships. When Cathy appears, a dissolve turns her into the Moon Queen and back, a visualization of Jeff mentally undressing her. "I can't believe it. You're here on Earth. I didn't lose you after all," he says, kissing her. The actress Marietta, in her double role, embodies alternative versions of the same woman: the highly competent, long-suffering office worker in love with her boss, and the relaxed,

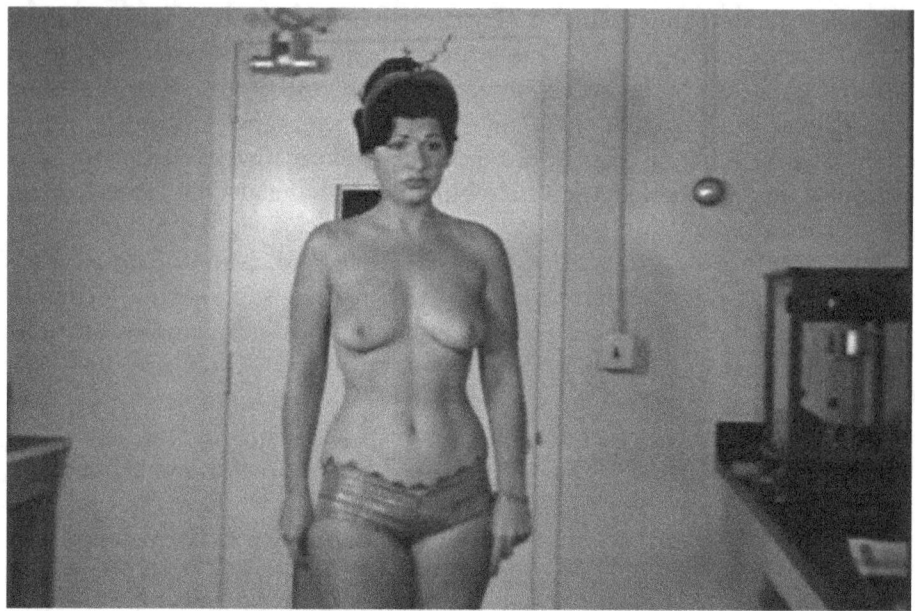

Figure 6.4 Cathy seen as the Moon Queen. Courtesy of Something Weird Video

desirable Queen of the Moon. In mundane reality, where there are jobs and responsibilities, the potential love interest is a rather dour-looking woman in a lab coat; seen through a prism of fantasy, she is an exotic, half-naked alien. It is a changed man who, recognizing that the nudity is just under her clothes, begins to see the normal woman as desirable.

Jeff's original masculine disinterest in marriage would not have been seen as entirely atypical in the early 1960s, a time when, for example, "there were few books for men about *how to be* happy while single because men, by definition, *were* happy while single."[35] The depiction of a man rejecting the pleasures of romance and sexuality altogether, in order to focus single-mindedly on his career and the life of the mind, is somewhat more unusual; the necessity for a woman to choose between a career and romance is a familiar trope, while there is less conflict for male characters, who are often allowed to have both without giving it a thought.[36]

Nonetheless, Jeff's single-minded focus on his career and intellectual endeavor aligns easily with traditional male gender roles, and "the rule of the basic double standard, according to which it is acceptable for a woman to 'give up everything' for love and unacceptable, even emasculating, for a man to do the same."[37] Having already abandoned his previous, heartfelt idea of love as incompatible with a career and scientific achievement, Jeff shows himself perfectly ready to give up everything related to those values, and even his life, to stay with the woman he loves. Back on Earth, with three million dollars spent and his professional life in limbo, he is able to honestly say, "I have no regrets." At this point, Wishman grants the character a romantic happy ending right out of a fairy tale, in a demonstration that, in this case, the man's true happiness hinges on the development of his emotional maturity.

In Jeff's narrative arc, the trip to the moon can be seen as an elaborate metaphor for a man's sexual awakening, operating as a kind of accelerated adolescence. He has channeled all his energy into strictly cerebral concerns, but once his attention is drawn to the beauty of the human body, in an environment of sensual pleasure, his previous harsh stance almost immediately softens, and he belatedly turns into a "love-struck teenager." By the time he returns to Earth, he has become a more mature person, able to see the value of the woman who already loves him. Cathy, on the other hand, has never visited a mysterious paradise, but her fantasies still come true. Contemporary space travel films like *12 to the Moon* and *Assignment: Outer Space* (both c. 1960) included romantic subplots involving women who were part of the space crews. Cathy's position as an Everywoman is partly a more realistic one for the time period, but it also marks her as an audience identification character. While she is physically identical to the idealized space woman, she is nonetheless down to Earth in every sense. Her passivity may open up no critique of the gender roles that constrain her, but the film takes her happiness into account; this cannot be said of many other films in the exploitation genre, generally thought as being dominated by male desires. Therefore, it is safe to posit that Wishman's "films were originally made for the largely male audiences seeking softcore thrills."[38]

Nude on the Moon displays a concern with the emotional life of its primary female character, and it depicts the man's emotional maturity as both a literal voyage for him and a reward for the woman's patience, themes that disrupt interpretations of Wishman targeting her work solely at male spectators. *Nude on the Moon*, then, provides evidence that "there is something more at work in her films than simply the act of exploiting women."[39] As science fiction, the film's emphasis on romance and male emotional maturation stands out as unusual in other genre works of the time, which often contain a token but mostly unexplored romantic subplot. The section of the film that deals with the preparation and voyage into space shares stylistic similarities with more straightforward films of the era, which remain focused on the science of space travel.[40]

The Phantom Planet (1961) probably has the most in common with *Nude on the Moon*. Its astronaut hero also makes a fairly realistically depicted space journey that takes a fantastic turn, leading to romance with an exotic alien woman. In the end, just like Jeff, he realizes that he can never prove the reality of his adventure, and the possibility that the experience was a dream or a hallucination is directly discussed. Unlike Jeff, though, his duty comes first, and he is stalwartly ready to leave the woman he loves behind: after their first kiss, he muses, "here in this place, I've found perhaps what I've been looking for all my life, and I must leave alone . . . it's my solemn duty."[41]

While *Nude on the Moon* distinctly differentiates itself from the space exploration genre of its time by turning into a nudist film, it also diverges from the tropes common to nudist films. For example, one of the genre's expected conventions was that "nudist exploitation films will explicitly or tacitly proclaim some important element of 'nudist philosophy.' This may include discussion of the physical, emotional, social, or spiritual benefits of practicing nonsexual social nudity," often in the form of a straightforward lecture about the benefits of a nudist lifestyle.[42]

It is all but unheard of for a nudist film of the period to avoid this kind of open didacticism, but *Nude on the Moon* bypasses the convention to such an extent that the astronauts never once comment on the nudity of the people they meet. The closest the film comes to addressing the topic of nudism per se is in a piece of subtle, self-congratulatory metafiction. Early in the film, en route to their historic trip, the Professor mentions that he went to a movie the night before. As they drive to the launch site, the Professor says, "the picture was well worth it," and at that moment, they pass the Variety theater, where a large marquee advertises Wishman's debut film *Hideout in the Sun*, in "Nudearama." The Professor does not directly identify this as the movie he saw, but it is strongly implied. This touch, visible in the background, is the only reference to social nudism of the kind promoted by other films in the genre. Instead, Wishman simply presents a civilized topless society without overt commentary, an unusual, and subtle, narrative strategy.

The implication that the Professor appreciates the nudist lifestyle, even before their journey, may be more than an in-joke. While his time on the moon is clearly enjoyable for him, the experience is not life-changing in the way it is for Jeff. The Professor encourages the younger man to date and eventually marry, evidence that the Professor, while not apparently married himself, has healthier ideas about the emotional and sexual sides of life, and does not see any contradiction between those possibilities and Jeff's scientific dedication. This is probably related to the connection, often depicted in the nudist genre, between open-mindedness about social nudism and a healthy, well-adjusted way of life.

The lunar utopia of *Nude on the Moon* is portrayed from the perspective of its male characters, which may contain an underlying symbolism, representing the idea that this kind of freeing sexuality is easier for men to experience, given societal constraints, but in another of Wishman's early films, *Blaze Starr Goes Nudist* (c. 1962), a visit to a nudist camp is similarly freeing for its female protagonist.

There are differences: in *Nude on the Moon*, Jeff is driven to explore and achieve in his career, and in so doing, accidentally discovers a paradise, where he can learn a more open-minded approach to the emotions and desires. In contrast, Blaze Starr begins the film overwhelmed by the demands of her career; she is "utterly exhausted," so worn out with "a million things to do" that her "nerves are frayed."[43] When she finds her earthly paradise, it is because she is seeking a sanctuary from the pressure of maintaining her career. Both characters do, however, find that their encounters with a nudist lifestyle make them happier than they have ever been, and lead to satisfying romantic relationships, ending on light, optimistic notes. *Nude on the Moon* differentiates itself in that its narrative leaps from any standard of cinematic realism, of the kind still on display in *Blaze Starr Goes Nudist*, to revel in a liberating fantasy world. This works more strongly to present "what utopia would 'feel like,'"[44] with an experience of an emotionally healthy paradise that can be brought to influence everyday interactions between the sexes.

CONCLUSION

This chapter has provided a fairly in-depth reading of *Nude on the Moon* in relation to overlapping issues of genre classification and gender norms within the film's text, which reveal more complexity than might be expected from its title, its place in the category of nudist films, or its fairly simple narrative. Doris Wishman was "a woman working in a virtually all-male domain,"[45] becoming one of only a few female cult film directors who "have been celebrated as exceptions made, against the odds, in an industry largely dominated by exploitation,"[46] particularly exploitation of the female form. If her work "simultaneously uses the exploitation genre and transcends it,"[47] *Nude on the Moon* exemplifies this flexibility. Its technical limitations do not preclude its winning a spot on film historian Mark Storey's "Top Twenty" films of the nudist genre.[48] Even as it borders other genres, it remains a singular work, and as a female artist working in a genre dedicated to the display of female nudity, Wishman unusually, and perhaps uniquely, utilized that genre to present a singularly imaginative case study of male emotional development.

NOTES

1. For example, Moya Luckett's essay in *Defining Cult Movies* is fourteen pages long, and the only reference is that nudism as a means of freedom for women goes "to its fantastic limits in *Nude on the Moon*, where the planet is harmoniously ruled by naked women" (144). Modleski's essay in *Sleaze Artists* is twenty-two pages, and includes a single paragraph (49). McKendry's sixteen-page essay in *From the Arthouse to the Grindhouse* includes seventy-six words on the film (58–9). See Moya Luckett, "Sexploitation as Feminine Territory: The Films of Doris Wishman," in *Defining Cult Movies: The Cultural Politics of Oppositional Taste*, ed. Mark Jancovich, Antonio Lázaro Reboll, Julian Stringer, and

Andy Willis (Manchester: Manchester University Press, 2003), 142–56; Tania Modleski, "Women's Cinema as Counterphobic Cinema: Doris Wishman as the Last Auteur," in *Sleaze Artists: Cinema at the Margins of Taste, Style, and Politics*, ed. Jeffrey Sconce (Durham, NC: Duke University Press, 2007), 47–70; Rebekah McKendry, "Fondling Your Eyeballs: Watching Doris Wishman," in *From the Arthouse to the Grindhouse: Highbrow and Lowbrow Transgression in Cinema's First Century*, ed. John Cline and Robert G. Weiner (Lanham, MD: Scarecrow Press, 2010).

2. Mark Storey, *Cinema au Naturel: A History of Nudist Film* (Oshkosh, WI: Naturist Education Foundation, 2003), 137.
3. Wishman herself rejected the label of sexploitation, saying that many of her movies "haven't any sex," or "very little . . . so they're not *sexploitation*." She specifically mentions *Double Agent 73*, *Deadly Weapons*, and *The Amazing Transplant*, but *Nude on the Moon* also contains no overt sexual activity. Andrea Juno, "Interview: Doris Wishman," in *Incredibly Strange Films*, ed. V. Vale and Andrea Juno (San Francisco: RE/Search Publications, 1986), 110–13.
4. McKendry, "Fondling Your Eyeballs," 63.
5. Writer Mike Quarles credits *Nature Girl*, a.k.a. *Blaze Starr Goes Nudist*, as Wishman's first film, followed by *Nude on the Moon*. Most scholars, including Rebekah McKendry and Moya Luckett, place *Hideout in the Sun* as her first film. Mark Storey attributes *Nude on the Moon* to the year 1960. Moya Luckett and Tania Modleski date it to 1962. See Mike Quarles, *Down and Dirty: Hollywood's Exploitation Filmmakers and Their Movies* (Jefferson, NC: McFarland, 1993).
6. Storey, *Cinema au Naturel*, 117.
7. Ibid.
8. Andrew Leavold, "Bad Girls Go to Dildo Heaven: An All-Nude Tribute to Doris Wishman," Senses of Cinema 23 (December 2002), <http://sensesofcinema.com/2002/feature-articles/doris/> (last accessed November 3, 2020).
9. According to Quarles, "she and her husband had moved to the Homestead, Florida area in the early 1960s." Quarles, *Down and Dirty*, 139.
10. Many theories, ranging from magnetism to real-life alien intervention, are found in work like Michael Kohler, *Coral Castle Explained: The Secrets of Edward Leedskalnin Revealed* (CreateSpace, 2013) and Praveen Mohan, *Coral Castle: Everything You Know Is Wrong* (CreateSpace, 2016).
11. The exception is McClure and Heffron's *Coral Castle: The Mystery of Ed Leedskalnin and His American Stonehenge*, which explains that "in 1961, filmmakers visited Coral Castle" for a movie in which "the erstwhile space explorers watch the 'Moon Goddess' bathe in Ed's tub and sit on Ed's throne chair. Other parts of the castle function at various times as perches for the moon's half-naked female inhabitants." Rusty McClure and Jack Heffron, Coral Castle: The Mystery of Ed Leedskalnin and His American Stonehenge (Dublin, OH: Ternary Publishing, 2009), 94–5.
12. Storey, *Cinema au Naturel*, 143.
13. The use of inexperienced, even amateur participants extends to the theme song, "Moon Doll." According to the credits, it was sung by Ralph Young, with words and music by Judith Kushner, Wishman's niece. Quarles credits Doc Severinsen of *Tonight Show* fame, then early in his career, with providing orchestration for the song. Quarles, *Down and Dirty*, 147. Young, also with only a handful of credits to his name, worked on all three of Wishman's early films, and even starred in *Blaze Starr Goes Nudist*. He went on to appear many times on *The Tonight Show*.
14. Storey, *Cinema au Naturel*, 138.
15. When the queen calls a gathering of her subjects, the confused looks of the characters, sometimes nodding and sometimes shaking their heads, with no real connection to her

speech, suggests that the actors had no idea what was happening in the scene. Doris Wishman, Marietta, William Mayer, Lester Brown, and Martin Caplan, *Nude on the Moon* (Seattle, WA: Something Weird Video, 2006).
16. Juno, "Interview," 110. Wishman seems to have become a less obscure figure in the history of cult filmmaking after being featured, with a brief interview, in this influential book.
17. Quarles, *Down and Dirty*, 142.
18. Brian Dunbar, "Mercury-Redstone 3 (18)," NASA, last modified August 7, 2017, <https://www.nasa.gov/mission_pages/mercury/missions/freedom7.html> (last accessed November 3, 2020).
19. Films such as *12 to the Moon* (1960) and *The Phantom Plane*t (1961) similarly include technical conversations that would be meaningless to the audience but establish the scientific credentials of its characters.
20. The script is vague about Cathy's job description: she types, answers phones, tidies up, and seems to act mainly as a secretary, but at the film's conclusion she is seen wearing a lab coat.
21. Lynn Peril, *Swimming in the Steno Pool: A Retro Guide to Making It in the Office* (New York: W. W. Norton, 2011), 127, 128.
22. Helen Gurley Brown, *Sex and the Single Girl* (London: New English Library, 1964), 35.
23. Juno, "Interview," 110. Rebekah McKendry agrees that, after having "complete control" on her first feature, "Wishman later said that she refused to work with anyone else because she could not hand over her total creative control to another person." McKendry, "Fondling Your Eyeballs," 58.
24. For example, *Destination Moon* (1950) and *12 to the Moon* (1960).
25. The film "was shot in one week." McKendry, "Fondling Your Eyeballs," 58.
26. Luckett, "Sexploitation as Feminine Territory," 145, 147.
27. Leavold, "Bad Girls Go to Dildo Heaven."
28. Many critics focus on this detail. McKendry says that "everyone in the film is naked except for some pipe-cleaner antennae." McKendry, "Fondling Your Eyeballs," 58. Modleski also refers to their "sporting antennae that suspiciously resemble pipe cleaners." Modleski, "Women's Cinema," 49.
29. Linda Williams, *Hard Core: Power, Pleasure, and the "Frenzy of the Visible"* (Berkeley: University of California Press, 1989), 154–5.
30. Storey, *Cinema au Naturel*, 138.
31. Ibid., 46.
32. Modleski, "Women's Cinema," 49.
33. Ibid., 69.
34. Laura Mulvey, "Visual Pleasure and Narrative Cinema," in *Feminist Film Theory: A Reader*, ed. Sue Thornham (New York: New York University Press, 2009), 59–60.
35. Lynn Peril, *Pink Think: Becoming a Woman in Many Uneasy Lessons* (New York: W. W. Norton, 2002), 150.
36. Peril, *Pink Think*, 196. One of Peril's examples is a magazine quiz that asks "Should you consider a career—or a husband?"—a strict either/or.
37. Molly Haskell, *From Reverence to Rape: The Treatment of Women in the Movies* (Chicago: University of Chicago Press, 2016), 28.
38. Luckett, "Sexploitation as Feminine Territory,"142.
39. McKendry, "Fondling Your Eyeballs," 68.
40. For example, the influential *Destination Moon* (1950) and more contemporaneous films like *12 to the Moon* (1960).
41. William Marshall, Dean Fredericks, Francis X. Bushman, Coleen Gray, and Tony Dexter, The Phantom Planet (1961; Medford, OR: Sinister Cinema, 2002), DVD.

42. Storey, *Cinema au Naturel*, 44.
43. Doris Wishman, Blaze Starr, Ralph Young, and Gene Berk, *Blaze Starr Goes Nudist* (Seattle: Something Weird Video, 2006).
44. Williams, *Hard Core*, 155.
45. Ernest Mathijs and Jamie Sexton, *Cult Cinema: An Introduction* (Malden, MA: Wiley-Blackwell, 2012), 109.
46. Modleski, "Women's Cinema," 65.
47. Juno, "Interview," 110.
48. Storey, *Cinema au Naturel*, 246, 249.

PART III

Comparative Approaches to Authorship

CHAPTER 7

Depicting Female Bodies: Doris Wishman, Carolee Schneemann, and Legacies of Subversion

Hannah Greenberg

Cinema has always been impacted by women's contributions.[1] Behind and in front of the camera, women have been innovators and pushed boundaries. As indebted as the film canon is to their influences, the standard recorded history of film has forgotten them as the industry has marginalized them. However, it is in these margins that women filmmakers have been able to explore the medium and exert influence. Underground genres ranging from American experimental cinema beginning in the late 1950s, to sexploitation cinema, to the Cinema of Transgression, and No Wave Cinema—while male-dominated—presented environments for women to work independently to express their points of view and depict women's experiences in ways not seen elsewhere. These small-scale movements were burgeoning spaces where women were able to push their way through and establish their voices.

Exploitation films, as Eric Schaefer has written, "purveyed the forbidden spectacle to moviegoers that the organized industry did not."[2] These topics included anything considered taboo, such as "prostitution and vice, drug use, nudity, and any other subject considered at the time to be in bad taste."[3] But these films were typically made by men and for men; sexploitation, as Tania Modleski identifies, is a mode that exemplifies "male-dominated culture and systems of representation."[4] Within this mode, women are victimized, they are raped, and they are displayed and objectified in the nude. For the very few women working in this mode, there were conventions—"systems of representation"—that needed to be upheld, but there were still opportunities to subvert and to critique within these conventions. Doris Wishman, one of the few women working in exploitation cinema, emerged in this atmosphere and established herself through her stark departure from this male-dominated mode. Wishman showed the dangers women faced in the world as targets of violence and unwanted attention, driven to self-defense and self-salvation. Wishman achieved this subversion under the guise of tawdry exploitation cinema, upending the genre's promise of salaciousness by delivering very little in the way of nudity, sex, or physical contact.

Exploitation was not the only underground genre built on male-dominated systems of representation. Independent movements blossoming in the postwar period mirrored the established film industry, predominantly anchored by men and artistically guided by them. Avant-garde film stands as an example of such a culture with a set of male-dominated conventions; like exploitation, other genres provided cracks that women could use to contribute their ideas. The independence fostered in experimental filmmaking provided an opportune environment for women to make films. Working contemporaneously, though not in dialogue with or being influenced by Wishman, Carolee Schneemann worked in a variety of mediums within the avant-garde and challenged the dominant male voice within that realm. Schneemann exposed the need for greater equality in art and in life through her performance art, visual art, and films. Arguably one of her most challenging, important, and enduring works, her film *Fuses* (1967) spoke not only to this need, but also to the nature of eroticism. With this film, Schneemann created a significant work for the erotic film canon—a film without a chronological structure, creating more of a collage of intimacy than a narrative about a sexual relationship, and depicted bodies, specifically a female body, with agency and not purely as sexy or a sex object.

In this chapter I will explore the work of these two women—minorities in their chosen mode of filmmaking—who used their personal perspectives to directly question, challenge, and expand the place of female bodies on screen and conventional views of women. Doris Wishman and Carolee Schneemann used their work to explore the implications of being a woman, and what it meant to inhabit a body coded female. Comparing their films and discussing their work together seems inappropriate or may seem jarring, as their work is stylistically, and even ideologically, very different. While I will address Wishman's work in the context of exploitation cinema, and her cinema's relationship to the more established avant-garde and the ways in which her work deserves placement in the avant-garde, I primarily aim to initiate a conversation between Wishman's and Schneemann's work by analyzing the ways they both centralize female bodies in their films and demonstrate the complexities of depicting female nudity. Aligning their work and indicating their legacies is one step in elevating Wishman's standing in experimental film scholarship, but most importantly it will establish an unlikely kinship between their bodies of work through their approaches to and interest in promoting new forms of women's representation.

THE FEMALE BODY AS METAPHOR

Doris Wishman had experience in film distribution,[5] and knew the kind of fast and cheap exploitation films that could be produced, booked in theaters, and most importantly make a profit; after her husband's death in 1958 she decided to make a career for herself in exploitation. Borrowing money from relatives, she immersed herself in filmmaking: directing, writing, producing, and editing. Her savvy ingenuity in creating a career for herself reflects important themes she brought to her films: stories about women trying to make their own paths in the world (though Wishman certainly fared better than most of her characters). Schaefer has contextualized the genre by explaining,

> The term exploitation film is derived from the practice of exploitation, advertising or promotional techniques that went over and above typical posters, trailers, and newspaper ads ... During the postwar years, the designation of exploitation film was gradually expanded to include almost any low-budget movie with a topical bent. During the 1960s and 1970s, the term was modified to indicate the subject that was being exploited, such as for "sexploitation" and "Blaxploitation" movies.[6]

Wishman's career can be approximately divided into three sexploitation periods: "Nudie Cuties," "Roughies," and her "Dangerous Bodies" films. Her lengthy career spanned from an early moment dictated by decency laws, which legitimized the nudist colony genre for its educational purposes, to a post-*Deep Throat* (1972) cinematic landscape, in which very little was off limits. In each of these chapters in her career, Wishman appropriated what male directors were doing and subtly radicalized it, challenging the male spectators and presenting a more nuanced woman's experience.

Wishman made several nudie cuties at the beginning of her career. These films promised to reveal the full experience of a nudist colony, but in fact revealed the bare minimum—specifically backsides and women's chests. Despite showing very little, that nudity was capitalized upon and nudists were shown in long shots, exhibiting life in a nudist camp. In writing about sexploitation more generally, Elena Gorfinkel has explained the nature of nudity in this subgenre in stating, "these nude bodies [fuel] the entire premise of the film and [enact] a series of hypostasized banalized actions, quotidian activities, as long as they are performed in the nude."[7] Though Wishman's work in this subgenre is not particularly revelatory when compared with her work in later periods, these early films introduce elements of her style and the ways she would challenge male expectations. Wishman biographer Michael Bowen notes that her depiction of nudist camps, filled with men and women playing games together, or just sitting and talking, points to Wishman's interest in "monogamous coupling,"[8] something at odds with the more modern lifestyle reflected in underground film movements. He further writes, "Wishman's monogamist overtones and romantic representations do not seem to satisfy traditional masculinist expectations."[9] Like all nudie cuties, Wishman's films achieve the goal of showing naked women, but maintain decency standards by desexualizing the relationships in her films, instead fulfilling the narrative closure with a happily coupled pair. But as Bowen observes, in narratively fostering monogamist coupling, without any level of depicted sexual gratification, these films challenge masculine pleasure by withholding any fetishistic depiction of female bodies.

Wishman's nudie cuties also reveal early inclinations to directly challenge male spectatorship, and her developing aesthetic approaches to filming female bodies. In *Blaze Starr Goes Nudist* (1962), women are filmed underwater swimming naked, canoeing, and shooting bows and arrows, but it is all blocked and filmed so precisely as to avoid revealing any female genitalia. Playing with expectations, Wishman withholds Blaze's nudity for much of the film, never revealing her fully nude until she is at the nudist camp, a moment Wishman even downplays by showing it in a long shot from behind. In this decision Wishman introduces her playfulness toward nudity and to her ways of alluding to the female body without revealing it. Beyond challenging men's hunger for female nudity by not showing much, she even challenges the simple fact of their spectatorship. In *Blaze Starr Goes Nudist*, she goes so far as to confront spectators on screen. In the film, Blaze is seen hiding at a movie theater where a nudist colony ethnographic film is playing. As Blaze takes her seat, several men visibly notice her entrance. They do not try to conceal the attention they pay to her breasts and body—true even of the man there with a woman—and one of the men even changes seats to sit directly next to her. Blaze, however, sees this attention, the objectification, and confronts their stares. Wishman is targeting her own audience, scolding them for their presumed behavior. As Moya Luckett observes, "She simultaneously offers an avowedly non-Mulvey-esque model of spectatorship, controlling the gaze, glaring back at the men to discipline them, to make them attend to the screen."[10] Blaze returns their stares, rejecting their voyeurism, while suggesting the absurdity of the seeming lack of a disconnect in men's minds between clothed women in public and nude women on display—Blaze asserts herself enough through her own gaze to make one man move. Luckett further notes that "The scene emblematizes Wishman's investments in women spectatorship and women's investments in looking at female bodies."[11] But more than that, this moment gives agency to women, in particular Wishman, to challenge their voyeurism in real life or in an audience.

Wishman's films evolved with the genre, and as decency laws wavered, exploitation developed into sexploitation by way of the "Roughie." Gorfinkel has explained this new designation as:

An offshoot of an older exploitation film tradition that spanned back to the late 1910s, sexploitation films were defined by their small economic means; an overweening focus on narratives that featured lured, sexual subjects; and their indulgence in erotic tease and innuendo in their marketing.[12]

The scheme of sexploitation moved beyond putting naked women in situations to putting women in situations to *make* them naked. Their displayed nudity became a signifier of their powerlessness, as men grappled with women's newfound agency as second-wave feminism was blossoming. Violence was introduced as a particular allure to this subgenre; depictions of women moved beyond a voyeuristic pleasure to fetishizing a sexualized woman and violence toward her. Further, as Modleski identifies, violence "provide[d] viewers with a fetishistic substitute for sexuality, the sight of which was both desired and—in terms of mainstream mores—feared."[13] Roughies, as an element of the subgenre, featured women being abused by men seemingly as a way of channeling a current male concern for women's growing societal empowerment. Gorfinkel writes,

> As a cinema inordinately preoccupied with the dangers posed by the sexual autonomy of women, particularly as they became unbound from domestic and reproductive space in a post-Kinsey era of the birth control pill . . . sexploitation often capitalized on the trope of the small-town girl in the big metropolis and, in a moralistic, leering register, would detail the depredations that would inevitably befall the naive and the unwitting when caught in the grip of the "naked city."[14]

Playing off the established aesthetics of contemporary realist cinema, these films were shot in a black and white documentary style, suggesting that the films' exploitive elements were natural and common within harsh, modern society. Bowen has described the aesthetic emerging in roughies, explaining that these films

> conformed to the economics of independent filmmaking of the period. Black and white film stock—more affordable than colour—typified the production standards of most low-budget filmmaking enterprises through the 1960s, particularly in the neo-realist and avant-garde modes. The look of cinema verité, the French New Wave and newsreel photography soon made black and white synonymous with the "realist" agendas associated with these forms.[15]

These films witnessed a shift in Wishman's focus from certain elements of nudie cuties to the new standards of sexploitation: the more revealing nudie cuties gave way to the implied sex and violence of roughies. Coupled with this independent, gritty aesthetic, these films seemed to shine a light on a problem, as Rebekah McKendry observes: "Though the roughies did not show nearly as much naked flesh as her nudist works, they were considered much more socially questionable because of their seedy subject matter, including lesbianism, rape, drug addiction, and blackmail."[16]

Wishman's roughies maintain her established interest in self-sufficient, determined women characters working against conventional male themes to make a statement about the experience for women, moving them out of the nudist camp and placing them in the dark, tough city streets. The protagonists of these films find themselves in the city, depicted as a ruthless place, after leaving, either by force or by choice, a space of safety and comfort. Their methods of survival become the crux of Wishman's films, more so than their victimization. As McKendry describes, "Just below the surface, these films present the 'radical feminist' ideals of women fighting for survival in a world full of male oppression."[17] Wishman's subtle breaks from genre conventions can be seen in the remarkable narratives she constructs, but even more apparent are the inventive ways she presents radical feminist ideals through narratives containing repercussions for male violence and devoid of unadulterated views of naked women.

Two of Wishman's roughies from this period, *Bad Girls Go to Hell* (1965) and *Another Day, Another Man* (1966), exemplify the narrative and aesthetic choices she made to subtly subvert established themes of violence and challenge male spectatorship. She achieves this though her focus on the bleak realities of the modern experience for women by depicting self-sufficient women as victims of male-led society. *Bad Girls Go to Hell* features a woman, Meg, who is left alone on a Saturday morning when her husband has to go into work. While she is taking some trash out to the hallway, the building's janitor rapes her on the steps. When he threatens to tell her husband what has happened if she does not come down to his apartment, she goes and he attempts to rape her a second time. She thwarts his attack by hitting him over the head with an ashtray, killing him. Shocked by what has happened to her and what she has done in return, she flees to New York City, a place where she can get lost in a crowd. She spends the next few weeks moving around Manhattan, facing continual abuse with every step. Eventually the film indicates that this has just been a dream, but as she wakes up and carries on with her morning, the film identically repeats the first act, indicating the prophetic nature of her nightmare.

This film is rife with sexuality, positive and destructive, but again very little nudity is actually shown. Instead, female characters in the film sit around in just their underwear or walk around in lace bodysuits. Perhaps the most significant sex scene in the film—the only one that shows loving, consensual sex—is only indicated by showing the two women's bare legs intertwined. The most explicit nudity in the film is during the second rape scene in which Meg kills the janitor, during which she is completely naked. While the choice of nudity in this scene may seem to make her defenseless, instead she represents an active and capable woman protecting herself. Playing against the potential pleasure (heterosexual) men glean from seeing the nude female body (and perhaps a naked woman being raped), Wishman disallows spectacle and enjoyment. The janitor visibly undresses Meg, but throughout the scene her body is never shown fully, or inactive long enough for the camera to fetishize her nudity in any way. The entire sequence is shot with a hand-held camera only moving to follow Meg's actions. The sequence is mostly shot with the janitor on top of Meg, obscuring her body. At one point, as he tries to remove her underwear, she breaks free and crawls on her stomach away from him, while the camera moves to follow her. In this portion of the scene, as she is positioned with her back to the camera, her nakedness is the most on display, though all of her motion is inelegant and desperate. Her movements in addition to the hand-held camera create an authentic sense of urgency; when he grabs her ankles and pulls her back to him, which would seem an opportunity to display her body and her subservient victimhood, she kicks and wriggles the entire time, disallowing an opportunity to fetishize her passive body. Further, once she is fully naked, Wishman's camera stays mostly still and only focuses on shots of aspects of her body through quick edits, such as the janitor's back with just Meg's legs writhing beneath; medium shots of Meg's tense, pained face in profile as she is pinned on the ground; and close-ups of her arms as she fights off the janitor and eventually reaches for the ashtray to smash on his head. While the camera is mostly steady, the editing and Meg's motion within the frame disables lingering stares and the potential for sexual fantasy and fetish. In this crucial moment, Wishman demonstrates her power to challenge male voyeurism and subvert disempowering genre conventions.

Wishman's aesthetic style in her roughie period accentuates her subversion, particularly in her trademark use of cutaways. She did not have the budget for much film stock and did not have a crew to record synchronous sound. Instead, she tended to shoot in long shot and recorded dialogue after shooting. The unsynchronized dialogue adds a significant element to her aesthetic. Whereas in her nudie cuties she crafted her narratives to be guided by characters' inner monologues to mask this deficiency, in her roughies she draws attention to the script's unpolished quality, enhancing the documentary feel of the films by leaving the dialogue out of sync. Most important to her chosen style, she filmed a lot of coverage. But she did not shoot traditional coverage, filming scenes from different angles and getting different character close-ups. Rather, she shot close-ups of objects in the room, aspects of the architecture around an apartment, birds and squirrels, or plants. Wishman relied on the coverage she shot for cutaways to hide continuity issues. These choices give her films a very particular and unusual look.

But her use of cutaways was more than an ingenious method to correct production problems. They work to visually create more depth in the narrative and ultimately tended to focus on female imagery. One instance of this in *Bad Girls Go to Hell* is a moment right after Meg arrives in New York and she decides to go to Central Park to plan her next steps. Wishman starts the sequence with shots of trees, pigeons walking in the grass, a pond, establishing her location. The editing of this sequence, while seemingly random and disparate, manages in fact to be symbolic of the narrative and give insight to Meg's character. As Meg cries in panic over the end to her former life and the terror of starting over, the film cuts to ducks in the pond, first a mother leading her children, indicating Meg's incomplete but finished life as a housewife. Following is a longer shot of many ducks swimming together on the pond, signifying the refuge she has found in New York and her attempt to escape and get lost in the crowd.

Figure 7.1 The San Remo apartment building stands out as a symbol of the female body on the horizon in *Bad Girls Go to Hell*. *Bad Girls Go to Hell*, Juri Productions/Sam Lake Enterprises, 1965

As Meg walks to a park bench, a long shot of a pond with buildings in the background reveals the San Remo apartment building, which hovers in the background throughout the rest of the sequence. This Art Deco apartment building on Manhattan's Upper West Side has a rectangular foundation with two pointed towers rising from this base. In contrast to Manhattan's mostly phallic skyline, this building stands out as a symbol of the female body on the horizon. A man joins Meg on her bench and sympathizes that her situation is a difficult one, and as he looks to Meg the camera cuts to the San Remo instead of to Meg, interrupting the expected shot-reverse-shot. The man eventually offers to take Meg home with him and the final image in the scene is again the San Remo. The editing of this scene constructs Meg and the San Remo as the same entity, enmeshing her within the landscape of the city while simultaneously hinting at the danger that it holds for her. The shot-reverse-shot between the man and the San Remo-as-Meg exposes the duplicitousness in his charity as the building's towers stand in for Meg's breasts. This editing pattern not only foreshadows the difficulties Meg will face while in the city, it also implicates the male gaze as Wishman withholds shots of Meg's breasts from the audience.

Wishman's follow-up film *Another Day, Another Man* (1966) maintains her focus on the difficulty of the modern woman's experience. *Another Day, Another Man* depicts the disenfranchisement of struggling working women and the systematic emotional violence and manipulation to which they are subject. The film centers on a woman, Ann, who has had to hide her marriage from her boss; he does not allow his women employees to be married. At the beginning of the film her husband announces that he has received a raise, making it possible for them to move in together and for her to quit her job. Shortly after they settle into their first home, her husband becomes very ill, rendering Ann responsible for supporting the two of them and paying her husband's medical bills. Since she cannot return to her previous job, she turns to prostitution. When her husband, who is unaware of her new career, recovers and tries to surprise her on the job, he catches her with another man. The devastation from this discovery forces him to commit suicide. In addition to this main story are examples of other small-town women who come to the city to pursue their dreams, but who are ultimately tricked into prostitution and ruined.

This film contains crucial examples of Wishman's use of cutaways, subverting anticipated spectatorship. Beyond just the violence toward women in roughies, the essential device in sexploitation was still ultimately to show women naked or semi-nude, generally relying on little narrative motivation for female characters to strip or to stay undressed. As Gorfinkel has indicated, "Spectacle in sexploitation is organized around the nude female body in states of strategic yet nonexplicit exposure."[18] Many of the women that she shows nude, though only ever partially naked, exude sex appeal, but are given freedom to be awkward or domestic. Repeated scenes of semi-nude women at home, frequently with other semi-nude women, enacting their banal daily routines and performing with a clear understanding that they are being seen, seems to function to indicate their sexuality, but Wishman manages to distance these depictions of women from sexualized fantasies, especially by showing them ungracefully undressing. For example, one scene begins with Ann's roommate, Tess, pacing in their living room. Tess is too distracted and nervous to talk when Ann arrives. In Tess's silence Ann shares the announcement of her husband's raise. They argue about their different lifestyles and then decide to go to bed, undressing simultaneously in different parts of the room. Throughout the scene, the film cuts to a number of inanimate objects. These objects act as stand-ins for the female body; for instance, a shot of a plant centerpiece on the coffee table is intercut with their discussion at the beginning of the scene, then just before Ann and Tess begin undressing the film cuts to a hanging plant in front of the window. They take off their tops and the camera cuts again to the hanging plant. The majority of action in the scene is shot in close-up, showing their bodies fragmented: just a thigh as a stocking is being unclipped and rolled down, or just a back as a bra is being unhooked. At the very end of the scene as the two women are nearing a state of complete undress, a sequence of shots shows Ann's bra being dropped and lying on the ground, then a shot of Tess unhooking her bra. The film cuts to a radio with a Playboy cigarette lighter on top, followed by a shot of Tess from behind as she slips off her bra, then Ann's bare lower legs walking past her high heels and out of the frame. When Tess walks out of the frame in profile, baring her naked chest, the film returns to the shot of Ann's bra on the ground to end the scene. In this scene, utilizing a hand-held camera and a perverted fly on the wall cinema verité style, both women attempt to seem unconscious of being watched while simultaneously undressing themselves, performing a sexless striptease.

Similar to *Bad Girls Go to Hell*, *Another Day, Another Man* takes for its subject matter the tragic and dangerous lives of urban women in modernity. This focus seems to be another way for Wishman to infuse her films with a challenge to male spectators, addressing them as violators and as abusers. Interestingly, the actress who played Meg in *Bad Girls Go to Hell* reappears in *Another Day, Another Man* as a prostitute working for the same pimp—an important narrative through-line identifying the tragedy faced by women who are abused. This theme points to the prevalent idea that women's survival depended on their own hard work and a rejection of traditional women's values. In both films, being in a traditional relationship leads to the women's downfall. The women depicted must use their own methods to try to survive and they must do so independently, but simultaneously, the independent attempt is still unsuccessful, evidence of women's social disempowerment. Experimental filmmaker Peggy Ahwesh, who professes a wholehearted admiration of Doris Wishman's work, wrote that Wishman's films are

> a rare blend of deep personal expression, gimmickry, and convenience. Her themes of sexual fear, good girls gone bad, warped desire, and various dystopic views of the body, power relations, and domesticity are a compelling dark vision in the history of women's experience.[19]

Wishman identifies these women so common to exploitation cinema and alters their narratives to reflect the stories of real women trying to exist in modernity, with narratives men could not write and perhaps would not want to watch.

By the 1970s, sexploitation's genre conventions had undergone another evolution, favoring more hardcore sex and overt nudity as censorship standards completely collapsed. As Bowen explains, Wishman did not like such blatant depictions of nudity and sex and chose not to pursue that direction.[20] Instead, the third period of her work focused on bodies, but rather than sexual and victimized bodies these bodies were dangerous, destructive bodies. The films of this period focused on violence more so than any of her other films: violence done to bodies and violence committed by bodies. Her "Dangerous Bodies" period is best understood through the two films she made featuring former exotic dancer, Chesty Morgan: *Deadly Weapons* (1974) and *Double Agent 73* (1975). As she aligns female bodies with disruption and destruction, these two films, capitalizing on Morgan's alleged seventy-three-inch bust, transform breasts into weapons. These two films qualify the latter part of her career as one of obscenity and grotesqueness, an area Wishman had not ventured into before. During this period Wishman gives the female body extraordinary power and strength while simultaneously depicting the female body grotesquely to undo the position of breasts as fetishized objects. This period seems to indicate an intention to divert from the typical trajectory of underground cinema, one that catered less to its male audience.

Both Chesty Morgan films provoke through associations between women's breasts and the male spectator, with men photographed staring at a woman's massive breasts as they die, or men being suffocated to death by a woman's breasts. This second relationship, the narrative focus of *Deadly Weapons*, viscerally plays off men's insecurities about women while depicting an empowered woman hero for sexploitation. In the film, Morgan stars as Crystal, whose gangster boyfriend Larry and his two accomplices break into a man's apartment, stealing a little black book. When Larry is killed by his accomplices for working behind their backs, Crystal takes it upon herself to avenge his death, going undercover as a burlesque dancer in Las Vegas to kill one man, then to Miami to kill the other. Crystal then discovers that her father is actually the criminal ringleader who ordered Larry's death, and in a final standoff between father and daughter, Crystal's father shoots her to prevent her from calling the police. Before she dies she manages to return fire and kill her father, dying with her head on his chest.

Deadly Weapons subverts codified views of masculinity. This film, perhaps the most challenging to men in Wishman's oeuvre, no longer permits men merely to stare at women's chests. From the first shot of the film, Morgan stands bare-chested with arms raised to attack, walking toward the camera. As she nears the camera the film's title, *Deadly Weapons*, appears on the screen, labeling her breasts to pronounce their threat. This image introduces the film and the impending threat to male spectators: breasts. The most fetishized parts of female anatomy are now grotesque and lethal. The opening of the film continues to alienate her breasts from fetishization. The title credits roll over kaleidoscopic images of Morgan caressing, shaking, and animating her enormous breasts by positioning Morgan in front of a surface made of domed mirrors. Her chest becomes more freakish as she continues to display herself very consciously for an audience. McKendry has described that

> through her use of "the gaze[,]" Wishman invites viewers to become voyeurs of her on-screen females. They pose right in front of the camera . . . they will smile or gesture sexually. At first glance, it seems that Wishman's women are inviting this gaze . . . but the gaze is undercut immediately when the camera shifts away from the beautiful female to some very unsexual object.[21]

Wishman uses this technique repeatedly in her films, showing women performing this being-looked-at-ness but never showing too much, but inverts the idea in her Chesty Morgan films. She instead chooses to over-show: Morgan looks at the camera, gestures sexually, and instead of cutting, Wishman will go in for a close-up, or in this case show Morgan's chest dozens of times in individual, miniature mirrors.

Figure 7.2 Chesty Morgan caressing, shaking, and animating her enormous breasts during the credit sequence of *Deadly Weapons*. *Deadly Weapons*, Juri Productions/Hallmark Releasing, 1974

For example, the first scene introducing Morgan's chest straightforwardly shows Crystal preparing for a bubble bath, splaying and shaking her breasts to herself in the mirror, drawing attention to her burden and their threatening enormity. Neither image of her breasts is easily enjoyed. As McKendry discusses, Chesty Morgan "was not and is not today viewed as a conventionally attractive woman. She is used primarily as a source of spectacle, gawked at for her freakishly large breasts—and her ability to kill people with them."[22] McKendry further identifies that there was a specific body image deemed sexy and desirable by society that Wishman rejected in her casting. She states that the fact that

> many of these women [Wishman's characters] come from different classes and ethnicities than the white blond that was considered sexy by society further complicates Wishman's denial of the audience's expectations, at least in terms of the body image they sought: hot, young, thin, and stereotypically feminine.[23]

Wishman doubles down in this rejection by casting Morgan. Not only is Morgan at odds with this desirable body image—chest is too big, not thin enough, too old, etc.—but, as exemplified earlier, Wishman constructs images of Morgan through framing and other effects to distort her image, exaggerating her differences from this desired body type and thus her lack of appeal.

When she turns murderous, Crystal's breasts can only be seen as threatening. In both instances she first removes a sedative tucked somewhere in her chest to slip to the men, and as they become impaired she moves toward them, bare-chested and arms raised above her head, repeating the pose from the opening, forcefully burying the men in her chest until they suffocate. In the second murder, the camera actually adopts her victim's perspective and the audience is once again forced to watch her enormous breasts move toward them. More so than any of her other films, Wishman directly implicates male spectators and their voyeurism by challenging their gaze and forcing them to imagine their own deaths. Wishman, through these many grotesque depictions, subverts any expectation for pleasure and manages to incorporate alternative depictions of female bodies. By aligning the female body with Morgan's larger-than-life form, Wishman works to move past representations fetishizing women's bodies, showing them instead as dangerous and threatening.

Wishman created films to fit a model but pursued her own version of this model and chose themes and aesthetics that were very much her own. In a zine Ahwesh created dedicated to Wishman's filmmaking, she wrote:

> the films reveal a one-of-a-kind filmmaker with the idiosyncrasies of the experimental world, the business savvy of the commercial world and the wit and imagination of some mysterious dream world ... a woman obsessed with the themes of women's social status and freedom, the contemporary drama of fear, mistrust and challenge between sexes.[24]

These "idiosyncrasies of the experimental world" that Ahwesh suggests warrant a discussion of Wishman's placement in film history and a broadened understanding of her work's categorization. A larger argument could and should be made to place Doris Wishman's work more firmly in the realm of experimental cinema in addition to exploitation cinema,[25] but I would like to address aspects of how her work, particularly in how I have analyzed it thus far, associates her films with experimental cinema, and begin to put her work in dialog with an artist as seemingly dissimilar as Carolee Schneemann.

In Bowen's essay "Doris Wishman Meets the Avant-Garde," he addresses the critical differences between avant-garde and exploitation cinema's cultural and scholarly standing. He states that exploitation films are "widely held to be inarticulate and aesthetically regressive; authorless and derivative, they pander to the worst impulses in human nature—violence and unregulated sexuality."[26] While, as he continues, avant-garde films "experiment consciously with the boundaries of experience, both personal and aesthetic; although often controversial, they strive for formal originality and deal with questions of widely recognized intellectual worth."[27] Accepting his definitions of this difference and my analysis of Wishman's work regarding the nature of her personal filmmaking and her formal experimentation, it is clear that Wishman was in fact challenging, not pandering to, these base human impulses like the male directors in exploitation might have been. She was in fact an auteur channeling her worldview and experiences into her films. Bowen sees one particularly pertinent overlap between exploitation cinema and experimental cinema: respectively, one shows a shocking depiction of something and the other shows a depiction of something shocking. Wishman's films remarkably do both. As Bowen states, "Both avant-garde and exploitation cinemas . . . comment equally upon the cultural organization of visuality, on the spectator's encoded experience of seeing."[28] The images Wishman captured prioritized unusual shots and seemingly unrelated objects over fetishizing female bodies, as observed earlier, challenging audiences by presenting banal imagery and difficult subject matter. Schneemann, too, confronted viewers' encoded experience of seeing and typical depictions of female bodies.

THE BODY AS MATERIAL, THE MATERIALITY OF THE BODY

Carolee Schneemann is an artist who has always defied labels. Trained as a painter and working in that medium at the start of her career, she has continued to evolve and expand, her work taking the form of kinetic theater, performance art, dance, photography, and film. Working as second-wave feminism was taking hold, she understood the importance of the personal becoming political. Her work depicts various aspects of a daily, lived experience. Through her depictions of relationships, bodies, everyday objects, and sex, she composed a complex understanding of the ordinary to achieve something much greater. A primary element of her work across mediums has always been the female body and the crisis of representation. In a photography series early in her career, *Eye Body: 36 Transformative Actions for Camera* (1963), she featured herself, covered in grease, paint, and chalk, in several photographs surrounded by Abstract Expressionist painted panels, broken glass and mirrors, umbrellas, fur, live snakes, and other objects. Through this work she developed her concept of the eye/body: "merging the inner eye of the artist/subject, the seeing eye of the artist/agent, and the eye of the viewer."[29] Schneemann wanted to explore the complexity of the passive woman subject by putting herself, as the art maker, in that position and creating and controlling her own image, an idea that guides her film career. Building upon that concept, Schneemann continued to experiment with her concept of the eye/body, and, through that, new and different ways of depicting female bodies.

In perhaps her best-known performance piece, *Interior Scroll* (1975, 1977), Schneemann delivered a work that summarized so much of what she as an artist and as a woman was confronted with in modernity. The piece was performed twice, the second time in 1977 at the Telluride Film Festival, where she was scheduled to introduce a program of erotic films by women. Frustrated to discover the program was titled "The Erotic Woman," demeaning the contributions of these filmmakers and their validity as artists, she decided to perform *Interior Scroll* in protest. In her introduction she stated:

> Having been described and proscribed by the male imagination for so long, no woman artist now wants to assume that she will define an "erotic woman" for other women—the very notion immediately reverts to the traditional stereotypes that this program of films vividly counters. Perhaps these films will redefine "The Erotic Woman," or to the contrary, the films will be found to be anti-erotic, sub-erotic, non-erotic. Perhaps the "erotic woman" will be seen as primitive, devouring, insatiable, clinical, obscene, or forthright, courageous, integral.[30]

Then she performed the piece, which requires her to stand naked, covered in mud or paint, as she slowly extracts and reads a scroll of paper she has placed in her vagina. In this second iteration of the piece she read a text from her film *Kitch's Last Meal* (1978), which stated:

> I met a happy man / A structuralist filmmaker / -but don't call me that / it's something else I do- / he said we are fond of you / you are charming / but don't ask us / to look at your films / we cannot / there are certain films / we cannot look at / the personal clutter / the persistence of feelings / the hand-touch sensibility / the diaristic indulgence / the painterly mess / the dense gestalt / the primitive techniques . . .[31]

As Schneemann addressed in her introduction and in the performance, women's contributions needed to be understood as their personal expression representing an individual perspective, not representing the collective experience of all women. Additionally, women had to fight to have their work seen as more than primitive, cute, or messy, to ultimately get respect. In her performance and film work she continually challenged the ideas and representations of women's identities and female bodies to chip away at these illegitimate attacks on women's work and female representation.

As Elise Archias has stated, "Carolee Schneemann focused her work on the everyday materiality of bodies, but in her case that meant first and foremost the materiality of sex,"[32] something that required more contributions from a woman's perspective. Before her *Interior Scroll* performances, Schneemann had expanded her work in another direction: filmmaking. Rather than her films serving as background pieces for her installation or performance art, she began making films as entities unto themselves. In line with much of her other work and its connection to respective male work in the medium, her first stand-alone film, *Fuses* (1967), was made as a reaction to two Stan Brakhage films. While living in New York, Schneemann developed a close friendship with Brakhage and was featured in multiple films he made. One of those films, *Loving* (1957), featured Schneemann and her boyfriend James Tenney, Brakhage's former roommate, as he documented their relationship sexually and domestically. She felt, though, that Brakhage did not properly capture the dynamic intricacies of their relationship. Despite his interest in the "erotic sensitivity and vitality"[33] between Schneemann and Tenney, she felt he was unable of capturing the eroticism of their relationship. *Fuses* arose as a project to truthfully document their relationship in both a sexual and sensual way. Schneemann also made her film as a response to Brakhage's *Window Water Baby Moving* (1959), in which he documents the birth of his first child. Schneemann found problematic the fact that Brakhage and his wife Jane shared the job of filming the birth, but she received no credit for being the co-director or co-creator of the film, making the film more about male ownership of a strictly woman's experience. As Schneemann describes it,

> I had mixed feelings about the power of the male partner, the artist subsuming the primal creation of giving birth as a bridge between male constructions of sexuality as either medical or pornographic . . . I know Stan and Jane passed the camera back and forth, but I was still very concerned that the male eye replicated or possessed the vagina's primacy of giving birth.[34]

She wanted to give the female body more agency by portraying a whole picture of the couple, and to explore what "'the fuck' is and locate that in terms of a lived sense of equity."[35]

Filmed and edited between 1965 and 1967, *Fuses* looks at the sexual and emotional relationship between Schneemann and Tenney. The film is disorienting and complex; without creating a narrative, she chronicles the intimate nature of her life with Tenney. She depicts everything from the minutiae of daily life to more explicit images of their lovemaking: lying around in bed, going on car trips, or watching the cat sit on a windowsill, which is then intercut with images of Schneemann performing oral sex. The frames are scratched, painted on, and cut, sometimes obscuring the filmic image and sometimes building up to a close-up of Schneemann or Tenney. The film gives the audience images of sex and intimate shots of nude bodies but is fragmented and never lingers long enough to feel intrusive or voyeuristic. It rarely depicts any erotic images straightforwardly, frequently showing nude images upside down or with superimpositions. Playing with the concept of defamiliarization, she fragments and obscures both bodies and posits an understanding of the film as experiencing from her cat's point of view. Taking turns holding the camera, the film depicts their lovemaking as a very equal action and gives equal attention to images of Schneemann's and Tenney's genitals, working to de-stigmatize and de-eroticize both while not allowing either to be a voyeuristic focus.

Exemplary of this new mode of feminist filmmaking with sexual politics clearly at the forefront, Schneemann films male and female genitalia, fellatio and cunnilingus, and male and female orgasms, and she does not depict herself or her partner as objects of voyeurism, or even fetishize their bodies. The film does include long shots of explicit intercourse, but without showing an extended sequence with buildup or climax and without sound, the image does not eroticize the act, but the context allows for an erotic feeling and a sense of the intimacy of their relationship. What the film so remarkably includes and prioritizes are numerous images of Tenney performing cunnilingus and close-ups of Schneemann's face as she experiences pleasure, something that was rarely ever shown in erotic cinema, or even publicly acknowledged in society. The film provoked outrage from men and women alike when it first began to show publicly for not delivering the expected, predictable pornographic narrative.[36]

In her work with *Eye Body*, her existence as both image and image-maker merged the points of view of the artist as participant, the artist as creator, and the spectator. With *Fuses*, she takes this idea even further by representing female bodies in ways they are so rarely shown. She has described her reasons for turning to this material in stating, "Women artists explore erotic imagery because our bodies exemplify a historic battleground—we are dismantling conventional sexual ideology and its punishing suppressions—and because our experience of our bodies has not corresponded to cultural depiction."[37] She understands the need to represent women as thoughtful, equal agents in society as well as in relationships, and particularly how images of powerful and sexual, but not sexualized, women were necessary in the cultural landscape. R. Bruce Elder addressed how *Fuses* visualizes the complexities humans face in society, perhaps women more so than others. His scholarship explores how we can see through the construction of the film and its multi-layering and how we live with two bodies, one that we display to the world, another that exists internally.[38] Schneemann grapples with the complexity of personhood and femininity by depicting intimate moments of both solitude and sexuality.

Schneemann works to convey the everydayness of sex and bodies in *Fuses*. There is an important performative element in the film, in that Schneemann and Tenney are always conscious of the camera watching and their being filmed. As opposed to traditional pornography wherein spectatorship is implied and the performers ignore the cameras, they interact with the cameras, filming each other, and creating a sense of closeness and sensuality. The film makes clear the interest in representing both mental and physical experiences during intercourse without falling back upon voyeurism and the male gaze. Not only does Schneemann challenge the male gaze in this film, she also challenges the camera's gaze as a more structured voyeurism and one that is completely illusionistic.

This strategy evokes a feeling of naturalism through the constructed performance, enhanced by prioritizing everyday objects in the frame. Much like Wishman, she focused heavily on feminine objects: the image of the cat, specifically as the possessor of the gaze, is an important symbol, as generally the feline is associated with the feminine. Similarly, the images of windows act as a strong signifier for women and female genitalia. Both filmmakers use these shots of animate and inanimate objects and architectural elements to infuse the action with a guiding feminine perspective. Schneemann uses these images to ground her film and to help convey the sense of everydayness and how personal the work was; she brings the spectator into her home and allows her cat to stand in as the guide for the intimate display of sex between her and her partner. These images imply a closeness that is then upended by the structured voyeurism and her consciousness of the camera. Wishman, too, uses her cutaways to imply more than is really revealed. Her characters are shown mostly nude, playing up their sex appeal and performing their being-looked-at-ness, but then she edits in another object, a close-up of a bra or a plant, to signify and replace what she chooses not to show.

The strong difference in their approaches to filming inanimate objects comes from their editing. In *Fuses* Schneemann powerfully juxtaposes images within single frames or edited in sequence, like showing a man's testicles resting on a table surrounded by colorful Christmas lightbulbs, or showing someone stroking a cat and then next stroking female genital hair, juxtaposing sex with objects of the everyday, working to de-spectacularize what is being shown and the act of sex itself. In this effort to show the ordinariness of a healthy sexual relationship and to depict a woman experiencing pleasure and fulfillment, Schneemann embraces her avant-garde aesthetics and challenges a desire to experience an emotionless erotic film. Wishman, instead, showed very little, cutting to inanimate objects as replacements for female nudity or sex. She is not making a statement to the audience like Schneemann's to force them to reconsider the spectacularization of sex in cinema and to see how ordinary a sexual life on film can be, but instead Wishman is forcing the viewer to confront their desire to see explicit nudity and sex on screen by disallowing its blatant presentation.

A LEGACY OF WOMEN'S OWN REPRESENTATION

Both Wishman and Schneemann had specific, though varied, approaches to what they were creating and through their chosen aesthetic challenged accepted representations of women and depictions of female bodies. Wishman, who was making films earlier than Schneemann, initiated her subversion of the established, male-led systems of representation by positing a new depiction of women. Because female characters in exploitation tended to be more types than actual women, her films altered the depiction of women in sexploitation more generally, but in a way that was based on the world she knew. These women, new to the city and forced to operate within the confines of the modern world, were shown to either succumb to the violence of this world or succeed by learning to operate within the system's confines. Wishman used her films as a commentary on the modern female experience: in her characters' success or failure was the implication that women were more than just victims or fetishistic objects. Wishman's women were assertive and fought back, challenging the desires of male spectators.

Later, when Schneemann began to make films, firmly operating from a feminist perspective, she was particularly concerned with framing her work as a representation of her individual perspective. She was not speaking on behalf of all women or depicting a collective experience, she was demonstrating her voice and depicting her personal experience as a woman. In doing so she challenged the attempts of men to simplify the complexity of a modern woman's experience in sex and in public life. She politicized the female body by placing hers into public consciousness and making it an object that both welcomed and defied voyeurism. She also upended the cultural landscape by subverting conventional male representations of female bodies and a woman's sexuality by representing a sexual but not sexualized woman.

The impact they made on the cultural landscape and in representations of female bodies helped usher in a more radicalized population of women spectators who saw these films and could appreciate the statements they were making. For instance, Peggy Ahwesh is one of the many filmmakers who has consciously continued their legacies by challenging genre, femininity, and sexuality through her filmmaking by working with themes like women's sexuality and the sexualization of women, and reimagining women's roles in genre films. In her Love-Sex Trilogy[39] consisting of *The Deadman*, *The Color of Love*, and *Nocturne*, she deconstructs exploitation, pornography, and horror genres and challenges their imagery and ideologies. These films each have narratives of sorts, but they defy resolution. Ahwesh states that she is interested in "presenting a problem and getting you into an emotional place where you understand the calamity or joy or desire within a person's life."[40] Just as Wishman and Schneemann presented women's experiences, Ahwesh's exploration of these different genres and styles challenges new and old forms of female representation and women's sexuality, but does so in a way that maintains an element of the personal in her voice and for her viewers.

By looking at Wishman's films in dialogue with Schneemann's work, a deeper resonance emerges. Their depictions of alternative views of female bodies and the subjective woman's experience broke ground for more progressive feminist cinema like Ahwesh's. Their narratives function to challenge the male gaze: Wishman's subverts the expectations of exploitation cinema by promising everything sexploitation has to offer and revealing nothing, not even the ability to vicariously experience violence toward women. Schneemann's similarly subverts expectations by creating an erotic film in which she obscures the pornographic elements in order to linger on the emotional aspects of a sexual relationship. Wishman's films are not merely outlets through which women might acclimate to the modern world, but rather they challenge preconceptions of a woman's experience and demonstrate its complexities, elements central to Schneemann's work. Their work in their respective margins proves the breadth of women's perspectives on a woman's experience, so needed in the cinematic landscape. Despite the differences in their films and approaches, they indeed were both working toward similar ends: representing women's experiences and radical depictions of female sexuality and female nudity, deconstructing pre-existing male depictions. Initiating this dialogue between Wishman's and Schneemann's work indicates the unlikely ties between their intentions and their bodies of work. This analysis not only shows how they worked to change the ways women were represented, but also demonstrates how their work has endured and been passed down to influence later filmmakers. Wishman is not just the last auteur in exploitation, as Tania Modleski labels her, she is part of a legacy of strong visions coming from cinematic margins challenging the status quo.

NOTES

1. In this chapter, I will be using both the terms "women" and "female," with the understanding that they are not synonymous. Aiming to avoid the narrow idea that a woman must be female, I will specifically use "female" when discussing a specific woman's sex (bodies coded female) or in the context of a woman's genitals.
2. Eric Schaefer, *"Bold! Daring! Shocking! True!": A History of Exploitation Films, 1919–1959* (Durham, NC: Duke University Press, 1999), 2.
3. Ibid., 4–5.

4. Tania Modleski, "Women's Cinema as Counterphobic Cinema: Doris Wishman as the Last Auteur," in *Sleaze Artists: Cinema at the Margins of Taste, Style, and Politics*, ed. Jeffrey Sconce (Durham, NC: Duke University Press, 2007), 56.
5. Her cousin, Max Rosenberg, was a low-budget film producer and distributor who later founded Amicus Films and was partners with Joseph E. Levine. Rosenberg offered her a job while she attended acting school. See Ted B. Kissell, "Screen Queen," *Miami New Times*, September 18, 1997, <https://www.miaminewtimes.com/news/screen-queen-6360415> (last accessed November 23, 2020); Christopher J. Jarmick, "Doris Wishman" (Great Directors), *Senses of Cinema* 22 (October 2002), <http://sensesofcinema.com/2002/great-directors/wishman/> (last accessed November 3, 2020).
6. Schaefer, *"Bold! Daring! Shocking! True!"*, 4.
7. Elena Gorfinkel, "The Body's Failed Labor: Performance Work in Sexploitation Cinema," *Framework: The Journal of Cinema and Media* 53, no. 1 (Spring 2012): 90.
8. Michael J. Bowen, "Embodiment and Realization: The Many Film-Bodies of Doris Wishman," *Wide Angle* 19, no. 3 (July 1997): 70.
9. Ibid.
10. Moya Luckett, "Sexploitation as Feminine Territory: The Films of Doris Wishman," in *Defining Cult Movies: The Cultural Politics of Oppositional Taste*, ed. Mark Jancovich, Antonio Lázaro Reboll, Julian Stringer, and Andy Willis (Manchester: Manchester University Press, 2003), 149.
11. Ibid.
12. Elena Gorfinkel, "Tales of Times Square: Sexploitation's Secret History of Place," in *Taking Place: Location and the Moving Image*, ed. John David Rhodes and Elena Gorfinkel (Minneapolis: University of Minnesota Press, 2011), 55.
13. Modleski, "Women's Cinema," 49.
14. Gorfinkel, "Tales of Times Square," 67.
15. Michael J. Bowen, "Doris Wishman Meets the Avant-Garde," in *Underground U.S.A.: Filmmaking Beyond the Hollywood Canon*, ed. Xavier Mendik and Steven Jay Schneider (New York: Columbia University Press, 2003), 117.
16. Rebekah McKendry, "Fondling Your Eyeballs: Watching Doris Wishman," in *From the Arthouse to the Grindhouse: Highbrow and Lowbrow Transgression in Cinema's First Century*, ed. John Cline and Robert G. Weiner (Lanham, MD: Scarecrow Press, 2010), 59.
17. Ibid., 63.
18. Gorfinkel, "Body's Failed Labor," 84.
19. This quote comes from program notes Ahwesh wrote for her curated film series "Peggy Ahwesh: Girls Beware!" in the Whitney Museum's *New American Film and Video Series* in July–August 1997. The series was made up of multiple lengthy programs pairing disparate yet connected work meant to demonstrate work that has influenced Ahwesh's approaches, ideas, and concerns. One program in the series featured Roger Jacoby's *Dream Sphinx* (1974), Ahwesh's *The Color of Love* and *Trick Film* (1996), Kurt Kren's *O Tannenbaum* (1964), trailers for films by Doris Wishman, and concluded with *Bad Girls Go to Hell*.
20. Bowen, "Embodiment and Realization," 79–80.
21. McKendry, "Fondling Your Eyeballs," 71.
22. Ibid., 70.
23. Ibid.
24. Peggy Ahwesh, "The Films of Doris Wishman," zine, February 1995.
25. Michael Bowen has begun this effort through his essay "Doris Wishman Meets the Avant-Garde," concluding that the comparison between Wishman's work and the formal avant-garde is "fruitful but precarious" (122) for both genres; ultimately, there is still more scholarship needed to address this crossover.

26. Bowen, "Doris Wishman," 110.
27. Ibid.
28. Ibid.
29. M. M. Serra and Kathryn Ramey, "Eye/Body: The Cinematic Paintings of Carolee Schneemann," in *Women's Experimental Cinema: Critical Frameworks*, ed. Robin Blaetz (Durham, NC: Duke University Press, 2007), 105.
30. Carolee Schneemann, *Imagining Her Erotics* (Cambridge, MA: MIT Press, 2003), 155.
31. Ibid., 159.
32. Elise Archias, *The Concrete Body: Yvonne Rainer, Carolee Schneemann, Vito Acconci* (New Haven, CT: Yale University Press, 2017), 77.
33. Schneemann in an interview with Scott MacDonald published in "Carolee Schneemann," in *A Critical Cinema: Interviews with Independent Filmmakers* (Berkeley: University of California Press, 1988), 142.
34. Carolee Schneemann, "Interview with Kate Haug," in *Imagining Her Erotics*, 26.
35. Ibid., 23.
36. MacDonald, "Carolee Schneemann," 141. Schneemann recounts the audience at Cannes that became destructive over the sexually political nature of the film, a fight at the University of Massachusetts for its lack of eroticism, and a group of lesbian separatists at the Art Institute of Chicago who complained about the film's lack of role model for them in this heterosexual relationship.
37. Carolee Schneemann, "The Obscene Body/Politic," *Art Journal* 50, no. 4 (1991): 28.
38. R. Bruce Elder, *A Body of Vision: Representations of the Body in Recent Film and Poetry* (Waterloo, ON: Wilfrid Laurier University Press, 1997), 234.
39. This title comes from Scott MacDonald, who uses it in his interview with Ahwesh published in "Peggy Ahwesh," in *A Critical Cinema 5: Interviews with Independent Filmmakers* (Berkeley: University of California Press, 2006), 140.
40. Ibid.

CHAPTER 8

Revolutionization of the Erotic Screen: The Films of Doris Wishman and Wakamatsu Koji

Molly Kim

> Everything in the world is about sex except sex. Sex is about power.
> — Popularly attributed to Oscar Wilde

This chapter examines the work of Doris Wishman, an American sexploitation filmmaker and Wakamatsu Koji, a Japanese filmmaker who specialized in Pink film (*pinku eiga*)[1]—the Japanese equivalent of theatrical softcore pornography which peaked in the 1970s. In both cases their active years as filmmakers overlap in the 1960s and 1970s. The peak of their careers coincided with dramatic changes that were taking place across multiple aspects of the film industry, audience reception, and the global cultural arena of sexual politics. Doris Wishman was one of the few female directors to work within the genre of exploitation film. Her nudie cuties in the 1960s and roughies in the 1970s defied the previous notion of (s)exploitation films and the ways that they served viewers by introducing a new kind of cinematic femininity. Her productions proved the influences of women and outside cinema that spoke to the changing dynamics within the film industry and politics of gender and sex.

If Wishman's works suggested new possibilities in the representation of female agency within male-dominated cinema, Wakamatsu demonstrated how politics could be voiced through the erotic conventions of Pink cinema. His films produced during the late 1960s and early 1970s, the overlapping period of political and cinematic revolution, demonstrated outrageous sexual display with an even more outrageous political critique. Moreover, the films of Wakamatsu were aesthetically sensational, a quality that is least expected for adult cinema in general, making his work highly distinctive within the field of Japanese "eroduction" (a concatenation of "erotic" and "production").

Most importantly, his productions candidly depicted polemic issues of the era, and offer useful testimony to the rise of leftist politics and the student movement within Japan. As a radical left-wing, Wakamatsu gradually became involved with the New Left movement in the 1960s, and soon felt compelled to introduce his own personal element of political activism into the world of Pink film. The founding of his own production company, Wakamatsu Production (1965), coincided with the peak of New Left student activism. Here he was able to dedicate himself to works filled with an "infectious energy and electrifying zeitgeist."[2] His films produced during this particular moment of revolution were regarded as the most frank politico-avant-garde statements of the time, and had a cult following by college students and young political activists.[3]

The works and filmmaking practices of Wishman and Wakamatsu are representative of how previously marginalized, low-budget independent filmmaking became significant on industrial, artistic, and cultural levels. Wishman's entry into sexploitation and Wakamatsu's pursuit of politically and artistically significant Pink films both indicate and are instigated by the shifting dynamics of the screen and television industry during the 1960s and 1970s.[4] On the thematic level, the subject matters they deal with and the ways they are represented echo the changing norms of gender and politics of the period. As a form and practice, they both pioneered and revolutionized the depiction of sex on the public screen in distinctive and remarkable ways.

In this regard, it would be meaningful to examine the oeuvre produced by Wishman during the early 1970s—*Double Agent 73* (1973) and *Deadly Weapons* (1974)—in conjunction with Wakamatsu's contemporary works *Season of Terror* (1969) and *Ecstasy of the Angels* (1972), to unpack how their concept of the "erotic" was cinematized to cater to the commercial, sexual, and political zeitgeist of the globe. Additionally, I trace how the works of Wishman and Wakamatsu, notwithstanding their origins within an "exclusive niche," came to represent not just erotic filmmaking, but anything that is full of rule breaking and progressive ideals in a way that mainstream cinema rarely achieved.

DE-EROTICIZING THE EROTIC BODY IN DORIS WISHMAN'S *DOUBLE AGENT 73* AND *DEADLY WEAPONS*

Hollywood had been in dramatic financial decline since the Paramount Decrees in 1948. The Supreme Court order mandated the eight major studios (Paramount, Fox Corporation, Loew's Incorporated, RKO, Warner Bros., Columbia Pictures, Universal, and United Artists) to relinquish their monopoly ownership of theater chains, substantially reducing their profit margins. This was worsened by the increasing pervasion of television across the U.S., which by the mid-1960s resulted in a large-scale recession within the film industry. The continual decline in audience attendance reached a low point of 15.8 million a week by the early 1970s, accompanied by a sharp decrease in the number of theaters.[5] The shrinking film industry, however, became an opportunity for many young directors and producers as the major studios began to seek out less expensive, younger talent.

On the other hand, previously marginalized players such as Poverty Row and other low-budget independent studios were quick to find alternative, niche venues among the steadily disappearing movie houses, including drive-ins and grindhouse theaters. They also found distribution easier and distributors increasingly amenable, finding that in the shrinking market, their product "no longer required the delicate handling typical of an exploitation roadshow."[6] Independent filmmakers also benefited from the gradual lifting of censorship toward the 1960s and the eventual termination of the Motion Picture Production Code (MPPC) in 1968. A new breed of exploitation film, "sexploitation," flourished, due in part to this abolition of the MPPC and the sexual revolution afoot during the 1970s.[7] Unlike classic exploitation films, low-budget (s)exploitation films of the 1960s and 1970s were no more "bound by the educational pretense" of their predecessors.[8] These films instead contained a heavy dose of nudity and sex scenes alongside graphic violence and the transgressing of numerous other social taboos.

This newly created phenomenon, which Brent Wood terms a new cycle of "sinema," witnessed the emergence of some of the most prominent figures in the field of exploitation.[9] Notable among these is Doris Wishman, one of the few female directors to work within the exploitation genre as it emerged around the late 1950s. Never professionally trained in filmmaking, but with some experience in stage acting and film distribution,[10] Wishman made her directorial debut with her first nudie cutie, *Hide Out in the Sun*, in 1960. For its opening two weeks, this played at the Stanton Art Theater alongside a revival of Kurosawa's *Rashomon* and Russ Meyer's *The Immoral Mr. Teas*, enjoying "comparable success" to the latter.[11] Her following films in the 1960s garnered reasonable sales that solidified her reputation as an expert in nudist pictures.[12] She produced fifteen nudie cuties in the 1960s alone and twenty-nine exploitation films over her entire career, a record that makes her one of the most prolific female filmmakers in history.

Wishman's second formative period starts with her roughies produced from the mid-1960s, including *Bad Girls Go to Hell* (1965) and *My Brother's Wife* (1966). Normally recognized as "the equivalent of a bona fide dirty movie," roughies signified nothing but a brief preparatory stage for the dawn of hardcore pornography in the 1970s.[13] However Wishman was reluctant to comply with the shifting focus of exploitation filmmaking toward more explicit representations of sex. Her works from this period bear out this predicament, witnessed through her combining the innocuous style of 1960s nudie cuties with that of sensational hardcore, as exemplified in films such as *Deadly Weapons* (1973), *Double Agent 73* (1974), and *Let Me Die A Woman* (1978).

One of the staples of Wishman's films in this transition period is the copious amount of nudity which was generally considered "a sexploitation cinema's box office success and promotional lure."[14] However, Wishman's employment of female nudity tends to be somewhat unconventional and "unerotic," departing from the typical construction of the female nude in sexploitation cinema. While the gratuitous use of female nudity is featured in those films, the degree of eroticism or sexual representation is rather curtailed, working against what is generally expected for hardcore pleasure. In her discussion of female nudity in sexploitation cinema, Elena Gorfinkel argues that female nudity does not always aim for a single duty of erotic arousal but serves multiple functions: "Nudity returns the performing body to a kind of fleshy documentary facticity that necessarily undermines but also exposes the conditions of working bodies and the body's work."[15] Likewise, a woman's bare body is seen neither eroticized nor theatricalized but is merely performed "as actions" in many of Wishman's works from the 1970s.[16] The nude scenes, for example, are displayed as part of mundane, quotidian actions such as shower scenes or bodily labor which frequently involves the main characters including prostitutes, madams, nude models, burlesque dancers, and strippers.[17]

This kind of de-eroticized construction of female nudity as "routine gesture" or "corporeal actions" simultaneously works in a way that excludes male pleasure. It is most apparent in Wishman's *Deadly Weapons* (1973) and *Double Agent 73* (1974), a two-episode espionage series, with both starring first-time actress Chesty Morgan, billed as a woman with "the World's Largest Naturally Occurring Breasts."[18] While the films centralize the nudity of Chesty Morgan, a primary source of spectacle, they are rarely erotically charged. More specifically, the framing of Morgan's (anticipated) bodily spectacle or erotic impact is always disrupted by out-of-focus shots and the absence of fragmented body close-ups/inserts and sexual sound effects, all of which counteract the ways that typically establish masculine pleasure. It is this latter point that distinguishes Wishman from her contemporaries within the sexploitation genre or in the larger context of filmmaking practice of the 1970s in which a feminist form of sexual representation would be close to impossible.

In the first episode, Morgan plays Crystal, a successful advertising executive. The film starts with a downright, frontal close-up of Morgan's/Crystal's breasts followed by out-of-focus shots of her breasts from multiple angles. After a lengthy sequence featuring numerous more shots of Crystal's bust, the story proceeds with her boyfriend, Larry, blackmailing someone on the phone. Soon after, he is shot to death by Italian mobsters and Crystal investigates his death. Crystal tracks down the murderers and takes revenge by smothering them one by one with her "deadly" breasts.

The most intriguing, and perhaps the most pivotal element of *Deadly Weapons* is that despite the ample close-ups of breasts, there is no sexually explicit depiction involved with Crystal. One example is Crystal's striptease scene in which she performs on stage as an "undercover" strip dancer to lure one of the murderers. Here, as opposed to the conventional construction of female strip dance on screen, eroticism is visibly muted or downplayed, particularly through the lack of the woman's fragmented body inserts and the male reaction shots. A striptease performance on cinematic screen traditionally magnifies and focuses on the woman's sexually charged gaze, actions, and/or fragmented (female) body parts, often delivered from the perspective from the male audience within the film. In the most-noted strip scenes in popular films such as *Striptease* (Andrew Bergman, 1996) and *Barbwire* (David Hogan, 1996) the woman's body simultaneously functions as the object of the male gaze and "cinematic spectacle," or, "the leitmotif of erotic spectacle that freezes the flow of action in the moments of erotic contemplation."[19] These images are often typified by the fetishizing of the female body shots that follow the lines of legs and arms, empowered close-ups in which the actress looks directly and seductively into the camera.[20]

Furthermore, the strip performance scene in *Deadly Weapons* subverts the staging of the erotic spectacle by obscuring the male gaze. The scene consists of shots of Crystal dancing as reflected on surrounding convex mirrors and a brief full shot of the audience consisting of both male and female spectators. The erotic impact is further downsized by the out-of-focus, mirrored shots of Crystal, whose body shape is barely seen. Here Crystal does not stand to serve "pleasure in being looked at" for male fantasy.[21] Rebekah McKendry is of the similar view that Wishman tends to undermine the idea of the male gaze: the gaze tends to be undercut when "the camera shifts away from the female to some very unsexual object for example, instead of seeing the completion of the striptease (full nudity), the audience sees a table leg."[22]

The similar exclusion of the male gaze and/or erotic climax occurs in the sequel, *Double Agent 73*. Morgan plays Jane, a spy with a camera implanted in one of her enormous breasts, sent on a mission to track down drug traffickers. In the process of killing one of her targets, she applies poison to one of her breasts before seducing him. Her target, hallucinating due to the poison, starts to caress and kiss Jane's breasts emotionlessly and soon dies. As the man starts to kiss her poisoned breasts, Jane goes out of frame. Jane becomes invisible throughout this scene, working against the popular convention that a femme fatale is expected to be depicted erotically to fulfill the voyeuristic desires of the audience. What remains visible is the deadpan face of the man, who is in no state of ecstasy but rather "in the dominance of the feminine body."[23] Moreover, the sound from both characters becomes muted throughout the scene, suppressed by a non-diegetic musical score. Again, this muting of the sound, generally considered crucial to a focused representation of sexual activity, works to subvert what would have been a moment of pure eroticism in a conventional sexploitation feature.

Figure 8.1 Crystal's breasts displayed non-erotically and seen from both female and male gaze. Courtesy of Something Weird Video

Overall, Wishman's employment of Chesty Morgan as the main protagonist serves two major functions. The predominant display of Morgan's breasts fulfills the commercial demand for a greater focus on female body parts than was featured in her prior nudie cuties. However, Morgan's nudity or breasts are rarely eroticized or "properly" staged throughout the series, as exemplified in the analysis of the striptease and poisoning sequence above. McKendry mentions that in Wishman's films Chesty Morgan was never really a sexy doll, rather she was the antithesis of the surgical beauty of the 1970s: her boobs were "natural, and drooped and hung pendulously during scenes" or were sometimes held "in an enormous white 'granny' bra just to keep her boobs above waist level."[24]

McKendry is accurate to say that Chesty Morgan's breasts or how they are visualized are far from those in the typical pornographic spectacle. What is more significant to me is that Wishman further articulates the breasts as an exclusively feminine quality, offering them as a powerful tool (at times literally a weapon) to contest and reverse male domination. While it is undeniable that the female breast has always been the centerfold of sexploitation films, Wishman transforms the convention to identify the breast as an element of female power. Excluding the explicit depiction of sexual engagement, the series caters to the expectations of the audience within the sexploitation genre premise "while reframing nudity and utilizing it to underline women's power and subjectivity," as Moya Luckett assesses, something both Wishman and Russ Meyer attempted in their works.[25]

The visual and narrative constructions in *Double Agent 73* and *Deadly Weapons* discussed above display a strategic and discursive complexity that far exceeds that of a mere alternative to the emerging hardcore market. The use of female nudity in both cases is noticeably de-eroticized and functions to liberate the female protagonist from the male gaze, which stands against the very generic premise of a "sexploitation" film. Wishman curtails the depiction of the erotic spectacle and it ironically results in the absence of male desire on screen, notwithstanding the films' staging within this most patriarchal cinematic realm. In this respect, *Deadly Weapons* and *Double Agent 73* provide crucial evidence to demonstrate how texts created by female directors reveal "the tensions and contradictions" that surround popular filmic conventions, and challenge their consistent orientation toward the masculine gaze.[26] I should note that not every Wishman sexploitation feature deserves distinction for attempting such a subversion, and Wishman may not have intended any of it after all during the actual production. Whether intended or not, however, her resultant works are valuable documents that embody disavowal of (male) pleasure and deconstruction of sexploitation conventions, as exemplified. For that matter, labeling Wishman "a kind of post-structural feminist" does not seem too out of place though it might sound paradoxical given her area of specialty.[27]

If Wishman's sexploitation films are emblematic of the wider oeuvre of feminist productions during the era of second-wave feminism, Wakamatsu's Pink films signaled cinematic activism that contextualized Japan's postwar anxiety instigated by the political and student movements of the late 1960s and early 1970s. Benefiting from the increasing transition of sexploitation cinema to television on a global scale, both Wishman and Wakamatsu had much more autonomy than other, studio-employed directors and were able to voice their authorial visions. In the domain of feminism and politics respectively, Wishman tweaks the traditional settings of cinematic eroticism which resulted in the reverse of gendered dynamics on screen, while Wakamatsu utilizes the conventions of Pink film and transforms them into political verse full of erotic allegories. In the resultant works of these two leading filmmakers in erotic cinema, Wishman and Wakamatsu proved that there are numerous possibilities of how sex can be screened and function in a cinematic context other than the carnal ecstasy that often configured the most critical discourses of the era.

KOJI WAKAMATSU'S PINK FILM OF REVOLUTION: *SEASON OF TERROR* AND *ECSTASY OF THE ANGELS*

Similar to Wishman joining the "wave" of sexploitation directors as the golden age of U.S. cinema passed into the era of television, Koji Wakamatsu debuted in Japan as television was starting to become the dominant medium in the national entertainment industry. After a peak year in 1958 which witnessed a record total of 1,127,000,000 attendees, Japanese cinema gradually lost audiences to television year on year, a process accelerated by the emergence of color television in 1964 and a boom in alternative leisure facilities in the wake of high economic growth.[28] By 1963, movie attendance was down to 511,000,000, decreasing to 373,000,000 by 1965 and then 253,000,000 by 1970.[29] The number of movie theaters fell along with attendance, from 7,457 cinemas in 1960 to 3,246 in 1970.[30]

The major film companies Nikkatsu, Daiei, Toho, Shochiku, and Toei had to come up with a solution that would enable them to remain afloat during this dramatic transition. To recover their losses, they started to produce Pink films, a niche domain previously occupied by only small, independent companies. In this regard, the oldest and most respectable film studio, Nikkatsu, shifted its entire production focus to Roman Porno (*roman poruno*), a Pink film label that Nikkatsu devised to compete against all other low-budget Pink films. Studio heads considered this move inevitable, and certainly relatively safe financially, because "in Japan, *eroduction* [wa]s the only type of picture that retain[ed] an assured audience."[31] Consequently, Pink films became the predominant genre of the time, constituting 45 percent of Japanese film productions in 1965.[32]

Consequently, many talented film directors at this time started their careers in Pink films, or shifted to the genre from other fields of filmmaking, including Tetsuji Takechi, Kiyoshi Kurosawa, Masayuki Suo, Takahisa Zeze, and Yojiro Takit.[33] Wakamatsu was also among those to emerge within this "Pink film" canon. Unlike Wishman, who had no filmmaking experience before her debut work, Wakamatsu had worked as a co-director/producer at a television company before his first picture, *Sweet Trap* (1963), a Pink film about killing a cop. *Sweet Trap* was produced by the independent production company Tokyo Kikaku for the small amount of $1,800.[34] Despite the film's extremely low budget, it garnered audience numbers far beyond those expected for a first-time director.[35] Over the next two years, Wakamatsu directed over eighteen Pink films and earned himself the title "A King of *Eroduction*."[36]

Apart from being one of the most prolific and successful Pink film directors, Wakamatsu is notable in many other respects. His productions were never "just" erotic films, as the orchestration of aesthetics and political themes within his work was a pivotal feature of Wakamatu's cinematic oeuvre. His films addressed social and political issues of the time through a visually arresting mis-en-scène, and in this regard, his work has become particularly associated with New Left student activism of the 1960s and 1970s. Alberto Toscano and Go Hirasawa highlight that the "uneasy combination of crude content and insidious beauty in Wakamatsu's images" and "the main axes of his aesthetics—sex, politics and violence" distinguish his films from "the commonplaces of 'extreme cinema.'"[37]

Because of their cinematic quality and political radicalism, qualities rarely seen or expected in the Pink genre, Wakamatsu's films became highly regarded not just by domestic Pink film patrons but across a wider realm of foreign film critics and intellectuals, a dynamic which certainly contributed to the global recognition of "the explosion of creative, independent filmmaking in Japan that followed in their wake."[38] *Secret Behind the Walls* (1965), for instance, was selected and screened at the competition section of the 15th Berlin International Film Festival. The story portrays a teenager who spends his time spying on a woman's sexual affair with a former radical activist suffering from the side effects of the atomic bombing of Hiroshima. The film metaphorizes the collective trauma of the Hiroshima bombing through the eyes of a boy who eventually transforms into a rapist and murderer. Sharon Hayashi has noted that this film "attest[s] to the permeability of generic boundaries that demarcate 'sex film' from 'art film.'"[39]

Following this production, Wakamatsu became known to a larger global audience, in part led by French film critic Noël Burch, who saw "great cinematic depth" in many of his films, including *Violated Angels* (1967).[40] Additionally, several other European festival screenings followed the Berlin screening of *Secret Behind the Wall*. For instance, *The Embryo Hunts in Secret* (1966) was screened at the 1968 Knokke-le-Zoute Experimental Film Festival in Belgium, and in 1971, Cannes invited Wakamatsu to screen two of his works—*Violated Angels* and *Sex Jack* (1970)—at Directors' Fortnight.

Perhaps most importantly, Wakamatsu's films have remained consistently focused on the theme of revolution. The peak years of his filmmaking and/or the films of his Wakamatsu Production company overlap with the era of the New Left student movement initiated by the renewal of the U.S.–Japan Security Treaty in 1959 (also known as "Anpo"). Under this new treaty, the U.S. military bases in Japan expanded, and the U.S. was able legitimately to use land in Japan for the storage of munitions to be employed in the Vietnam War. In response to this, hundreds of thousands of civilians demonstrated, demanding Prime Minister Kishi's resignation, new elections, and the cancellation of the upcoming Eisenhower state visit to Japan.[41] Many of the demonstrators were college students, and this critically contributed to the formation of New Left student activism.

Wakamatsu was deeply inspired by this movement and supported its actions. He directly expressed that he could not bear the stupidity of the Japanese political system and politicians, a statement that reflected his desire to align with student demonstrators and activists.[42] Working under the banner of Wakamatsu Production since 1965, he became increasingly involved with the theme of social revolution both inside and outside his life as a filmmaker.[43] Within his films, his subject matter became increasingly radical, featuring stories about political groups such as the Communist League Red Army Faction (*Ecstasy of the*

Angels), and the Japanese Red Army and the United Red Army (*Red Army/ PFLP: Declaration of World War*, 1971).[44] Beyond filmmaking, Wakamatsu's personal political interests are reflected in actions such as giving over his production offices to house members of the far left, or visiting Lebanon right after the screening of his film at the Cannes Film Festival.[45]

In his films produced through Wakamatsu Production, Wakamatsu consistently employed a rebel or an activist as the major character. Examples of such include, as the leader of a revolutionary group (*Ecstasy of the Angels*), a Red Army Faction member (*Sex Jack*), or young terrorists (*Season of Terror*). This framing of political characters and narratives within the genre of Pink movies proved to be enormously popular with Japanese college students.[46] Yuriko Furuhata describes that the spectatorship that formed around Wakamatsu's films was directly linked to "the ideological positioning of . . . Pink Film as defiant and oppositional to . . . mainstream cinema."[47] This anti-establishment orientation enabled Wakamatsu's work to appeal to both intellectuals and student activists alongside the normative patrons within the Pink film circuit. On this point, Wakamatsu himself acknowledges that his work was celebrated by two very different kinds of audiences, a student, avant-garde public interested the theme and artistry of his films, and a public that "loves [Pink] cinema."[48]

Ecstasy of the Angels and *Season of Terror* are often considered to be examples of precisely the sort of work that demonstrates Wakamatsu's synchronicity with young intellectual audiences and his own desire for political revolution relative to the genre framework of Pink film. Both directed in 1969, a year after the All Campus Joint Struggle Committee (Zenkyōto) movement was at its peak,[49] these films feature stories about student rebels and their lives filled with sex, politics, and violence, all central aesthetic themes within Wakamatsu's work.

Season of Terror, a black and white feature, begins with "real" newsreel footage and newspaper photos concerned with the student and police standoffs that occurred at many of the demonstration sites. This introduction is followed by a sequence in which two fictional undercover policemen pursue a former member of the Red Army. They suspect he will soon engage in terrorism against Prime Minister Sato, who is planning to visit the U.S. (a reference to the background context of the imminent renewal of the U.S.–Japan Security Treaty). From the opposite side of the apartment complex, the police watch the man through binoculars day and night. However, the man's daily life seems insignificant except for the fact that he is a sex addict living with two female partners. After voyeuristically watching his polyamorous sexual activities for several evenings, the police conclude that the suspect is not dangerous after all, and they soon decide that their mission has been unfruitful. At the same time that they report that he is not a threat, he heads out on a suicide mission to the airport to stop the prime minister's visit to the U.S.

Throughout the film, the male protagonist is portrayed as a defeated, unemployed former rebel, and the only thing he can do with his life is have meaningless sex with two women day and night. The man's seemingly endless engagement in threesomes is understood as a sign of his wider social inability, and he is constantly mocked and derided by the two undercover policemen. However, in the later part of the film, when the two policemen finally leave to go back to their headquarters, in a shocking twist the man starts to pack what appear to be Molotov cocktails. At this point, the film dramatically transforms from black and white to a full color close-up of Japanese and American flags flying against the sky, and between the flags is a superimposed image of the man and his partners in a threesome sex scene from earlier in the film. The power of this imagery is further heightened by an eerie musical score, intermixed with the moaning of the two female partners.

The male protagonist's terrorist attack in the film is designed to mirror an actual event of a stone-throwing mass protest against U.S. delegates, which happened at Haneda airport in 1960 and was led by leftist student activists and anti-American demonstrators.[50] The abrupt transition from the scene showing the man packing Molotov cocktails to the monumental (clearly exaggerated) close-up of Japanese and American flags seems somewhat comical, especially with the superimposition of a sex scene between them. Here, the threesome sex scene reappears to allude to the previous connotations of shame and mockery, allegorizing the impending, nonsensical, shameful alliance of Japan and the U.S.

The wedding of political activism and sexual activities is similarly portrayed in *Ecstasy of the Angels*. Loosely based on the Japanese Red Army's terrorist bombing campaigns of 1971, politics and sex go hand in hand in the film, as the story follows a student resistance group called "The Seasons." "October," the leader of a faction within The Seasons, breaks into a U.S. military base with several men and steals bombs that the group plan to use for a terror attack in Tokyo. Several of the men are killed during the operation and October goes blind. A leader of another group, "February," raids October's soldiers and takes the stolen bombs into their possession after hours of torture and interrogation. After the incident, October's soldiers suffer a crisis of faith in him and the revolution generally. Days of internal debates and fights follow, after which the members reconcile to proceed with their original plans. Still blinded, October goes out to the street with the remaining bombs to complete his mission for revolution.

Again, sexual activity and political activism form the twin themes in *Ecstasy of the Angels*. However, as opposed to *Season of Terror* where the male protagonist's sex acts and political activism were separate up until the moment of the climactic flag scene, in *Ecstasy of the Angels* the sex acts and political acts are continuously intermixed.

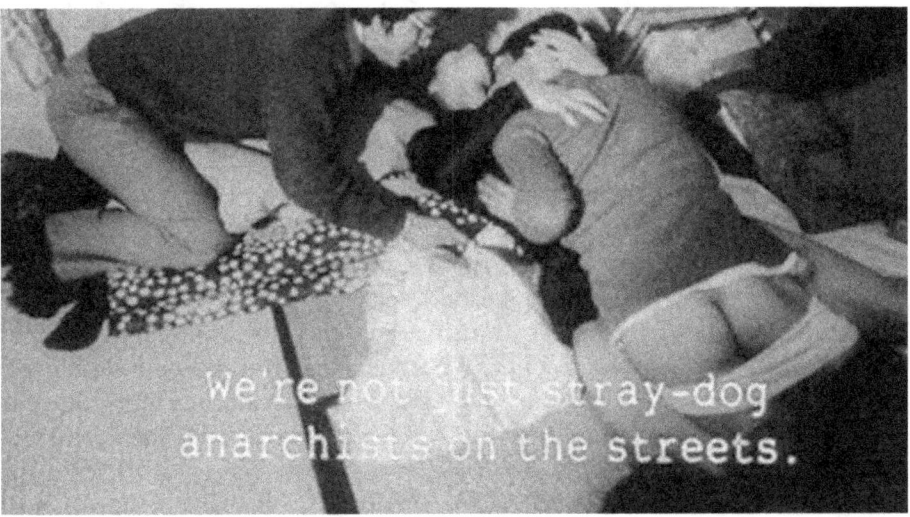

Figure 8.2 Sex among rebels

For example, sex between two members of The Seasons randomly takes place in the middle of group meetings. Likewise, the dialogue during these moments of sexual activity between the members is entirely concerned with the plans for revolution, or other political issues. As such, in both films, the sex depicted is never staged in an erotic sense, or for the purpose of titillation. Overlapping with politics, it instead functions to mark the moments of political turmoil with exploding tension and futile ecstasy.

Both Wishman's and Wakamatsu's entry into the realm of erotic cinema was affected by the expansion in independent filmmaking and boom in alternative distribution and exhibition networks during the industrial shift toward television.[51] Sexploitation in the U.S., or Pink film in the Japanese context, boosted the mainstream film industry through their frank, yet innovative, low-budget strategy of screening sex as the main draw for audiences. Although the names Wishman and Wakamatsu hold a level of importance within erotic cinema, their work does not fit into the run-of-the-mill softcore film genre, particularly in the ways that they thematize and visualize sex.

In the examples of Wakamatsu's political Pink films and Wishman's roughies of the 1970s discussed in this chapter, sex is the undercurrent, but the depiction of sexual activity is rarely used to provoke pleasure. Wishman's *Deadly Weapons* and *Double Agent 73* with Chesty Morgan utilize the female body as a centerpiece; however, they simultaneously use the body within the narrative as a "radical weapon," in the Mulveyan sense of that which establishes a woman's power.[52] I have also discussed how the masculine gaze and dominant power is either absent or deactivated in the examples of the striptease scene and the bedroom murder scene, both of which can be considered as a form of feminist intervention to deconstruct the patriarchal view common to the exploitation genre. If Wishman revolutionized screening sex by negating male pleasure in an exclusively male-dominated domain, in contrast, Wakamatsu created "the image of politics" using the very generic elements of Pink film—a plethora of nude bodies and pornographic construction of sex. The sexual activities visualized in Wakamatsu's *Season of Terror* and *Ecstasy of the Angels* serve as a metonym for politics, signifying the tensions, contradictions, and impotency keenly felt by many within 1970s Japanese society.

Ultimately, despite the great difference in their subject matter, style, and level of critical and popular reception, Wishman and Wakamatsu both suggest how sex or pornography can be deployed as a new visual language within the cinematic medium, and more specifically, a language that can usefully combat the very stereotypes and forms of power it is used to represent. Beyond the constraints of their respective local niche genres, or perhaps empowered by such exclusivity, the films discussed above were effectively able to transgress and subvert cultural, social, and political ideals and norms, something which has remained almost impossible within mainstream cinema. Taken together, they offer meaningful glimpses of an alternative cinematic history; one that powerfully focused the medium's revolutionary potential to its fullest.

NOTES

1. The term *pinku* is an English loanword for the color "pink." According to Roland Domenig, "its Japanese equivalent *momoiro* (meaning the color, peach) had sexual or erotic overtones in Japan for quite a while. From the 1960s on the English loanword '*pinku*' (pink) started to gain ground, often with an even more explicit sexual innuendo as for instance with '*pinku kyabare*' (pink cabaret) or '*pinku saron*' (pink salon) . . ., pink became very popular and a Japanese film critic, Murai Minoru first came up with the label 'Pink Film.'" Roland Domenig, "The *Market of Flesh* and the Rise of the 'Pink Film,'" in Abé Mark Nornes (ed.), *The Pink Book: The Japanese Eroduction and Its Contexts* (New Haven, CT: Kinema Book Club, 2014), 28–9.
2. Jasper Sharp, *Behind the Pink Curtain* (Godalming: FAB Press, 2008), 79.
3. Philip Brophy, "The Way Wakamatsu Chose His Own Fate: Political Mortality and Radical Dramaturgy," *Senses of Cinema* 65 (December 2012), <https://www.sensesofcinema.com/2012/feature-articles/the-way-wakamatsu-chose-his-own-fate-political-mortality-and-radical-dramaturgy/> (last accessed November 3, 2020).
4. Michael J. Bowen, "Doris Wishman Meets the Avant-Garde," in *Underground U.S.A.: Filmmaking Beyond the Hollywood Canon*, ed. Xavier Mendik and Steven Jay Schneider (London and New York: Wallflower Press, 2002), 109.
5. Yannis Tzioumakis, *American Independent Cinema: An Introduction* (New Brunswick, NJ: Rutgers University Press, 2006), 170.
6. Brett Wood, *Forbidden Fruit: The Golden Age of the Exploitation Film* (Parkville, MD: Midnight Marquee Press, 2009), 190.

7. Eric Schaefer, *"Bold! Daring! Shocking! True!": A History of Exploitation Films, 1919–1959* (Durham, NC: Duke University Press, 1999), 326.
8. Ibid.
9. Wood, *Forbidden Fruit*, 190.
10. Michael Bowen, *The Art of Insignificance: Doris Wishman and the Cinema of Least Resistance* (doctoral dissertation, New York University, 2015), 1.
11. Ibid., 117.
12. Ibid., 156.
13. Ibid., 114.
14. Elena Gorfinkel, "The Body's Failed Labor: Performance Work in Sexploitation Cinema," *The Journal of Cinema and Media* 53, no. 1 (Spring 2012): 85.
15. Ibid., 86.
16. Ibid.
17. Ibid.
18. Rebekah McKendry, "Fondling Your Eyeballs: Watching Doris Wishman," in *From the Arthouse to the Grindhouse: Highbrow and Lowbrow Transgression in Cinema's First Century*, ed. John Cline and Robert G. Weiner (Lanham, MD: Scarecrow Press, 2010), 61.
19. Laura Mulvey, "Visual Pleasure and Narrative Cinema," in *Feminism and Film Theory*, ed. Constance Penley (New York: Routledge, 1988), 57–60.
20. Teri Silvio, "Lesbianism and Taiwanese Localism in The Silent Thrush," in *AsiaPacifiQueer: Rethinking Genders and Sexualities*, ed. Fran Martin, Peter Jackson, Mark McLelland, and Audrey Yue (Chicago and Urbana: University of Illinois Press, 2008), 222.
21. Mulvey, "Visual Pleasure," 57.
22. McKendry "Fondling Your Eyeballs," 71.
23. Previously Moya Luckett has made the point that the representation of breasts in Wishman's films functions differently from those of male directors. In Wishman's case, images of breasts tend to be "not handled fetishistically but instead, represen[t] the dominance of the feminine body." Moya Luckett, "Sexploitation as Feminine Territory: The Films of Doris Wishman, in *Defining Cult Movies: The Cultural Politics of Oppositional Tastes*, ed. Mark Jancovich, Antonio Lázaro Reboll, Julian Stringer, and Andy Willis (Manchester: Manchester University Press, 2003), 151.
24. McKendry, "Fondling Your Eyeballs," 61.
25. Luckett, "Sexploitation as Feminine Territory," 150.
26. Pam Cook, *Screening the Past: Memory and Nostalgia in Cinema* (New York: Routledge, 2005).
27. McKendry, "Fondling Your Eyeballs", 68.
28. Se-sub Oh, "A Study on the Film and Life of Wakamatsu Koji—From the Perspective of A. Van Gennep's 'Rites of Passage,'" *Film Studies* 57 (Fall 2013): 262; Domenig, "*Market of Flesh*," 18.
29. David Desser, *Eros Plus Massacre: An Introduction to the Japanese New Wave Cinema* (Bloomington: Indiana University Press, 1988), 9.
30. Ibid.
31. Donald Richie, "The Japanese Eroduction—Inside Out," in *Pink Book*, ed. Nornes, 334.
32. Domenig, "*Market of Flesh*," 33.
33. Abé Mark Nornes, "Introduction," in *Pink Book*, ed. Nornes, 9.
34. Yuriko Furuhata, "The Actuality of Wakamatsu: Repetition, Citation, Media Event," in *Pink Book*, 155.
35. Oh, "Study," 262.
36. Ibid., 268. For his detailed filmography during this period see the website for the retrospective screening of Wakamatsu Koji 2020 at IFFR (International Film Festival

Rotterdam) at <https://iffr.com/en/persons/wakamatsu-koji> (last accessed November 3, 2020).
37. Alberto Toscano and Go Hirasawa, "Walls of Flesh: The Films of Koji Wakamatsu (1965–1972)," *Film Quarterly* 66, no. 4 (Summer 2013): 41.
38. Nornes, "Introduction," 7.
39. Sharon Hayashi quoted in Furuhata, "Actuality of Wakamatsu," 153.
40. Noël Burch quoted in Sharp, *Behind the Pink Curtain*, 79.
41. "Japan and the United States: Diplomatic, Security, and Economic Relations, Part I, 1960–1976," National Security Archive, <https://nsarchive.gwu.edu/japan-united-states-diplomatic-security-economic-relations-part-i-1960-1976> (last accessed November 3, 2020).
42. Oh, "Study," 278.
43. Aaron Gerow notes that Pink film "is almost an ironic epitome of the director system." In the 1960s, this was the entry ticket for an experimental filmmaker and political activist like Adachi Masao, who eventually joined the Red Army and spent decades with the Popular Front for the Liberation of Palestine in Lebanon. Aaron Gerow quoted in Nornes, "Introduction," 5.
44. Sharp, *Behind the Pink Curtain*, 79.
45. Toscano and Hirasawa, "Walls of Flesh," 46.
46. Oh, "Study," 268.
47. Furuhata, "Actuality of Wakamatsu," 155.
48. Toscano and Hirasawa, "Walls of Flesh," 46.
49. The All Campus Joint Struggle Committee (Zenkyōto) was founded at Nihon University, where the "suppression of students' democratization movements regarding the welcoming of new students in April 1968 and the issues of the university's illicit accounting practices and tax avoidance issues were coming to light." "1968: A Time Filled with Countless Questions," National Museum of Japanese History, October 11, 2017, <https://www.rekihaku.ac.jp/english/exhibitions/project/old/171011/index.html> (last accessed November 3, 2020).
50. On June 10, 1960, Presidential Press Secretary Hagerty and Appointments Secretary Stephens, in Japan to prepare for Eisenhower's visit to commemorate the centennial anniversary of the U.S.–Japan Friendship and Commerce Treaty, are mobbed at Haneda airport by some 60,000 stone-throwing, anti-American demonstrators. Along with Ambassador MacArthur, they are besieged in their car for an hour and twenty minutes, then rescued by a U.S. Marine Corps helicopter. No one is hurt, although the car is damaged. Ambassador MacArthur later receives an apology from the Japanese government. "Japan and the United States," National Security Archive.
51. Pam Cook, "The Pleasures and Perils of Exploitation Films," in *Screening the Past: Memory and Nostalgia in Cinema* (London and New York: Routledge, 2005), 52.
52. Mulvey, "Visual Pleasure," 59.

CHAPTER 9

"You can't say you're not getting a horror film here!": Authorship, Genre, and the Accidental Avant-Garde in Doris Wishman's *A Night to Dismember*

Jamie Hook

Doris Wishman's *A Night to Dismember* (1983) is itself a film dismembered, and one that is routinely relegated to passing mention in overviews of its director's filmography when not excised from it altogether. Tania Modleski's excellent essay on Wishman, for instance, erases *A Night to Dismember* by citing *Let Me Die a Woman* (1978) as Wishman's last film.[1] Rebekah McKendry acknowledges the film as a "1980s gory slasher," only to disavow it as one of the "enigmatic pieces that don't fit into [Wishman's] larger body of work."[2] Mike Quarles mentions the film in his survey of Wishman's career, but claims it was never released.[3] While it is true that the film never enjoyed theatrical exhibition in the manner of Wishman's earlier output from the 1960s and 1970s, it has remained more or less accessible to those motivated to track it down. The film's earliest release was likely through Video Search of Miami, a gray market mail order collector's service, who "acquired [their] copy directly from Wishman herself"[4] sometime in the 1980s. The film also had commercial releases on VHS in 1989 by MPI Media Group, and on DVD in 2001 by Elite Entertainment. At the time of this writing, the DVD remains out of print,[5] unlike the licensed home video releases of most of Wishman's other films, which remain relatively easy to purchase through niche distributors like Something Weird Video. In short, *A Night to Dismember* occupies a tenuous position both in the home video market and in the body of popular and scholarly literature that exists about Wishman's career.

On the one hand there is a discernable logic at work here given how as an ostensible horror film it is, technically speaking, generically singular within Wishman's oeuvre.[6] On the other hand, virtually all the authorial tropes that make one of Wishman's films a "Wishman film" are present in *A Night to Dismember*, albeit activated in a different generic-iconographic register. This is in addition to the fact that a number of Wishman's non-horror titles heavily encroach on the horrific. *Indecent Desires* (1968) centers on the ultimately tragic effects a makeshift voodoo doll has on a young woman. The titular appendages of *The Hands of Orlac* (Robert Wiene, 1924) are reimagined as the grafted penis in Wishman's *The Amazing Transplant* (1970). The shower scene from Hitchcock's *Psycho* (1960) is given a direct homage in *Double Agent 73* (1974). Even the titles of such non-horror efforts as *Bad Girls Go to Hell* (1965) and *Satan Was a Lady* (1975/2001) call to mind the increased intermingling of sex, exploitation, and horror in post-World War II European cinema, as documented by Cathal Tohill and Pete Tombs.[7] To this end, most scholars who have written on Wishman make note of the pervasive sexual violence and violent eroticism that define her "roughies," usually marked as the second major phase of her career after the pastoral nudie films with which she got her start. All of this is to say there are very clear textual and contextual reasons why *A Night to Dismember* can be considered a "Wishman film" proper rather than simply a film literally made by Doris Wishman.

Essential to note is the lore surrounding the film's bizarre fate during post-production—its own dismemberment—that features in most discussions of it.[8] After shooting was complete, MovieLab, the company hired to process the negative, went bankrupt and an irate employee destroyed footage from various films including over half of *A Night to Dismember*.[9] By Wishman's own estimate, the finished film uses only 60 percent of the original footage.[10] Wishman met such extreme post-production difficulties with doggedness and irrepressibility, mythologizing her experience through later recollections of not eating or sleeping for eight months while trying to complete the project.[11] The film was ultimately finished using outtakes, footage from other films, and generous voiceover narration, giving it what I argue is an accidental avant-garde aesthetic. Many of the film's formal elements—the privileging of conceptual montage, asynchronous sound, color filters and superimpositions, confused spatial and temporal continuities—heavily evoke the distinguishing properties and poetics of avant-garde and experimental modes of filmmaking. As an exploitation maverick, however, Wishman never aligned herself with the ethos or politics of an avant-gardist. Thus, the film refuses the expectations set both by the horror genre and that dizzying array of practices consolidated under the label of experimental filmmaking.

Nevertheless, this chapter considers *A Night to Dismember* through each of these three distinct lenses: as a Wishman film and its attendant engagement with the hallmarks of her earlier filmography; as a piece of paracinematic horror that draws on and departs from trends of the contemporaneous slasher cycle; and, finally, as an accidental evocation of avant-garde aesthetics. Individually, these readings will demonstrate what is conventional and exceptional about the film when situated in each of these contexts and, collectively, will indicate the impracticality of ever fully disentangling its respective authorial and generic influences. First, however, because the film often remains unseen even by Wishman aficionados, I offer a summary with the caveat that what follows is sure to visit its own reductive violence upon the intricacies and more unintelligible aspects of Wishman's stupefying narrative.[12]

After a rambling prologue that attempts to narrate the hopelessly convoluted past crimes surrounding the Kent family, the film enters the present tense as Vicki Kent is released from a mental asylum into the custody of her parents, Adam and Blanche, much to the vexation of her jealous siblings, Mary and Billy. The world outside the asylum feels strange and destabilizing to Vicki, who immediately begins to experience hallucinations. Mary and Billy only exacerbate things, as they scheme to find a way to have Vicki re-institutionalized. Despite Mary's insistence that he no longer loves her, Vicki attempts to reignite a relationship with Frankie, her former boyfriend. While Frankie is making love to another woman, an unseen intruder arrives and decapitates them both. Detective Tim O'Malley (who narrates the prologue) receives a call from an unknown caller with a disguised voice instructing him to go over and investigate the carnage.

Meanwhile, in an attempt to escape the hostility at home, Vicki tries to visit her Uncle Sebastian and Aunt Ann who have always been fond of her. They reject her unceremoniously, remarking that she and her siblings are crazy. Later, when Sebastian, Ann, and Ann's sister, Bea, hurry into their car to escape the rain, someone lurking in the back seat slaughters them all. Down by the lake, Vicki is terrorized by a creature who rises out of the water and pursues her though the woods. Back home, she sees Billy washing mud off his body in the bathroom and is shocked to overhear him conspiring against her with Mary. Adam and Blanche refuse to speak to O'Malley when he arrives at the house, leaving him to try to return a dropped scarf to a despondent Vicki outside. After she returns indoors, O'Malley watches through her bedroom window as she performs a striptease for him. Her exhibitionism induces a psychedelic sex dream in which Vicki imagines a faceless man making love to her. Her erotic reverie is cut short when she wakes up alone. She puts herself to bed, but her sleep is interrupted when Billy appears standing over her in a frightening mask. After he terrorizes her and she goes back to bed, O'Malley returns to the house and again peers through her window as she sleeps.

Concurrently, Mary has a nightmare in which she dreams her family mutilates her. In another attempt to convince his parents that Vicki is "up to her old tricks," Billy pours fake blood around the sink. The plan works and Adam calls O'Malley back to the house. The lights suddenly go off and Adam is stabbed through the neck while investigating the cellar. Blanche is axed to death in her bed. Billy finds his mother's body and runs into the woods, only to be hit over the head by the unseen assailant and buried alive. Back at the house,

Mary—who is revealed to be the true murderer—has a breakdown, believing she sees her own head in a hatbox. She runs into the woods where the demons of her victims confront her. Vicki discovers the bloody ax and is mistaken for the killer when O'Malley sees her holding it. After a pursuit he corners her, and she strikes him with the ax until he strangles her to death in self-defense. Mary leaves with a suitcase in hand. When we last see her, she is preparing to strike a taxi driver with her ax as the cab drives off into the darkness of the city.

All of this is packed into a frenetic sixty-nine minutes.

A NIGHT TO DISMEMBER AS A WISHMAN FILM

Even when reluctant to confer such status upon her, most authors in their writings on Wishman eventually discuss her career in terms of auteurism. Since it is most common to find articles analyzing Wishman's films in relation to one another (as opposed to, say, others within the same genre), the Wishman-as-auteur idea has been reified discursively regardless of whether the term is formally bestowed. Irrespective of her work's lack of adherence to traditional norms of quality, like many of the directors in Andrew Sarris's contentious pantheon, Wishman has a recognizable, highly flamboyant extra-filmic persona ("When I die, I'll make movies in Hell!" is one particularly memorable quotation attributed to her). She is also associated with a generally agreed upon catalog of visual and thematic tropes observable across her filmography, a partial list of which might include: cutaway shots that privilege inanimate objects, post-synchronous dialogue, the use of untrained actors, sexually charged and violent melodramatic situations, a reliance on stock footage to signify specific geographical locations, "Muzak"-style scoring that is often incongruous with the images on screen, and an inconsistent adherence to continuity editing. What precisely her authorship means in socio-cinematic terms, however, is another question entirely. Beyond being credited as the "most prolific American woman filmmaker of the sound era,"[13] "one of cult film's most reknowned [sic] auteurs,"[14] and "the Godard of low-budget genre films,"[15] she has been called everything from "a positive woman's role model"[16] to a "radical feminist's worst nightmare."[17]

If not conversant in the language of auteurism as it has been academically theorized, on the commentary track included as a supplement on the DVD release of *A Night to Dismember*, Wishman herself repeatedly casts the film as her personal artistic property. When, for instance, her co-commentator, her longtime cinematographer C. Davis Smith, attempts to correct her about a shooting location, Wishman impatiently shoots back, "Don't tell me about my movies!" Later, when Smith asks about Blanche's absence during a Kent family dinner scene, Wishman snaps, "Chuck, don't tell me what to do with my characters." It is in fact Smith himself who describes the film through language

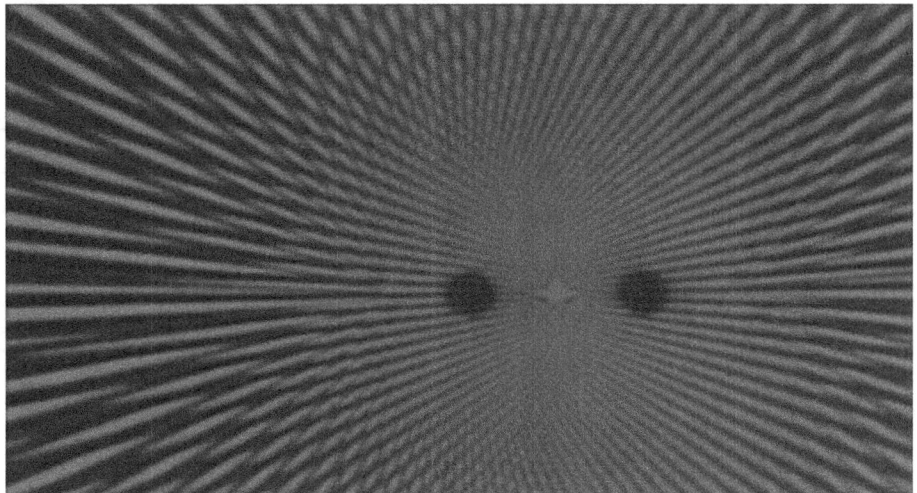

Figure 9.1 An out-of-place optical or "a Doris Wishman touch"?

that expounds a playful sense of auteurism. He describes a shot of pacing feet as "very Wishman-esque," and when Wishman concludes that an optical effect near the end of the film "really has no place here," Smith justifies its inclusion by contextualizing it as "a Doris Wishman touch" (Figure 9.1).

To be sure, with few exceptions, the tropes routinely identified as contributing to Wishman's authorial style are present in *A Night to Dismember*, oftentimes magnified to an even greater extent than what can be observed in many of her earlier works. Formally, the editing in several sequences of the film is so disorienting that it makes the intermittent departures from classical norms found in her earlier films, such as the occasional jump cut or violation of the 180-degree rule, seem surprisingly subdued.[18] In most of Wishman's 1960s and 1970s films, such gaffes certainly bespeak their "low-budgetness" but rarely hinder *narrative* clarity, whereas *A Night to Dismember* truly throws the viewer into an off-kilter world wherein certain moments are just plain hard to follow. It is difficult to say if this is ultimately a result of editing choices dictated by whether certain footage did or did not exist, Wishman's personal conception of horror as a genre, or something else entirely. Whatever the cause of this narrative illegibility and extreme disturbance of spatial and temporal continuity, the effect contributes to the production of the film's avant-garde affect, which will be addressed in a later section.

Thematically, the film features traces of Wishman's familiar interest in eccentric or "perverse" sexual display. The specter of incest is raised by the close physical proximity of adult siblings Billy and Mary as the undressed Billy washes mud from his body in the bathroom after his attempt to frighten Vicki.

The violent and erotic quite literally merge when Mary imagines her family mutilating her body, during which she lets out what can only be described as sensual moans of pleasure. Several instances in the film in which we watch Vicki dress or undress have no real narrative function but do affirm the continuation into this later film of what Moya Luckett reads as an ongoing element of Wishman's "feminine authorial presence."[19]

Beyond the general formal and thematic tropes that recur across Wishman's filmography, *A Night to Dismember* also features the repetition of specific elements from earlier films, giving these moments an uncanny, already-seen quality for viewers acquainted with Wishman's work. The shaky-camera, approximated point-of-view low-angle shots of trees used to represent Arthur's psychosis as he goes home with a prostitute in *The Amazing Transplant* are replicated here to signify Vicki's mental state as her parents first drive her home from the asylum. The technique of shooting characters running up the same set of stairs multiple times in order to elongate the space and prolong the action is used in an early scene of *Deadly Weapons* (1974) and reappears during the climactic chase between Vicki and O'Malley. Even stock music is reused; the same musical buildup heard when Chesty Morgan's Jane Tennay ingeniously uses ice cubes to murder an underworld type in *Double Agent 73* is redeployed throughout *A Night to Dismember*. Since Wishman's budgets necessitated an uncommon resourcefulness, the same shooting locations frequently become various settings in different films, not the least of which is Wishman's own apartment, herein used as the Kent home. There comes a point when after seeing enough films this apartment begins to feel like an inanimate but central player in the Wishman stock company.

In this way, Doris Wishman's authorial imprint takes the form of inter-film palimpsests, hazy but still-legible traces of earlier elements pulled from her directorial catalog and redeployed in new contexts. This becomes quite literal when Wishman turns to outtakes or alternate shots from her previous films in order to compensate for *A Night to Dismember*'s lost footage. For example, Wishman identifies some of the shots at Frankie's apartment as originating with *Hideout in the Sun* (1960), repurposed here having never been used in the earlier film.[20] Another example is a shot of Nancy's body from *The Immoral Three* (1975), which finds new "life," ironically, as a murder victim during the opening prologue that enumerates the acts of death and destruction which have long plagued the Kent family.

Finally, brief consideration must be paid to extratextual factors in the construction of Wishman-as-auteur. Specifically, it is telling how approaches for marketing *A Night to Dismember* changed dramatically from its debut on VHS to its reappearance on DVD. The VHS case features an artist's rendering of Billy in his fright mask and an unidentified woman's head thrown back in shrieking terror, much in the style of the popular Paragon and Vestron video releases that were a staple of video store horror aisles in the 1980s and 1990s. Wishman's name is only listed requisitely as the director and the back cover copy entreats the viewer to read the film as a routine slasher, asking, "What really happened that bloody night at Woodmeyer lake? . . . Viewers will be trembling as the senseless slaughter grows into a disgusting body count. Who will get wiped off the map next?" In contrast, the DVD cover is emblazoned with an affirmation of Wishman as the creative force behind the film: "Doris Wishman's cult classic *A Night to Dismember*." Far from a pedestrian body count film, it is now (more accurately) described as "a horror film that approximates the twisted logic of a narcotic laced carnal nightmare," with Wishman credited as "a one woman gang who wrote, produced, directed and edited her films in a career spanning four decades." This articulates how the continued construction of Wishman as a cult auteur in the post-grindhouse/drive-in era changed the strategies through which her films have been marketed and recommodified on home video.[21] All of this is to say that when one stops to actually look at the film, only the most unyielding understandings of Wishman as a *sexploitation* auteur would be unable to accommodate *A Night to Dismember* in an appreciation of her total filmography.

A NIGHT TO DISMEMBER AS A HORROR FILM

At least as far back as John Carpenter's pioneering *Halloween* (1978), which is commonly accepted as inaugurating the slasher cycle of the 1970s and 1980s, many films produced in this vein have advanced the trope of the escaped mental patient as an agent of violence. As the subgenre developed, films such as *Happy Birthday to Me* (J. Lee Thompson, 1981), *The Slayer* (J. S. Cardone, 1982), *Curtains* (Richard Ciupka, 1983), *The Initiation* (Larry Stewart, 1984), and *April Fool's Day* (Fred Walton, 1986) began to tinker with the relationship between the final girl, the identity of the stalker, mental insanity, psychiatry, and/or institutionalization. Plot twists and viewer misdirection in these films play off the question of whether or not the final girl and the insane killer stalking her friends might not in fact be one and the same. In this way, *A Night to Dismember* participates in, and even anticipates (given its year of production),[22] a trope that would emerge as a recognizable plot device of the genre by the mid-1980s. While Vicki Kent does not embody the qualities of the final girl as famously described by theorist Carol Clover,[23] she is positioned as the film's protagonist-victim, the question of her sanity motivates most of the dramatic action around her, and she is narratively configured as a sympathetic figure— even if this is not the affective response most viewers would likely have toward the character given the bizarre nature of the film at large and the scenery-chewing performance by Samantha Fox.

Although much of the film runs afoul of the paradigmatic stalker formula as outlined by Vera Dika, it does abide by what she calls the subgenre's "single most distinguishing characteristic," that is, "the representation of the killer as an off-screen entity, one knowable only by a distinctive set of visual and aural markers."[24] To this end, Wishman structures the film so her killer too remains more or less off-screen, allowing Vicki to be set up as the obvious (or perhaps too obvious) force of carnage. To take one example, the triple murder of her extended family members occurs in the scene immediately following their rejection of Vicki when she visits them for sympathy. The kind of "Is she or isn't she?" guessing game this encourages puts the film squarely in line with the aforementioned titles in which the question of the heroine's sanity becomes a crucial engine driving the narrative.

Unlike these films, *A Night to Dismember* denies the agency both Dika and Clover note the genre often bestows upon the final girl. Especially pertinent for Clover's conception of this archetypal figure is the "active investigating gaze" through which the final girl looks *for* and *at* the killer, "bringing him, often for the first time, into our vision as well."[25] It makes sense then that Vicki, a character who is more conventionally acted *upon* throughout the film, has little to do with the revelation that signals its denouement. The film's "twist" comes after the murders of the Kent parents and Billy, when Mary is seen wiping blood from her face as O'Malley narrates:

> Mary thought she was well-rid of her family. Her mother, father, and Billy tried to murder her. They had all deserved to die. She was sorry about Billy, but what could she have done? He would have told the authorities that she had committed all of the murders and that Vicki was innocent.[26]

Therefore, rather than through a discovery on the part of Vicki as the film's final girl, this information comes from Detective O'Malley in his capacity as the film's male authority figure. In this moment of revelation, his authority within the diegesis is pushed into the *authorial* through the omniscient narration that demonstrates knowledge over and above what can be discerned from the narrative action alone. O'Malley soon re-enters the scene and discovers the mutilated bodies of Adam and Blanche at more or less the same moment Vicki happens upon the bloodied ax. Momentarily, they share the final girl's active, investigating function, but a gendered hierarchy of power is soon reasserted when O'Malley misreads Vicki's possession of the ax as proof of her guilt, an error that instigates the pursuit that culminates in her death.[27] Although O'Malley's voiceover has already confirmed Vicki's innocence, this narration is a retrospective conclusion drawn only after he has killed her in self-defense. As if anticipating this potentially confusing structural (dis)order, O'Malley's final voiceover explains, "If you were wondering how I came upon all these intimate details, the Kent family had one thing in common: they all kept diaries . . . Poor, innocent Vicki."

The film's rambling narrative is punctuated by numerous set pieces that offer up spectacle by way of gore and, well, dismemberment as this constitutes its subgenre's *raison d'être*. Decapitations, stabbings, ax murders, and the like are all on display. "You can't say you're not getting a horror film here!" crows Wishman about the film's triple murder sequence,[28] which features such grisly (yet patently artificial) effects as a hand pushed through a chest to extract the heart, a head run over by a car, and fingers hacked off by an ax (Figure 9.2). While it has been reported that Wishman had no penchant for horror and pursued the genre primarily due to the value she understood it to carry in the post-*Halloween* marketplace,[29] there are undeniable precedents for this generic iconography earlier in her work, especially that made only shortly before *A Night to Dismember*. While ostensibly a sexploitation film for the James Bond era, many of the violent sequences in *The Immoral Three* (a loose sequel to her two spy thrillers starring Chesty Morgan) anticipate slasher imagery, offering a throat slitting, an impaling by multi-pronged poker, and a stabbing. This indicates Wishman had already developed the how-to necessary to achieve practical gore effects even before the slasher film's ascendance and found such images to have exploitable value.

While it is then useful to consider *A Night to Dismember* in relation to the slasher or stalker film—given this was the generic formula rapidly coming to define horror at large in the moment, a fact clearly not lost on Wishman—in the final estimate the film offers anything but the "predictability of the stalker film's soon-conventionalized elements."[30] Rather than feature the interpersonal, freewheeling dynamics of a group of teenagers in an isolated location like a summer camp or after-hours party, *A Night to Dismember* is a familial melodrama at its core, recalling from Wishman's earlier work the sisterly relationship between two roommates in *Another Day, Another Man* (1966), the fraternal violence of *My Brother's Wife* (1966), or the literal

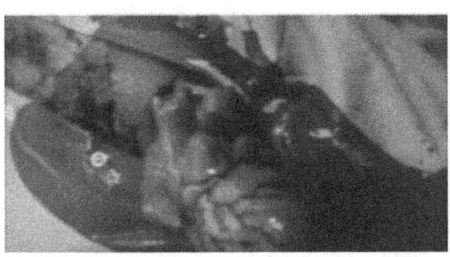 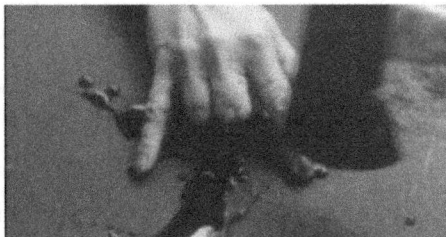

Figure 9.2 Grisly, yet artificial, gore effects

competition between three siblings in *The Immoral Three*. As in these films, the sibling rivalry that plays out among the thirty-something brother and sisters of *A Night to Dismember* places it far closer in tone to John Waters than Douglas Sirk, the campy melodrama pushing it outside the unremarkable everydayness that typically permeates the slasher's generic milieu. This extends to the film's treatment of sexuality. Unlike the casual and coyly shot teenage trysts that often serve as a prelude to violence in the slasher film, *A Night to Dismember* maintains the outré kinkiness of Wishman's earlier films. For example, the highly stylized sex fantasy catalyzed by Vicki's striptease for O'Malley is given the effect of having been shot through multicolored filters and superimposed over crashing waves, psychedelic imagery that would not be out of place in a *giallo* by Mario Bava or Dario Argento, what with their highly stylized merging of the erotic and the macabre. Wishman herself understood her film's generic boundaries as much less permeable. On the DVD commentary track, when goaded by Smith about the absence of nudity during a scene where Vicki disrobes, Wishman corrects him, "It wasn't that type of movie . . . it was a horror film." She later repeats, "This is not a skin flick. This is a horror film."

Even so, as mentioned earlier, the film refuses to ever settle into the highly routinized plot structure of the slasher film, denying viewers the possibility of "playing along" with what Dika describes as the game of the stalker film. Instead of asking, "Where is the killer?" and "When will he strike?"[31] a viewing of *A Night to Dismember* is likely to trigger questions of what in fact is even happening on screen. Operating without logic rooted in clear cause-and-effect as well as oscillating between levels of reality (in the form of Vicki's and Mary's hallucinations, which are not always formally demarcated as such), the film's violence erupts in an especially chaotic and unpredictable manner, which is only undercut by its blatant artificiality. It is no wonder that since Wishman apparently turned to gore only in an attempt to keep up with the times, *A Night to Dismember* can often feel less like a horror movie by design than a horror movie by default. The film frequently spills over—and runs rampant within—the perceived generic boundaries of horror. Recalling the film's unsteady position in writings on Wishman and her other films, this has led to its not infrequent devaluing by horror fans, when it is not once again ignored entirely. Such is the case in *The Mammoth Book of Slasher Movies*, which concludes its review by stating, "The effects were cheap, the storyline almost impossible to follow and the acting wouldn't have made it to the village hall theatrical society. . ."[32] Of course, there is another mode of filmmaking in which blatant artificiality, non-linear plotting, and non-professional acting are approached with a different set of reading strategies and it is to a consideration of this realm that I now turn.

A NIGHT TO DISMEMBER AND THE ACCIDENTAL AVANT-GARDE

The starting point for any discussion of Doris Wishman's relationship to underground and experimental film cultures is Michael J. Bowen's 2002 essay "Doris Wishman Meets the Avant-Garde," which establishes continuity between Wishman's work and the distinguishing properties of 1960s underground filmmaking. For Bowen, both a friend and biographer of Wishman's, the confluence of the avant-garde and exploitation in her films ultimately "remains an uneasy alliance."[33] Still, Bowen is quite right to acknowledge the existence of this alliance, given how in important respects the "low" cinematic culture with which Wishman is identified and the avant-garde in its various guises together represent two different sides of the same cultural coin.[34] Both are notorious for their capacity to shock, for instance, although Bowen maintains they diverge with exploitation's "recourse to the obscene" and the avant-garde's radical defamiliarization of the "visual experience itself."[35] Yet the avant-garde canon certainly contains its share of "obscene" images and, while a film like *A Night to Dismember* may not entirely upend the visual experience to the same degree as, say, a Brakhage short, it does demand viewers negotiate its visual terrain in a way that is markedly different from more conventional exploitation fare. In terms of foregrounding the material networks that link the cultural spheres of "low" culture and the avant-garde, it is especially helpful how Bowen accounts for the roles played by exhibition and the politics of space in understanding how Wishman's films have shifted along hierarchies of taste since their initial runs on the grindhouse circuit. He notes that since video artist Peggy Ahwesh first programmed Wishman at the Whitney Museum, her films have gone on to screen in such high art environs as Harvard Film Archive and The Andy Warhol Museum.[36]

Many of the traits Bowen and others call on to position Wishman in proximity to the avant-garde—genre mixing, affinities with punk, and her singular aesthetic style—are heightened in *A Night to Dismember* and pushed to an excess that surpasses the disruptive potential they carry in many of Wishman's earlier works. Students of paracinema will remember that excess becomes the linchpin by which Jeffery Sconce argues that through

> concentrating on a film's formal bizarreness and stylistic eccentricity, the paracinematic audience . . . foregrounds structures of cinematic discourse and artifice so that the material identity of the film ceases to be a structure made invisible in service of the diegesis, but becomes instead the primary focus of textual attention.[37]

This is precisely what is happening in Bowen's description of how watching Wishman can sometimes feel like watching "the record of a film being made more than . . . a film itself."[38]

As previously indicated, the disjointed editing, eccentric cinematography, and reliance on voiceover in *A Night to Dismember* begin to subsume the diegesis under the demanding weight of its all too visible artifice. Following Sconce and Bowen, it is herein that an additional layer of meaning, a lurking record of the film's own making and post-production calamity, registers most forcefully. For viewers, this has to be negotiated—either through ridicule, paracinephilic ecstasy, or some combination thereof—if one is to endure all sixty-nine of the film's gloriously unhinged minutes. The film's paracinematic visual texture is heightened in moments such as when a shot of Vicki looking at a vertically rectangular photograph of her old boyfriend (reminiscent of an actor's headshot) cuts to what reads as a frozen close-up of the actor that entirely fills the horizontally oriented screen.[39] Nothing about the image or its framing imparts the sense we are looking at the selfsame photograph as Vicki (Figure 9.3). More disjointedly, a moment in which Vicki screams is represented by a still photographic image of an open mouth, while a scream is heard on the soundtrack. Despite its brevity, the total arrestation of movement in this moment is distanciating, while the signification of the jarring image (i.e. a scream) remains literal and obvious. Even moments of more traditional continuity editing are often interrupted by non-sequitur shots that reveal things or locations appearing nowhere else in the film or are overtaken by Wishman's love of visual gimmicks. One bizarre series of morphing geometric superimpositions toward the film's climax suggests something designed by a slapdash Saul Bass, herein broken free from the usual perimeters of the opening credit sequence and come to invade the diegesis.

Thematically, little in the film is organized around character psychology or even narrative progression per se. Rather, it is often the other way around, insofar as the disjointed narrative feels as though it has emerged only after the fact, a story haphazardly trying to cohere around a series of disparate tropes:

Figure 9.3 Vicki looks at a photograph of Frankie

sibling rivalry, infidelity, sexual tension between an investigator and the subject of his investigation, a killer on the loose, and the return of the repressed. While this certainly gives the film a berserk quality rivaled only in truly aggressive underground filmmaking, there are additionally specific formal choices that ease the film onto a continuum with the avant-garde, at least as it has been more broadly understood in the decades following the work of the Dadaists and historical surrealists.

As incohesive as its visuals is the film's soundtrack, which Stephen Thrower aptly describes as "like some *musique-concret* nightmare by Pierre Schaeffer, John Cage, or Kenny Everett."[40] Ambient noise is often audible behind the post-synchronized dialogue (when Adam explores the cellar and calls upstairs, for example, it sounds as if he is in a war zone), suggesting Wishman may have lifted it from other sources. Music cues frequently feel erratic and misplaced, such as when an intense buildup is heard and repeated three times in direct succession during an otherwise innocuous meeting between Vicki and Frankie.

Whether or not to compensate for the lost footage, Wishman borrows a technique from film noir and, as discussed earlier, lays Detective O'Malley's voiceover narration over much of the film. Poorly integrated, the voiceover dialogue is recurrently cut off too early or begins too late so it is not always clear what O'Malley is saying. The voiceover's traditional function is further subverted insofar as the information it provides does little to clarify the confused narrative, as it is alternately insipid or superfluous to the visuals. Such is the case when the villainous Billy plots to send Vicki back to the insane asylum, O'Malley helpfully suggesting that "maybe he could get some ideas from the newspaper" as we see Billy on a park bench intently perusing the pages. Later, we are given no fewer than three shots from Vicki's point of view as she watches the disguised Billy emerge from a tranquil lake *before* the voiceover tells us, "Suddenly, a figure started to come out of the water." Alternately, the voiceover can be premature, thus undercutting the film's shocks. When O'Malley describes Billy's "truly hideous" mask over a shot of Vicki asleep, we know exactly what to expect before the film then cuts to a low-angle shot of the looming, masked Billy.

Were it not for the lack of self-reflexivity or political import, the effect of all this would be not entirely unlike the Situationist technique of détournement as in *Can Dialectics Break Bricks?* (René Viénet, 1973), in which new dialogue consisting of Marxist polemics and axioms is dubbed over the soundtrack of an extant Hong Kong kung fu film, the continental philosophy defamiliarizing the violent genre film and obscuring the details of its original narrative. While the voiceover in *A Night to Dismember* is certainly not true détournement (defined as a subversive transformation of the meaning of a "hijacked" text), there is a way in which the hyperbolic literalness and obviousness of O'Malley's words produce a distanciating redundancy between what he says and its on-screen visual realization, suggesting the existence of two counterpoised systems of obvious meaning inexplicably struggling for dominance within the selfsame text. The aforementioned psychedelic sex scene is superfluously described and quickly rationalized through a voiceover stating, "Vicki felt as though someone faceless was making love to her in bright, flashing colors that were changing from one second to the next." Wishman's desire to obtrusively literalize and place this visual novelty in the character's mindscape only aggrandizes and foregrounds its conspicuous artifice; the narrative is allowed to run amuck, but an aesthetic choice such as this is brought firmly in check, the film itself becoming a battleground where the rationalizing voiceover attempts to subdue the thoroughly irrational things it describes.

Voiceover has more typically functioned throughout Wishman's career to bring otherwise illegible visual elements into alignment with their narrative function, which makes sense given how Wishman herself identifies resolutely as a narrative filmmaker and has been cited as extoling the supremacy of continuity editing, claiming, "There's nothing worse than a jump cut."[41] Regardless of Wishman's contra-avant-garde views, her films frequently feature discontinuities far more conspicuous than mere jump cuts. The editing of *A Night to Dismember* occasionally lapses into something that heavily encroaches on montage in the Eisensteinian sense of the word. Consider the nightmare sequence in which Mary imagines herself the victim of a group of killers. Color shots alternate with those shown in photographic negative. Extreme close-ups reveal bladed weapons being driven into Mary's bloodied body by unrecognizable assailants. However, Wishman declines—or perhaps was unable—to utilize traditional match-on-action cuts to link the shots of assault with those depicting their grisly results. For the spectator, this produces an altogether surreal sequence. We see a knife aimed at Mary's back and then a close-up of her bloodied shoulder, disrupting a sense of spatiotemporal continuity as we seem to be witnessing another moment of the attack. Continuity is further suspended as Mary may appear to fall in one shot only to reclaim her upright stance in the next. Virtually identical shots reappear throughout the sequence.[42] Despite the material causes giving rise to what certain rubrics may name incompetent editing, the overall effect is a scene that can be appreciated for its energy, experimental sense of time, and jarring juxtapositions: for all intents and purposes, the traits of montage.

While the historical avant-garde has long maintained a complicated stance toward the question of intentionality, in *Nightmare USA: The Untold Story of the Exploitation Independents*, Thrower argues that "bad" filmmakers "may stumble upon techniques normally associated with the *avant-garde*, while remaining stubbornly—or helplessly—cut off from the safe haven of art theory."[43] He goes on to choose Doris Wishman as a counterpoint to Luis Buñuel when claiming, "the only difference is self-consciousness, and since the surrealists were desperately seeking to evade rational thought, we can hardly be blamed for assessing those incapable of it just as favourably."[44] Thus in the foregoing I have not attempted to argue *A Night to Dismember* is somehow essentially avant-garde in any practical sense of the term, be it historical, colloquial, or otherwise. Rather, its idiosyncratic formalism is such an extreme departure from any known codification of cinematic norms that the film does not read so much as a "failed" deployment of Hollywood style (meant here as metonymic of narrative, continuity-driven filmmaking) as it does something with a different frame of reference and truly singular (il)logic altogether, that of an accidental avant-garde. This understanding of the film necessarily departs from a reading rooted in Wishman's auteurist intentionality. To hear her describe *A Night to Dismember* so insistently as a horror film is to believe she earnestly sought to deliver a film made in a generic-Platonic ideal, horror with a capital 'H' in a manner of speaking. In a roundabout way, however, if the elements that give the film its avant-garde resonances are best described as accidental, they are also simultaneously all too deliberately and prototypically the product of Wishman's self-willed, no-holds-barred approach to filmmaking.

CONCLUSION

As evidenced by the foregoing, discussions of *A Night to Dismember* through the lenses of auteurism, genre, or its encroachment on, and accidental evocation of, the avant-garde invariably lead to a kind of categorical slippage as an observation germane to one attempted framework so often finds its cause or effect rooted in another. To analogize in the film's own terms, this is a strangely multi-bodied work that frequently finds its constituent impulses bleeding through and leaving residue upon the other operative elements. This is precisely why the film remains something of an "other" in Wishman's filmography, why it is illegible if not completely ridiculous when viewed as a "genuine" slasher exercise of the late 1970s/early 80s, and why it possesses an avant-garde textuality divorced from the sociopolitical project such an aesthetic system typically functions to support. Stephen Thrower is a rare commentator who has championed *A Night to Dismember*; he declares it, in fact, to be "Doris's finest hour."[45] Unsurprisingly, he is also the critic who most readily accepts the film's "plent[iful] blood and violence" as well as its "aesthetic transgressions" in equal measure.[46]

Bowen discusses the "irremediable hybridity" of Wishman's films, although argues in distinction to Thrower that the irony this produces "is complicated... by evidence that her transgressions were not intentionally ironic."[47] At least in the case of *A Night to Dismember*, it is unclear to me where intentionality begins and ends. Certainly, it was not Wishman's intention to see a large fraction of her film destroyed, but the fact the film exists in a finished form at all can only be understood as the realization of Wishman's resolve to overcome what other filmmakers might have understandably written off as an insurmountable setback. Who else except possibly an Ed Wood (a director to whom Wishman is often compared) or an avant-gardist would complete a film from mere fragments? The decisions Wishman made to actualize the project at any (aesthetic) cost—those which give the film its accidental avant-garde qualities—find some degree of license in the precedent set by the idiosyncratic films through which she had already established her reputation. Recycled footage, compensatory voiceover narration, and lack of a firm commitment to continuity norms far predate *A Night to Dismember*, as they already pervade her oeuvre albeit to a less relentless degree. Magnified to the point of overkill and made to function within the framework of the slasher, an emerging genre as immensely popular as it was disreputable, however, these features make *A Night to Dismember* an exceptional product of Wishman's authorship, a filmic record of Wishman ironically and unknowingly writing herself out of familiar territory just as the film would go on to be written out in too many accounts of its intrepid director's career.

NOTES

1. Tania Modleski, "Women's Cinema as Counterphobic Cinema: Doris Wishman as the Last Auteur," in *Sleaze Artists: Cinema at the Margins of Taste, Style, and Politics*, ed. Jeffrey Sconce (Durham, NC: Duke University Press, 2007), 60.
2. Rebekah McKendry, "Fondling Your Eyeballs: Watching Doris Wishman," in *From the Arthouse to the Grindhouse: Highbrow and Lowbrow Transgression in Cinema's First Century*, ed. John Cline and Robert G. Weiner (Lanham, MD: Scarecrow Press, 2010), 63.
3. Mike Quarles, *Down and Dirty: Hollywood's Exploitation Filmmakers and Their Movies* (Jefferson, NC: McFarland, 1993), 149.
4. Tim Lucas, "A Night to Dismember," *Video Watchdog* 25 (September–December 1994): 24.
5. As of December 2019, the film has reappeared in a seemingly unofficial release from Frolic Pictures as part of a double feature with *Effects* (Dusty Nelson, 1980) on DVD-R (manufactured on demand).
6. This is with the exception, perhaps, of *Each Time I Kill* (2007), the final film Wishman shot before her death in 2002 and which was only completed and released posthumously by her collaborators.
7. Cathal Tohill and Pete Tombs, *Immoral Tales: European Sex and Horror Movies 1956–1984* (New York: St. Martin's Griffin, 1995).
8. Much of this exists in the form of online reviews and blog entries.
9. In a remarkable twist in the continuing saga of *A Night to Dismember*'s ultimate fate, on August 8, 2018, the YouTube channel Hamilton Trash Cinema (self-described as "Uploads of obscure and hard to find horror movies that only ever existed on VHS") posted an earlier cut of the film with its heretofore presumed forever-lost footage intact and captioned with the provocative pronouncement, "You probably thought this was destroyed in a fire." Running just shy of an hour and twenty minutes and following a completely different narrative than both that of the released film and its promotional trailer, this

AUTHORSHIP, GENRE, AND THE ACCIDENTAL AVANT-GARDE 175

version hews more closely to a "typical" Wishman outing, especially in its first half, which is driven by the familial drama surrounding a daughter's pregnancy out of wedlock. While scenes of gore and carnage still feature prominently, additional narrative elements that concern Mary Kent's possession of Vicki (here her illegitimate daughter) from beyond the grave bring it far more in line with a work of supernatural horror than the released version's affinity with the then burgeoning slasher subgenre, as discussed later in this chapter. According to an article on *Film Trap*, Ben Ruffett, the programmer of Hamilton's Trash Cinema in Hamilton, Ontario, received a VHS copy of this alternate cut directly from cinematographer C. Davis Smith. In a note from Smith duplicated in the article, he states:

> *You have in your hands a rare copy of the "LOST" version of "A NIGHT TO DISMEMBER."*
>
> *I only know of three other existing copies of the film. One to a friend in Manhattan, one to another friend in Pennsylvania and the copy I have. Now you are among the elite (sic) to join the club. (There are no benefits!) (Unless it is possible nightmares!)*
>
> *The story according to the Gospel of Doris is that a disgruntled employee of MovieLab, (the film processing company in which all the processing and printing work was accomplished) ruined much of the negative to the original version. "WHY" has never come to the forefront of our knowledge. (Or even IF!)*
>
> *HOWEVER....*
>
> *Somehow the film was distributed in Europe in the original version. A lot of people are unaware of this. I have a friend who saw it in Europe years ago when it first came out. (A film nut!) My information could possibly be conjecture. But I have seen paperwork from the distributor of the film showing that at least one print was sold as European Rights.*
>
> *Diana Cummings was the lead in the original "LOST" version. She* was replaced *by Samantha Fox .... not the English singer but the American Porn Star. Doris told me that she (Doris) needed money and that to "salvage" the results of the disgruntled MovieLab worker she* re-edited *the film from the undamaged negative. I'm not sure that I believe this as I know that Samantha gave Doris $2000 to be the lead in the* updated *version. The questions are #1. Did it need to be updated or #2 Did Doris need some cash?*

No matter the veracity of Smith's information, the unanticipated reappearance of this earlier version can be said to raise more questions than it answers. Justin Decloux, "WATCH: The LOST version of Doris Wishman's A NIGHT TO DISMEMBER," *Film Trap*, August 8, 2018, <https://filmtrap.com/watch-the-lost-version-of-doris-wishmans-a-night-to-dismember/> (last accessed November 3, 2020).

10. *A Night to Dismember* DVD commentary track.
11. Ibid.
12. It should be noted that a markedly different narrative is outlined in the film's promotional trailer (Wishman often produced her trailers in the early stages of a production as a way to raise additional funding). Here, in a supernaturally driven plot, Mary Kent (played by

an actor who does not appear in the finished film) is an only child possessed by a creature that gives her destructive powers, which she eventually uses to murder her entire family. Sometime later, the Monroe family moves into the abandoned home where daughter Vicki (played by the actor who plays Mary in the finished film) suffers visions of what previously took place there.

13. Michael J. Bowen, "Doris Wishman Meets the Avant-Garde," in *Underground U.S.A.: Filmmaking Beyond the Hollywood Canon*, ed. Xavier Mendik and Steven Jay Schneider (London and New York: Wallflower Press, 2002), 111.
14. Moya Luckett, "Sexploitation as Feminine Territory: The Films of Doris Wishman," in *Defining Cult Movies: The Cultural Politics of Oppositional Taste*, ed. Mark Jancovich, Antonio Lázaro Reboll, Julian Stringer, and Andy Willis (Manchester: Manchester University Press, 2003), 142.
15. Christopher J. Jarmick, "Doris Wishman" (Great Directors), *Senses of Cinema* 22 (October 2002), <http://sensesofcinema.com/2002/great-directors/wishman/> (last accessed November 3, 2020).
16. Andrea Juno, "Interview: Doris Wishman," in *Incredibly Strange Films*, ed. V. Vale and Andrea Juno (San Francisco: RE/Search Publications, 1986), 110.
17. Modleski, "Women's Cinema," 48.
18. Speaking anecdotally, I had what I sense is the uncommon experience of coming to *A Night to Dismember* first. When I later explored the rest of Wishman's filmography, much of it seemed formally tame by comparison to what *A Night to Dismember* had primed me to expect.
19. Luckett, "Sexploitation as Feminine Territory," 143, 150.
20. *A Night to Dismember* DVD commentary track.
21. For an in-depth, theoretical explanation of how the material identity of a film intersects with its status as a cult object see David Church, *Grindhouse Nostalgia: Memory, Home Video and Exploitation Film Fandom* (Edinburgh: Edinburgh University Press, 2015).
22. At least one source lists the production year as early as 1979. See Michael J. Weldon, *The Psychotronic Video Guide* (New York: St. Martin's Griffin, 1996), 402.
23. For Clover, the final girl is intelligent, levelheaded, and sexually reticent, and embodies a femininity to some extent "qualified" by traditionally masculine interests and behaviors. See Carol Clover, *Men, Women, and Chain Saws: Gender in the Modern Horror Film* (Princeton, NJ: Princeton University Press, 1992), 21–64.
24. Vera Dika, *Games of Terror:* Halloween, Friday the 13th, *and the Films of the Stalker Cycle* (London and Toronto: Associated University Presses, 1990), 123.
25. Clover, *Men, Women, and Chain Saws*, 48.
26. Attentive viewers may in fact have already noticed when Mary's face is briefly visible in the montage that depicts the deaths of Sebastian, Ann, and Bea.
27. Although they are not killed, the endings of *Happy Birthday to Me* and *Intruder* (Scott Spiegel, 1989) intimate that their respective final girls will be apprehended by law enforcement for crimes they did not commit.
28. *A Night to Dismember* DVD commentary track.
29. In an interview prior to the film's release Wishman stated, "There's a lot of blood in this, but that's what the public wants, and if you're in the business you have to give them what they want, if you have the courage." Juno, "Interview," 112. See also Jarmick, "Doris Wishman."
30. Dika, *Games of Terror*, 22.
31. Ibid.
32. Peter Normanton, *The Mammoth Book of Slasher Movies: An A–Z Guide to More Than 60 Years of Blood and Guts* (London: Constable & Robinson, 2012), 37.

33. Bowen, "Doris Wishman," 122.
34. For fuller theorizations of this idea see Jeffrey Sconce, "'Trashing' the Academy: Taste, Excess, and an Emerging Politics of Cinematic Style," *Screen* 36, no. 4 (Winter 1995): 371–93; Joan Hawkins, *Cutting Edge: Art-Horror and the Horrific Avant-garde* (Minneapolis and London: University of Minnesota Press, 2000).
35. Bowen, "Doris Wishman," 109.
36. Ibid., 116; When I attempted to program *A Night to Dismember* at the Indiana University Cinema as part of our Underground Film Series, we were unable to track down the current rights holder. At the level of distribution too, *A Night to Dismember* seems to sit at the periphery of the Wishman canon.
37. Sconce, "'Trashing' the Academy," 386.
38. Bowen, "Doris Wishman," 115.
39. This may be a result of the DVD transfer. One review of this release noted, "With their complete disregard for conventional composition, Wishman's movies play better on video in fullscreen; Elite's 1.85:1 formatting makes things look more cramped and unbalanced." John Charles, "DVD Update: A Night to Dismember," *Video Watchdog* 81 (March 2002): 8.
40. Stephen Thrower, *Nightmare USA: The Untold Story of the Exploitation Independents* (Godalming: FAB Press, 2007), 485.
41. Quoted in Bowen, "Doris Wishman," 118.
42. And, of course, there *is* a certain narrative logic behind what we see here, given that the events are occurring in Mary's nightmare. If anything, this sequence might defamiliarize for us just how frequently characters in Hollywood (and independent films that follow its protocols) even dream according to continuity norms.
43. Thrower, *Nightmare USA*, 43.
44. Ibid., 43.
45. Ibid., 485.
46. Ibid., 486.
47. Bowen, "Doris Wishman," 114.

CHAPTER 10

My Teenage Cinematic Love Affair with Doris Wishman

Rebekah McKendry

When I was in high school my obscure cinematic predilections often made me feel like an outcast. Resultingly, I came to think of my viewing choices as mischievous discretions, often keeping my adoration of bizarre media, including horror, exploitation, and sexploitation, as something I should not discuss with my friends. Without fully realizing it or grasping the co-habitual nature of the movies I was viewing, I was subconsciously battling questions about whether these movies were highbrow art that were overflowing with artistic merit or lowbrow smut I should keep hidden and chastise myself for enjoying.

I first encountered Doris Wishman in the book *RE/Search #10: Incredibly Strange Films* which was published as part of the paracinema-infused *RE/Search* book series in 1985. This tome was my gateway to many fascinating and transgressive artists and filmmakers. But as a teenage girl in small-town where few others even shared my interest in filmmaking, let alone my love of questionable movies, no person in this book fascinated me like Doris Wishman. Her chapter and interview presented a strong woman who had fought to be part of the exploitation world and in no way resented or had ill feelings about any of the products she had created, no matter how smutty they were. You could feel her love for the filmmaking craft. She spoke highly of her own films, and even after thirty years (at the time of publishing), the book discussed how Doris was still making movies. If Doris Wishman was proud of the films she had created, then I could be proud of viewing them. I suddenly felt validated in my love of what others would call "questionable" movies. But in the late 1990s, when Blockbusters dotted the suburban landscape, I had to hunt for most of her titles.

I started using mail order VHS services from the back of magazines like *Fangoria* and *Psychotronic Video*. Fellow peculiar film connoisseurs posted classified ads listing that they had copies of eccentric, obscure movies. You would "snail mail" the person a request for the list of the titles they had, and a few weeks later, a mimeographed sheet would arrive in the mail listing the available movies' titles along with brief summaries and prices. You would then send a hand-written note detailing what films you wanted, and include a check made out for the correct amount. And finally, after a few long weeks, freshly dubbed bootleg VHS tapes would arrive in the mail. It was a painstakingly long process, but for cinephiles and lovers of peculiar media, these were just the necessary steps to feed our passions.

It was in this form that I watched the bulk of Doris Wishman's movies, and the "underground" nature of this filmic black-market transaction only made them seem more divine, a curious mix of "home-grown" and "forbidden." As I slowly worked my way through Wishman's library, I began to understand a bit more about the constructs of filmmaking, often finding myself questioning the elements of cutaways and sync sound before I ever understood the technical sides of moviemaking. Wishman's films became some of my earliest film classes, as I thought about why scenes would suddenly cut to shots of house plants during fight scenes or why the acting always seemed so artificial and plastic.

I also began to make mental connections about the history of exploitation cinema as I joined hands with Doris and ventured through the early nudist camp films, into the sexploitation roughies, onward to 1970s sex-action flicks and shock cinema, and then early the 1980s slashers. Through her, I traversed decades of film history and discovered endless marketing trends, historical styles, trending subgenres, and budget-slicing techniques. Doris Wishman had unknowingly become my exploitation film school.

During these formative years, some filmmakers I encountered perplexed me more than the rest. I still to this day do not know where to place the likes of Herschell Gordon Lewis, Lloyd Kaufman, and yes, Doris Wishman. They seem to exist on both sides of the filmic coin and yet somehow cannot rest comfortably on either. They clearly have a vision, style, and voice, but was this just a constraint of the time period or perhaps a mad dash for profit that happened to turn out quite unique and ground-breaking? Are the boundaries or rationales under which the films were made important, or do we merely examine the final cinematic projects?

Though I am now decades separated from my sixteen-year-old self and my clandestine viewings of *Bad Girls Go to Hell* (1965), the questions about message and meaning still plague me, causing me to re-evaluate my own approach every few years. I know I love Doris Wishman, and I know there are fascinating gender politics at work in her films, but how can one begin to separate historical timeframes, trends, budgets, less-than-stellar acting and shooting conditions, and needing to turn a profit to find a nugget of gender identity, which was likely not one of Wishman's goals? The truth is, it is not possible to separate all the many elements at work in these films, and it has taken me decades to come to terms with this fact.

Over the years, my appreciation of Doris Wishman has only increased. I grew to view her more as a female forerunner fighting a male-driven industry, as an artist adapting to ever-evolving cinematic trends, and as a transgressive subversion to mainstream cinema. Doris Wishman may still not have the full recognition she rightfully deserves, but history has only increased the general awareness of her work and equally opened questions about the constructs and dilemmas under which she thrived.

DORIS WISHMAN VS GENDER IDENTITY

After spending years pugnaciously struggling with how to approach Doris Wishman, I began to question if she was in fact a "feminist." Did it even matter? Would the label or her intentions change the way I viewed the films?

Doris Wishman spent her entire career largely exploiting her own gender. This was, after all, exploitation filmmaking, films that used a particularly controversial or risqué topic to sell tickets, in this case, sex. Doris was doing her job. Over time I have come to approach the gender politics in sexploitation films in much the same manner I approach many tropes in horror. There are certain formulaic social constructs that exist within specific subgenres. There were, and often still are, basic requirements to get a movie made within these subgenres and sell tickets to audiences. Throughout horror history, there has often been a requisite amount of nudity and sex expected in movies, all in the name of distribution and ticket sales. Many of these requirements are still in place today. I have been told by an investor that they required a nude scene or a heavy gore scene within the first thirty pages, and as a filmmaker, I willingly abide by this rule just to get the project made. This is also my approach to the historically controversial element of the final girl which became a slasher staple and persists in areas of the genre today. It is an expectation of genre, a trope that serves purposes better in than out.

Doris Wishman traversed several decades, but her work usually rooted itself into the specific exploitation subgenre that was trending at the time. Each of her films occupies a subgenre that has very specific rules and formulas. The exploitation of women and sexuality was a requirement to sell the films in every one of these subgenres. Therefore, I do not see Doris Wishman as exploiting her gender, but more of her finding a way to work and thrive within the constraints of the exploitation industry. She was a commercialist. Yet somehow, no matter how trendy and profiteering she aimed to be, a little bit of the artist always ended up in the mix. Doris understood what was needed to sell the films, and this is the prime factor that allowed her to keep making films for so long.

Accepting that exploitation of women is a given in this arena, we as viewers are then left to siphon and separate what filmic elements are part of the genre requirements and what portions are pure Doris. For this, I shall start by examining the writing. While Doris had many budgetary constraints on set, we must assume that when it came to writing Doris firmly held the reins. The characters, crazy plots, and wild twists were mostly her own creation.

It is important to highlight here that, even in the male-dominated climate of exploitation filmmaking, the bulk of Wishman's protagonists are women. Whether it be stripper extraordinaire Blaze Starr, the victimized ladies of the roughie years, or the self-reliant and well-endowed Chesty Morgan, Doris often let women control the helm. Even when Wishman did not have a central character that was a woman, she still maintained powerful female roles. Going back to one of her earliest films, *Nude on the Moon* (1961), we find a Moon Queen as well as other women with governance over males. This femininized power reoccurs in other titles like *My Brother's Wife* (1966) and *Satan Was a Lady* (1976). Although these movies take place in male-dominated societies, the women wield their power with ease and grace.

Perhaps the most problematic feminist quandary is created by Wishman's roughie phase. These films follow a formulaic blueprint: an innocent girl is put into a desperate situation and forced into a moral dilemma at the hands of man. For example, a wife's husband can no longer support them, so she is forced to find other, less socially respectable, means to make money. A wife is sexually attacked by her building's janitor and flees to a city full of inescapable sin. Right from the title credits, the audience is not only seeing the story from the woman's perspective but is also immersed in a specific point of view: the world full of domineering males, portrayed as brutish and abusive. The women are the subjects of unwanted sexual advances at the hands of these shady men (and occasionally women too) who respond violently when their sexual advances are declined.

To determine Doris Wishman's messages and intention within her work, one must also examine the entirety of the roughie subgenre in comparison with Wishman's films. Do her films function in the same manner as other roughies from this period? Do they function in the same manner as male-helmed films of the same ilk? Doris Wishman's roughies are notably different.

Russ Meyer's movie *Lorna* (1964)—largely considered to be the film that kicked off the roughie trend—features a young housewife whose husband ignores her. He works long hours in a mine during the day and is studying to become a CPA at night. Lorna has a sexual awakening through violence and then begins cheating on her husband. But, though she is portrayed in parts as a victim, her husband is shown as a victim as well. The movie asserts that he is fighting for a better life for them when Lorna becomes bored and follows more wanton ways.

Just a few months after *Lorna*'s release, Doris made *Bad Girls Go to Hell*, which, following the exploitation trend, seemed to be in response to the success of *Lorna*. Yet Doris bucked the formulaic element of having a hard-working man and wanton woman. Instead, in *Bad Girls Go To Hell*, Doris presents an innocent girl who is sexually attacked by her building's janitor, and she accidentally kills him during the fight. Fearing prison, she flees to New York City and is forced to befriend more abusive sexual predators to survive. The leading lady is always innocent, and the men are always sinister. The entire world is full of sexual predators, and women must be constantly fighting them off.

Looking at other low-budget roughies that came out in 1965, Doris was clearly doing something different. *The Defilers* (1965), a sordid tale about two men who kidnap women and keep them locked in a basement, is largely told from the perspective of the guys. And though several other roughie films during this time have female protagonists as the victims (*Scum of the Earth* from 1963 comes to mind), Wishman's films delve more deeply into complex concepts like coping with sexual attacks and women as victims of a male-dominated society, topics that the bulk of her exploitation comrades do not broach. Yet Doris did. Though she doubtfully would never call herself a feminist or say that she was making films from a female perspective, there are gender politics at play in her movies that are absent in other films from this time.

DORIS WISHMAN: THE FILMMAKER

Over the years, I have heard countless theories, both critical and academic, on Doris Wishman as a filmmaker. Many of the thoughts fall into the "her films are so bad that they are good" category. Others view Wishman as a highly skilled artist who was just forced to work in a less than respectable genre of films. To unpack these theories and explore Wishman's craft of filmmaking, I feel we need to begin by briefly examining what generally comprises a good filmmaker. The answer is not budgets, nor is it the genre in which she worked.

Often, genre labels are determined by budget. For example, a sex-filled drama at a higher budget level becomes just a drama. But in a low budgetary realm, the same plot is deemed sexploitation. We must begin our exploration by coming to terms with the fact that Doris worked under very strict budgetary conditions. She was severely limited in equipment, time, quality of actors, locations, and costumes. These obviously kept her restricted in the scope of films she could make. Even Doris herself stated that she always felt her films would have been much better if she had had larger budgets.[1] She also said the same about her actors and actresses, lamenting that she was not always happy with the quality of performances.[2]

Knowing that Doris was well aware of her own budgetary restraints and understanding that these were not accidents or hallmarks of bad filmmaking, we can begin to examine what elements were not hindered by budgets. There is still a style and distinct mis-en-scène that is used in each one of the films. And throughout the course of her life there is growth, changes in style, and an increasing complexity of shots and storytelling.

Doris was an artist. Her movies have conviction, and they feel distinctive and unique. Whether it be the strange cutaways or her working plots into nudist films when they had previously just been a collection of non-linear footage, Doris enjoyed experimenting and truly loved the craft. To repeat a well-worn but terrific quote from Doris Wishman, "When I die, I'll make films in hell." In Doris's eye, this is what she was born to do. She loved the process! It is reported by her biographer Michael Bowen that Doris even left the room when they were shooting the hardcore sex scenes of her later pornographic films, simply because it made her uncomfortable. It was not the exploitation side that she loved, but the act of filmmaking.[3]

It is also important to realize that Doris Wishman was a one-woman band; as such, she was truly a pioneer. She never made the decision to head to Hollywood to work for a studio, and she even turned down work to direct films for other exploitation companies. Doris loved the control of her own projects and wanted to do things her way. She was an auteur (a word I don't use lightly). She was her own writer, director, editor, and producer. Doris was also largely responsible for her own marketing, an entirely additional area of exploitation filmmaking in which she truly excelled. She crafted trailers that cleverly used voiceover and placards to entice the viewers without ever delivering on the full goods. She often handled the distribution side of her films as well, selling the movies and coordinating the transport of the film strips and the marketing assets to theaters. She coordinated the payments and sometimes had to get tough with distributors. In a world where women were not welcome behind the camera, Doris Wishman excelled.

FROM SEXPLOITATION TO ARTHOUSE

By all accounts and interviews, Doris never expected her films to gain much respect, let alone have a resurgence. And it is hard to determine why a specific project will resurface and find a different audience decades later. Of course, Doris's being a female exploitation filmmaker made her an isolated, glittered-covered unicorn in a sea of white male exploitation colleagues. But it seems like there is much more than that going on. Contemporary audiences could overlook (or perhaps accept) the sexploitation money-making game of these films, pushing beyond that into the quirky filmmaking. I also believe part of her contemporary appeal stems from the authenticity to be found in Doris's films. Viewers can see the constructs that went into making the projects. The cuts are deliberate and often jarring. The acting is just artificial enough to feel like a small pebble in the viewer's shoe—not painful exactly, but something they are always aware of. In a way, the movies are beguiling because the viewer is constantly aware of the master's hands at work, rarely losing oneself in story or plot, but always being aware that this is a peculiar construct of fiction. And as audiences have become savvier to filmmaking tricks over time, the allure of these films has only become stronger, entrapping viewers of a newer generation in strangely artistic and artificial constructs.

Doris was tenacious right up until her final days. Even as she was being rediscovered by audiences, she was still trying to raise funds for more films. And she never really stopped working, barely completing the production of her final film *Each Time I Kill* when she passed away from lymphoma in 2002.[4]

SUMMATIONS

While I was completing my Ph.D. in 2016, a large portion of my research centered on the theory that cult media as a concept was circling the drain. My theory was that a core portion of cult media was the quest and rediscovery of past projects which would then be reinitiated by new audiences. But how does cult media persist in an internet age, when all media from cinematic history available is at our fingertips in a matter of seconds, legally or illegally? I theorized that when everyone has access to all media, then the idea of the underground will diminish, causing labels like "cult" to no longer be applicable in a digital world beyond maybe a marketing term. Still . . . Doris Wishman makes me question my own working concept. As women are now pushing more and more into all areas of the film industry, I am witnessing Doris Wishman emerge yet again, being hailed not just as a quirky filmmaker who also happened to be a woman, but as a female filmmaker who survived in a male-driven industry and never once gave up. Though most of her work can now be accessed online, it has not changed the underground and transgressive ways in which she created her projects and distributed them, and ultimately the transgressive way in which she lived her life. So perhaps, in some instances, cult media is not about re-emergence of projects or the quest to locate elusive rare films, but sometimes about the parameters under which the art was created and how the art can be revisionist, meaning something different to each generation of viewers. In this, Doris has become immortal.

NOTES

1. Myrna Oliver, "Doris Wishman; Exploitation Film Director, Cult Favorite," *Los Angeles Times*, last modified August 21, 2002. https://www.latimes.com/archives/la-xpm-2002-aug-21-me-wishman21-story.html (last accessed November 3, 2020).
2. Ibid.
3. Alison Nastasi, "'She Was An Outsider Artist': Doris Wishman Biographer Michael Bowen on the Sexploitation Filmmaking Queen's Life and Career," *Flavorwire*, last modified June 2, 2016. https://www.flavorwire.com/578455/she-was-an-outsider-artist-doris-wishman-biographer-michael-bowen-on-the-sexploitation-filmmaking-queens-life-and-career (last accessed November 3, 2020).
4. The film was posthumously completed and released in 2007 at the New York Underground Film Festival.

Index

#MeToo, 35–6
12 to the Moon, 113

Abrams, Jack, 5
Ahwesh, Peggy, 131, 134, 140–1, 169
All Campus Joint Struggle Committee, 153
Amazing Transplant, The, 5, 160, 164
American Film Institute Catalog, 7
American Sunbathing Association, 103
Another Day, Another Man, 5, 126, 129–30, 167
April Fool's Day, 165
Archias, Elise, 137
archives, 1
Argento, Dario, 168
Assignment: Outer Space, 113
auteurism, 17, 34, 37, 73, 74–6
avant-garde cinema, 122, 134–5, 139, 160, 163, 169–74; see also experimental cinema

Bad Girls Go to Hell, 5, 126–30, 146, 160, 179, 182

Barbwire, 148
Bass, Saul, 170
Bava, Mario, 168
Behind the Nudist Curtain, 4
Benjamin, Roxanne, 36
Berlin International Film Festival, 152
bisexuality, 78–100
Blaze Starr Goes Nudist, 4, 114, 124, 181
Blockbuster Video, 178
body horror, 35
Bond, James, 167
Bowen, Michael, 3, 123, 125, 134–5, 169–70, 183
Brakhage, Stan, 137, 169
Brown, Lester, 103, 131
Buñuel, Luis, 172
Burch, Noël, 152

Cage, John, 171
camp, 168
Can Dialectics Break Bricks?, 171
Cannes Film Festival, 152–3
Carpenter, John, 165
censorship and content regulation, 3–4, 124, 131, 146

Chesty Morgan, 15–31, 33, 69
Cinema of Transgression, 121
close-up, 23–5, 55, 61, 71, 88
Clover, Carol, 165–6
Color of Love, The, 140
Come with Me My Love, 5
Coral Castle, 103, 109, 111
cult
 cinema, 33, 34, 37, 75, 78
 media, 2, 6, 102, 110–11, 115, 145, 162, 165, 184
Curtains, 165

Dadaism, 171
Daiei, 151
Deadly Weapons, 5, 131–4, 145–8, 150, 155, 164
Deadman, The, 140
Deep Throat, 123
Defilers, The, 182
desire, 22, 26, 28, 29, 49, 52–4, 57–60, 72, 79–81, 84–7
Destination Moon, 104
détournement, 171–2
Diary of a Nudist, 4
Dika, Vera, 166, 168
Dildo Heaven, 6
documentary films, 6, 18, 37, 47–64, 102, 125, 127
Double Agent 73, 5, 131, 145–50, 155, 160, 164
drive-in theaters, 146
Ducournau, Julia, 38

Each Time I Kill, 6, 184
Ebert, Roger, 6
Ecstasy of the Angels, 145, 152–6
edging, 56–8
editing, 17, 54–62
Eisenhower, Dwight, 152
Eisenstein, Sergei, 172
Elder, R. Bruce, 138

Elite Entertainment, 159
Embryo Hunts in Secret, The, 152
Entertainment Industry Magazine Archive, 1
eroduction, 144, 151
ethnographic films, 4, 124
Everett, Kenny, 171
experimental cinema, 121–2, 134–5, 160, 169; see also avant-garde cinema
exploitation films, 1, 7, 101–3, 121–3, 131, 134–5, 140–1, 144, 146, 156, 160, 169, 178–80, 183; see also sexploitation films
Eye Body: 36 Transformative Actions for Camera, 135–6

Fangoria, 178
feminism, 125–6, 135, 140–1, 147, 150, 156, 180–2
feminist film theory, 15–31, 32–46, 72–3, 95
film noir, 171
film promotion, 21–2, 89–95
filmic histories, 1, 3, 121
final girl, 165, 180
Findlay, Michael, 4
Findlay, Roberta, 1, 35–7, 68, 75
Fox, Samantha, 165
Furuhata, Yuriko, 153
Fuses, 122, 137–9

Garden of Eden, 3
gender in the workplace, 105–6, 111–12, 129
gender norms, 101–2, 106, 109–15, 123–4, 126, 128, 130–1, 134, 141, 145
genre, 16, 18, 20–2, 33, 35–8, 41, 47–8, 56, 68, 71–2, 78–9
Gentlemen Prefer Nature Girls, 4
giallo films, 168

Gorfinkel, Elena, 1–2, 5, 123–5, 129, 147
grindhouse theaters, 5, 146, 169

Halloween, 165, 167
Hands of Orlac, The, 160
Haneda Airport, 154
Happy Birthday to Me, 165
hardcore, 37, 55, 67–77, 85
Harvard Film Archive, 169
Hayashi, Sharon, 152
Hideout in the Sun, 2, 102, 114, 146, 164
Hirasawa, Go, 151
Hiroshima, 152
Hitchcock, Alfred, 160
Hollywood cinema, 20, 55, 95
home video, 6, 159, 162–5, 168, 178–9
horror films, 2, 6, 18, 32–46, 140, 160–1, 164–8, 173, 178–80; see also slasher films
Hot Month of August, The, 5

identity, 29, 34, 38–44, 48, 50, 53, 54, 58, 60, 79, 80, 84, 85, 92
Immoral Mr. Teas, The, 146
Immoral Three, The, 6, 164, 167–8
incest, 163
Indecent Desires, 5, 160
Initiation, The, 165
Interior Scroll, 136–7
Internet Movie Database, 7

Japanese Red Army, 152–4

Kaufman, Lloyd, 179
Keyholes Are for Peeping, 5
Kishi, Nobusuke, 152
Kitch's Last Meal, 136
Knokke-le-Zoute Experimental Film Festival, 152

Kurosawa, Akira, 146
Kurosawa, Kiyoshi, 151
Kusama, Karyn, 36

Lacan, Jacques, 19, 26–9, 48–60
Late Night with Conan O'Brien, 6
Lebanon, 153
lesbianism, 126
Let Me Die a Woman, 6, 146, 159
Levine, Joseph E., 3
Lewis, Herschel Gordon, 26, 179
Lorna, 4, 181–2
Love Toy, 5
Loving, 137
Luckett, Moya, 4, 124, 149, 164

Mahon, Barry, 4
male gaze, 102, 110–11, 113, 122–7, 129–41, 147–8, 150, 153, 155–6, 161
male spectatorship *see* male gaze
Mammoth Book of Slasher Movies, The, 168
Margulies, Juliana, 6
Marietta, 103
marriage, 105–6, 108–10, 112, 114
masochism, 20–3, 25–7, 29–30, 90
Mayer, William, 103
McKendry, Rebekah, 126, 132–3, 148–9, 159
Media History Digital Library, 1
Metzger, Radley, 1, 68, 69, 85n28
Meyer, Russ, 1, 4, 68, 146, 149, 181
Millard, Nick, 84
mirror(s), 33, 35, 40–3, 55, 91–3
Modleski, Tania, 121, 125, 141, 159
Morgan, Chesty, 5, 131–4, 147–9, 155, 164, 167
Motion Picture Production Code, 146
Movielab, 160
MPI Media Group, 159

Mulvey, Laura, 124, 155
My Brother's Wife, 5, 146, 167, 181

NASA, 104
naturalism, 139
negativity, 47–52, 54–8, 60
New Left, 145, 151–2
Night to Dismember, A, 6, 159–74
Nikkatsu, 151
No Wave Cinema, 121
Nocturne, 140
Nude on the Moon, 4, 101–15, 181
nudie cuties *see* sexploitation

ontology, 49–51

Paragon Video Productions, 164
Paramount Decrees, 145
Passion Fever, 5
Peril, Lynn, 105
Phantom Planet, The, 113
photogenie, 23–5
Pink films, 144–5, 150–6
Pink Pussycat Boutique, 6
Playgirls International, 4
pornography, 2, 5, 109–10, 131, 138–41, 144, 146, 149–50, 155–6, 183
Poverty Row, 146
Prince and the Nature Girl, The, 4
prop, 18, 22
Psycho, 160
psychoanalysis, 15–31, 47–64
Psychotronic Video Guide, 7, 178

Quarles, Mike, 159
queer studies, 72, 73, 79–95
queer theory, 48–50

rape *see* sexual violence
Rashomon, 146
realist cinema, 125

Red Army Faction, 152–3
Red Army/PFLP: Declaration of World War, 152–3
remake, 39, 76
RE/Search #10: Incredibly Strange Films, 178
Rocco, Pat, 69
Roman Porno, 151
Rosenberg, Max, 3
Rothman, Stephanie, 20, 67
roughies *see* sexploitation

sadism, 86, 90–2
sadomasochism, 79, 89–95
Sarno, Joseph W., 1, 4, 39, 68, 84, 85n28
Sarris, Andrew, 162
Satan Was a Lady (1976), 5, 160, 181
Satan Was a Lady (2001), 6, 160
Sato, Eisaku, 153
Schaefer, Eric, 2, 121
Schaeffer, Pierre, 171
Schneeman, Carolee, 122, 134–41
science fiction, 101, 103–7, 111
Sconce, Jeffrey, 169–70
Scum of the Earth, 182
Season of Terror, 153–4, 156
Secret Behind the Walls, 152
Sex and the Single Girl, 105
Sex Jack, 152–3
Sex Perils of Paulette, The, 5
sex work, 5, 129–30, 147, 164
sexploitation
    films, 2, 102, 121, 125, 129, 140–1, 144, 146–50, 155, 164, 167, 178, 180–3
    nudie cuties, 2–4, 101–4, 109–11, 114–15, 123–6, 149, 160, 179
    roughies, 2, 4–5, 33, 69, 72, 73, 78–100, 102, 123–6, 146, 155, 160, 179, 181–3
    see also exploitation films

sexual violence, 4–5, 102, 121–2, 125–7, 152, 160, 181–2
Shochiku, 151
Silverman, Jack, 3
Sin in the Suburbs, 4
Sirk, Douglas, 168
slasher films, 159–60, 164–8, 173–4, 179; *see also* horror films
Slayer, The, 165
Smith, C. Davis, 39, 73, 162–3
Something Weird Video, 3, 6, 15, 75, 96, 159
space travel, 101–13
spectacle, 22, 33, 35, 37, 49, 55, 59, 85, 86
Sprinkle, Annie, 70–3, 75–7
Striptease, 148
striptease performance, 148, 155, 161, 168, 181
subjectivity, 24, 32–5, 39, 53, 87
sublimation, 47–60
Suo, Masayuki, 151
surrealism, 171–3
Sweet Trap, 151

Takita, Yojiro, 151
Talalay, Rachel, 42–3
Taste of Flesh, A, 5
television, 145, 150, 155
Telluride Film Festival, 136
Tenney, James, 137–9
terrorism, 152–4
Thrower, Stephen, 171–3
Times Square, 5
Toei, 151
Tohill, Cathal, 160
Toho, 151
Tokyo Kikaku, 151

Tombs, Pete, 160
Too Much Too Often!, 5
Toscano, Alberto, 151
trans
 -gender, 6
 -sexuality, 47, 49, 50, 61
 studies, 47–64

U.S.–Japan Security Treaty, 152–4
United Red Army, 152–3
United States Supreme Court, 145

Vestron, 164
Video Search of Miami, 159
Vietnam War, 152
Violated Angels, 152
visibility, 22, 23, 35, 68, 72, 80, 81, 94
voiceover, 33, 40, 74, 85, 87, 93
voyeurism, 19
Vraney, Mike, 3

Wakamatsu, Koji, 144–5, 150–6
Wakamatsu Production, 145, 152–3
Warhol Museum, 169
Waters, John, 168
Weldon, Michael J., 7
Whitney Museum, 169
Wikipedia, 7
Window Water Baby Moving, 137
Wodening [Brakhage], Jane, 137
Wollman, Leo, 54, 55, 57, 61
Women in Horror, 35–8
women's subjectivity, 5, 141, 149
Wood, Brent, 146
Wood, Ed, 174

Zeze, Takahisa, 151

EU representative:
Easy Access System Europe
Mustamäe tee 50, 10621 Tallinn, Estonia
Gpsr.requests@easproject.com